C000048132

Open access edition supported by the National Endowm
Andrew W. Mellon Foundation Humanities Open Book ɪ ɪ ʊɡ ɪ ɑɪɪɪ.

© 2019 Johns Hopkins University Press
Published 2019

Johns Hopkins University Press
2715 North Charles Street
Baltimore, Maryland 21218-4363
www.press.jhu.edu

ISBN-13: 978-1-4214-3315-8 (open access)
ISBN-10: 1-4214-3315-X (open access)

ISBN-13: 978-1-4214-3313-4 (pbk. : alk. paper)
ISBN-10: 1-4214-3313-3 (pbk. : alk. paper)

ISBN-13: 978-1-4214-3314-1 (electronic)
ISBN-10: 1-4214-3314-1 (electronic)

This page supersedes the copyright page included in the original publication of this work.

THE JOHNS HOPKINS UNIVERSITY STUDIES IN HISTORICAL AND POLITICAL SCIENCE

Under the Direction of the Departments of History,
Political Economy, and Political Science

SERIES LXI   NUMBER 3

STUDIES IN THE HISTORY OF THE ENGLISH FEUDAL BARONY

By

SIDNEY PAINTER

OCTAGON BOOKS

A DIVISION OF FARRAR, STRAUS AND GIROUX

New York   1980

Reprinted 1980
by special arrangement with The Johns Hopkins Press

OCTAGON BOOKS
A DIVISION OF FARRAR, STRAUS & GIROUX, INC.
19 Union Square West
New York, N.Y. 10003

Library of Congress Cataloging in Publication Data

Painter, Sidney, 1902-1960.
    Studies in the history of the English feudal barony.

    Reprint of the 1964 printing of the ed. published by Johns Hopkins
    Press, Baltimore, which was issued as ser. 61, no. 3 of the Johns
    Hopkins University studies in historical and political science.
    Includes bibliographical references and index.
    1. Feudalism—England. 2. Great Britain—Baronetage. 3. Great
    Britain—Politics and government—1154-1399. I. Title. II.
    Series: Johns Hopkins University. Studies in historical and political
    science; ser. 61, no. 3.
JN137.P3   1979   321.3   79-17294
ISBN 0-374-96177-8

Manufactured by Braun-Brumfield, Inc.
Ann Arbor, Michigan
Printed in the United States of America

To

SYDNEY KNOX MITCHELL

PREFACE

This book grew out of research that was undertaken in connection with another project. I have been working for several years on what I hope will become a comprehensive history of England during the reign of King John. In attempting to write a chapter on the English baronage in this period I discovered that the questions that seemed to me important could not be answered without far more knowledge than I had of the periods before and after John's reign. On scanning the standard secondary works I soon discovered that some of my questions had never been asked and many had never been answered. After the period covered by Professor F. M. Stenton's *The first century of English feudalism*, the field of baronial history was almost untouched. Hence I embarked on the research which led to this study. I have not tried to deal with all aspects of the subject—many are already sufficiently well known. Many of my questions still await a satisfactory answer. But several authorities on this period of English history whom I have consulted agree with me that it is worthwhile to publish this book in the hope that the tentative answers it supplies may be of aid to other scholars and that more students may be tempted to follow such men as Stenton and Denholm-Young into the study of baronial history.

No historian can ever pretend to express adequately his debt to his predecessors in his field of study. I must, however, point out that I might never have considered writing a chapter on the baronage if I had not read *The first century of English feudalism*. I consider it the most valuable and stimulating work on mediaeval England produced in the last two decades, and I take great pleasure in acknowledging my deep obligation to Professor Stenton. Of the many who have aided me directly and personally my gratitude is particularly due to Professors Sydney Knox Mitchell and William Huse Dunham of Yale University and Professor Johannes Mattern of Johns Hopkins University. These three friends read the entire manuscript and made many valuable suggestions. Professor Dunham's counsel was especially welcome because he is at work on a rather similar study covering the fifteenth century. My colleagues in the departments of History, Political Science, and Political Economy, and the members of the Johns Hopkins Historical Seminar have all given me useful criticism. If the chapter on manorial revenues is of any value, it is largely due to the assistance given me by Professor George Heberton Evans, Jr., of the department of Political Economy. Finally if past experience is any criterion, before this book is through the press I shall be under very great obligations to the editorial and proof-reading abilities of Miss Lilly Lavarello.

SIDNEY PAINTER

THE JOHNS HOPKINS UNIVERSITY
July, 1943

CONTENTS

CHAPTER I

BARONS AND BARONIES

From the point of view of the historian the English feudal barony presents two closely interrelated yet quite different aspects. It was a feudal subdivision of the realm with important political, military, and social functions, and it supported the baron. The first of these two aspects of the barony has been extensively studied. To speak in very general terms the majority of writers on English mediaeval history have tended to consider the barony primarily as an impediment to the development of a strong central government. Even Mr. Round to whom we owe so much of our knowledge of the barony in the eleventh, twelfth, and thirteenth centuries clearly had this rather limited view. This tendency of historians to concentrate their attention on the development of the central government has done much to illuminate the origins of English political institutions, but it has also seriously distorted our view of the government of mediaeval England. Not until the appearance of Mr. Stenton's *The first century of English feudalism* was the subject exposed in broader terms.[1] He pointed out the vital part played by the baron and his fief in English government. As Stenton's study stops at 1166, much work remains to be done before the history of the barony as an intrinsic part of the English feudal monarchy can be finally written. One can only hope that the task so well commenced by Mr. Stenton will soon be carried to complete fruition.

The second aspect of the history of the feudal baronies of England—the account of their development from the point of view of the barons themselves—has been almost entirely neglected. While several writers, notably Mr. Ault, Miss Chew, and Mr. Denholm-Young, have dealt with various phases of the subject, no one has attempted a general survey.[2] It might

[1] F. M. Stenton, *The first century of English feudalism, 1066-1166* (Oxford, 1932).

[2] W. O. Ault, *Private jurisdiction in England* (New Haven, 1923); *Court rolls of the abbey of Ramsey and of the honor of Clare* (New Haven, 1928);

11

be argued that any such attempt would be premature until many more detailed studies have appeared, but I am inclined to agree with M. Bloch that there is much to be said for a broad preliminary survey even if many of its conclusions must be tentative.[3] Such studies can often furnish scholars with a common method of approach to the subject and may indicate fruitful fields for further research.

The history of the utilization of the baronies by their lords should be of great interest to the student of the Middle Ages. It is a vital element in the economic history of the upper class. As such it is a necessary foundation for the study of the political and constitutional history of the period. In so far as the baronial policy toward the king and his administration was governed by economic self-interest, the explanation of that policy must be sought in the economic history of the baronies. Finally any information that can be accumulated about what a baron sought to obtain from his fief will be of assistance to the scholar who is interested in the social history of the feudal class.

Men have always sought to utilize the resources at their disposal so as to satisfy their desires to the greatest possible extent. Hence the historian who traces the policy of an individual or a group is forced to construct an hypothesis in respect to basic motives. Even if it serves no other end than to point out to the reader that it is an hypothesis, I wish to state the assumptions as to baronial motives which will underlie my discussion. The first point that requires consideration in this connection is the matter of individual tastes. The biographer may speculate about the personal eccentricities of his subject, but the student of a group must assume that they do not exist. Suppose for instance that a baron clears two hundred acres of his demesne woods. Although it is perfectly possible that his motive was to improve the view from his chamber window, the historian must assume that he wanted more arable land. When

Helena M. Chew, *The ecclesiastical tenants-in-chief and knight-service* (Oxford, 1932); N. Denholm-Young, *Seignorial administration in England* (Oxford, 1937).

[3] Marc Bloch, *Les caractères originaux de l'histoire rurale française* (Cambridge, 1931).

a royal favorite who has obtained the privilege of marrying an heiress exchanges his fiancée for another, we cannot consider the possibility that the second was more charming but must conclude that he believed her fief more valuable. Only when a personal taste can be conclusively shown to be a general trait of the feudal class—such as the love of hunting—can it be used as one of our hypothetical motives.

Individual eccentricities must be banned from consideration because there is no effective method of dealing with them. Various other motives can be ruled out on the ground that they are not pertinent. Obviously a baron was interested in food, clothing, and shelter, but as he was a member of the highest economic group of his day, he was assured of these necessities. No barony was so lacking in resources that it could not supply its lord with plain food, home-made clothes, and a castle of earth and wood. In addition the baron was assured of ample resources for the satisfaction of the desires that were common to the feudal class. He could afford to buy the best military equipment known to his day. He had woods to hunt in and meadows for hawking. Perhaps most important of all he could provide for the salvation of his soul by gifts to the church. In short the baron could live—and live as a gentleman.

If the above reasoning is sound, the motives governing baronial policy must be sought in the desire for luxurious living, power, prestige, and outstanding services to the church. It is, of course, impossible to classify these motives definitely. A man may want a fine silk robe because he likes the feel of silk or to impress his associates. He may want the right to hang thieves because he loves power or to increase his local prestige. From what is known of the interest of the feudal class in honor and glory one might with some justice conclude that a baron's dominant motive was the desire for prestige in this world or the next. But this problem does not concern me. I am simply assuming that a baron's policy in regard to the utilization of his fief was dictated by one of these desires.

My purpose then is to trace the methods by which the feudal barons of England sought to draw from their fiefs the resources needed to satisfy the desires mentioned above. The period to be covered extends from the Norman Conquest to about the

middle of the fourteenth century. By 1350 the feudalism that
had been introduced by the victorious Norman duke had ceased
to exist in any real sense. Although the barons of the fourteenth century wore armor and lived in castles, there was little
that was feudal in their position. Their relations with their
tenants by knight service were purely financial. Homage itself
had become merely an occasion for collecting relief. The men
who fought for them and administered their households and
estates were hired retainers. The relation between the baron
and the crown had become equally non-feudal. The title of
baron no longer meant possession of a certain fief, but marked
a man who received a summons to Parliament as a baron. Few
if any royal taxes were collected or assessed on a feudal basis.
As far as the crown was concerned the baron was simply a
great landholder who had certain dignities and privileges
because he sat in Parliament as a baron.

One more introductory question remains to be considered—
the meaning of baron and barony. The content and use of
these terms at various times have been the subject of extended
scholarly discussion. It would be pleasant to be able to say
categorically that a baron was a man who held a barony, but
this was not always true. Mr. Stenton has pointed out that in
the Norman period the word baron designated a social and
political status, and this usage continued into Angevin times.[4]
A man might be a baron because he held a barony or because
he was a man of importance for some other reason. Thus the
lord of a barony was a baron, but a baron might hold a fief
that his contemporaries would not describe as a barony. King
John announced that he had taken Geoffrey Wac under his
protection *tanquam dominicum baronem nostrum.*[5] Geoffrey
held a fief of one knight's fee in chief—far too small to be
called a barony. While the term demesne baron is obviously
intended to distinguish him from the great lords whom John
called his *capitales barones,* the king was clearly applying the
term baron to Geoffrey.[6] But as cases of this sort seem to have
been rare, they cause little confusion. The real difficulty begins

[4] *English feudalism,* pp. 83-113.
[5] *Rotuli chartarum* (ed. T. D. Hardy, *Record commission*), p. 170b.
[6] *Rotuli litterarum clausarum* (ed. T. D. Hardy, *Record commission*), I, 85b.

with the appearance of barons by writ of summons to Parliament. The men so honored might or might not hold fiefs which contemporary usage called baronies. Moreover the holder of a barony was not necessarily summoned to Parliament as a baron.

The history of the term barony in England is extremely complicated. Stenton has suggested that in the Norman period any fief that was held for the service of five knights or more was considered a barony.[7] Certainly in the eleventh and early twelfth centuries the more important tenants *in capite* of the crown called their chief vassals barons.[8] A passage in the *Leges Henrici* indicates that this practice was recognized by the royal government.[9] But by the end of the twelfth century official usage restricted the term barony to fiefs held in chief from the crown.[10] The only exception seems to have been in favor of the major vassals of the palatine lords such as the bishop of Durham and the earls of Chester and Pembroke.[11] An interesting case is that of the Shropshire tenants-in-chief whose predecessors had been vassals of Robert de Bellême. The *Dialogue of the exchequer* and *Magna Carta* both distinguish carefully between the king's tenants *de corone* and those who held of him as mesne tenants of an escheated barony.[12] The latter were not considered barons. Yet the feeling that the major tenants of a palatine lord were barons seems to have moved the compiler of the Shropshire returns to the inquest of knights' fees of 1212 to designate as barons such men as Robert Corbet and Hugh Pantulf.[13] Fourteen years later the royal government officially declared that Hugh Pantulf held of the escheated fief

---

[7] *English feudalism*, p. 95.

[8] See evidence collected by Stenton, *ibid*, pp. 85-93. I should like to add to his cases the references in *Exon Domesday* to the barons of the count of Mortain. *Domesday book* (*Record commission*), IV, 66.

[9] *Leges Henrici*, c. 7. 7 in F. Liebermann, *Die Gesetze der Angelsachsen* (Halle, 1903).

[10] *Dialogus de scaccario* (ed. Hughes, Crump, and Johnson, Óxford, 1902), pp. 134-135.

[11] Stenton, *English feudalism*, pp. 85-87. The chief fiefs held of the bishop of Durham were called baronies on the pipe roll of 1196. "Pipe roll 8 Richard I," *Pipe roll society*, XLV, 260-261.

[12] *Dialogus de scaccario*, pp. 134-135; *Magna carta*, c. 43.

[13] *Book of fees* (*Rolls series*), I, 144.

of Robert de Bellême and was not obliged to pay relief as a baron.[14]

Miss Reid has discussed in detail the nature of tenure by barony in the thirteenth century. Two features distinguished a barony from other fiefs. *Magna carta* set the relief for a barony at £100 no matter how many knights' fees it contained. Other fiefs paid at the rate of £5 per fee. Then a barony had a recognized chief seat, a *caput*, which could not be alienated, granted in dower, or divided among co-heirs.[15] To Bracton the possession of a *caput* was the distinguishing mark of a barony.[16] Yet as late as 1214 two mesne lords were claiming that the *caputs* of their fiefs were inalienable.[17]

In the light of the confusion in contemporary usage of baron and barony, it seems essential to adopt an arbitrary terminology for the purposes of this study. I shall confine the use of barony to fiefs held in chief of the crown. The baron will be the lord of a barony. When it is necessary to speak of similar estates not held *in capite*, I shall use the expressions mesne baron and mesne barony. The men summoned to Parliament as barons will be called Parliamentary barons.

Finally before embarking on a detailed examination of the history of the English feudal baronies it seems pertinent to give some idea of what they consisted of at the beginning of our period. When Duke William of Normandy conquered England, he kept some land in his own hands, left the church most of its extensive possessions, and distributed the rest in lay fiefs. *Domesday Book* supplies much information about these fiefs. It gives us the name of each estate held, the county and usually the hundred in which it lay, the number of hides at which it was assessed for danegeld, various details about the land and its inhabitants, and an estimate of its annual value. Mr. Corbett believes that some 170 of the fiefs held in chief of the crown described in *Domesday* were large enough to be called

---

[14] *Ros. claus.*, II, 111.

[15] Miss R. R. Reid, "Barony and thanage," *English historical review*, XXXV (1920), 162-163.

[16] Bracton, *De legibus et consuetudinibus Angliae* (ed. George E. Woodbine), II, 269.

[17] *Curia regis rolls* (*Rolls series*), VII, 138-139.

baronies.[18]   On the basis of the information furnished by
Domesday these baronies can be described geographically in
terms of number of estates, fiscally in terms of hides, agri-
culturally in terms of plow teams, and economically in terms
of annual value. For our purposes here the first and last seem
most useful. The question of what *Domesday* valuations
actually represented will be discussed later in connection with
baronial revenues. Here they will be used as by Mr. Corbett
for purely comparative purposes.

Let us then glance at the extent, geographical distribution,
and annual value of some Domesday baronies. The largest
and richest of the fiefs granted by the Conqueror went to his
half-brother, the count of Mortain, who received some 793
estates worth over £2,500 a year.[19] He was practically the only
tenant-in-chief in Cornwall, and he was one of the three largest landholders in Buckinghamshire, Devonshire, Dorsetshire,
Northamptonshire, Somersetshire, Sussex, and Yorkshire. In
the first rank of those outside William's family came Earl
Roger de Montgomery who received 544 estates worth about
£1,750 a year.[20] Earl Roger was master of Shropshire where
lay 350 of his estates, was the largest landholder in Sussex, and
held scattered lands in ten other shires. Count Alan of Brittany held 442 estates.[21] The bulk of these were in Yorkshire,
but he was the greatest landholder in Cambridgeshire and
Lincolnshire and an important one in Norfolk and Suffolk.
Below these mighty lords who were dominant figures in many
counties came a group of men who were important in single
regions. Baldwin of Exeter had 4 estates in Somerset and 162
in Devon where he was by far the largest tenant-in-chief. His
lands were valued at £321 a year. Walter Giffard with 44
estates in Buckinghamshire was the chief landholder in that

[18] *Cambridge medieval history*, V, 508.

[19] This estimate of the value of the count of Mortain's fief is based on
Corbett's statement that the lands given to him and the bishop of Bayeux
totaled £5,050. *Ibid.*

[20] This too is Corbett's estimate of value. *Ibid.*, p. 510.

[21] Except for the valuations noted above the statistics in this paragraph are
mine. The estates were counted and the values added up, but as exactness in
this case seemed unimportant, I did not do it very carefully. It would be
unsafe to use the figures for a less general purpose.

2

shire. In addition he had 6 estates in Oxfordshire, 2 in Cambridgeshire, 1 in Huntingdonshire, 7 in Bedfordshire, 1 in Berkshire, and 10 in Norfolk. The value of his lands came to £375. Then there were barons of importance whose fiefs were too scattered to give them a dominant position in any one shire. Walscin de Douay held 32 estates in Somerset, 24 in Devon, and 2 each in Wilts, Dorset, and Essex. Their total value was £210. Ernulf de Hesding had 17 estates in Wilts, 7 in Gloucester, and 15 scattered in eight other shires with a total value of £268. Roger de Ivry held 22 estates in Oxfordshire and 17 in five other counties with a total valuation of £259. Alured of Marlborough had 18 in Wiltshire, 8 in Herefordshire, 2 each in Somersetshire and Hampshire, and 1 in Surrey. They were worth £182. Finally let us glance at two small baronies. Gilbert de Breteville possessed 7 estates in Wiltshire and 6 each in Berkshire and Hampshire. Their total value came to £64. Robert d'Aumale held 15 estates in Devon worth £26 a year—a very small barony later to be subordinated to the great fief of Plympton.

While a barony can best be visualized in geographical terms, this mode of description is essentially misleading. In reality it consisted of a mass of varied rights over lands and men. The baron had manorial demesne lands—arable, meadow, pasture, waste, and woods—to exploit as he saw fit. He was entitled to the rents in money, kind, and service paid by the inhabitants of his fief. He could erect mills and fisheries and levy tolls. Through his manorial courts he enforced the economic regulations which bound the inhabitants of his lands. As a franchise holder he wielded more or less extensive police powers over his people. But the baron could not use the gross surplus productivity of his fief to satisfy his personal desires. In return for the rights granted him by the crown he owed various feudal services. Moreover except in the case of the palatinates the king did not grant the baron all the perquisites which came from his fief. Certain rights over lands and men were retained by the royal government and its agents. Hence the barony was burdened with feudal services and with various non-feudal public obligations. It was the net revenue after these obligations were performed that was at the disposal of the baron.

Any adequate account of how the barons of England exploited their fiefs must take into account the complex factors mentioned in the last paragraph. I shall first consider the means employed by the barons to perform or avoid the feudal and non-feudal obligations imposed on them and their fiefs. Then I shall examine the nature and size of their revenues. Lest this outline seem too simple and too purely economic in its viewpoint let me point out that I am not using the word revenue in the sense of money return. The satisfaction received by the baron from holding a rare franchise was just as much a part of his revenue as the actual profits which came from its exercise. I am interested in how the barons used their fiefs to satisfy their desires. Sometimes a profit in money was the intermediary between a right and its enjoyment by the baron— very often it was not.

CHAPTER II

FEUDAL OBLIGATIONS

The most important obligation owed by a vassal to his lord was military service. This was particularly true in eleventh-century England. King William and his barons found themselves ruling a conquered country which had long lain under the threat of Scandinavian invasion. Hence their first care was to establish an effective military system. This system was bound to be feudal in nature. While it would be extremely difficult to prove that the economic condition of England in the eleventh century would not have been able to support a mercenary standing army, it seems unlikely that there was sufficient money in circulation to make it feasible. But even if there had been sufficient resources to maintain an adequate hired army, the fact that William and his men were deeply steeped in feudal tradition would have made the adoption of such a military system out of the question. When the Conqueror granted the barons their fiefs, he imposed on each a quota of knights for his host.

Both royal and baronial interests demanded that this public obligation be provided for quickly and effectively. There were obviously two methods by which a baron could furnish the knights he owed the crown. He could collect the requisite number of knights and feed and clothe them from the produce of his estates. In short he could travel from manor to manor with as many knights as his quota called for, consuming the produce of the estates. This would not necessarily mean a period of residence on every manor. Produce could be carried short distances, and the estates of most barons fell into geographical groups. Hence supplies could be gathered at one manor of each group and there consumed by the baron and his knights. Nevertheless this method involved a large amount of transportation at a high cost in labor of man and beast. It made small isolated estates almost useless. It required the baron to have rather large residences on a number of manors. The effective supervision of so many estates would be a very serious administrative problem. But I suspect that the most important

20

argument against such a system was the difficulty in getting knights. Feudal tradition urged a young knight to serve in a baron's household, but it was in the hope that he would eventually receive a fief. Social prestige and economic security demanded that a knight have a fief. No doubt some knights never attained this end and spent their lives serving as household knights, but it is hard to believe that many would enter a service where there seemed no hope of acquiring a fief. In all probability it was not difficult for a baron to keep four or five knights in his household. For a minor baron this might be an important part of the quota owed the crown. But the great lords could hardly hope to maintain indefinitely household forces large enough to furnish any great proportion of their obligations.

The other method of providing a contingent of knights for the royal army was the one favored by feudal custom—the granting of fiefs in return for service. If a baron owed twenty-five knights, he could grant twenty-five fiefs large enough to support a knight or he could give five knights fiefs able to support five knights and let each of these vassals find his quota as he saw fit. Then the mesne tenant was faced with the same problem his lord had had and in general solved it by granting sub-fiefs. By the time of the Domesday survey most barons of any importance had granted out part of their lands in fiefs. Using once more Domesday values Baldwin of Exeter had granted £195 of his total of £321, Walter Giffard £226 from £375, Walscin de Douay £110 out of £210, and Roger de Ivry £100 from £259. But Ernulf de Hesding had given in fiefs only £45 from his total of £268.[1] In general these baronies I have used as samples lay in the region where sub-enfeoffment had progressed farthest. In the North and the Midlands the baronies would probably show a smaller proportion in the hands of mesne tenants. Unfortunately *Domesday Book* says nothing about knights' fees, and hence it is impossible to say what portion of his quota a baron had provided for by means of the fiefs granted.

Obviously any generalizations that can be made about sub-infeudation as shown in *Domesday Book* would be of great

---

[1] All these figures are mine.

value as indicative of the ideas that governed the barons in granting fiefs. Unfortunately very few such general statements can be made. The only principle that seems to have been applied in almost every barony was to keep in demesne the more valuable estates while granting the smaller ones as fiefs. Thus the demesnes of Walter Giffard included three manors valued at £20, one at £14, two at £12, one at £8, two at £7, and two at £5. On the other hand out of fifty-one estates granted as fiefs only sixteen were valued at £5 or above and six of these belonged to his fellow baron and chief mesne tenant, Hugh de Bolbec, who held in fee about a quarter of the Giffard barony. Nine of the twenty demesne estates of Baldwin of Exeter were valued at over £5 while only seven of the 146 estates granted by him to his men reached that valuation. The reasons for this practice seem obvious. A large estate was little more trouble to administer than a small one. Moreover it could supply the produce required for a period of residence by the baron and his household without the cost and trouble of transportation. From the baron's point of view one manor yielding £20 was far more useful than ten worth £2 each.

One might expect that such considerations of convenience in utilizing the produce of his demesnes would move a baron to concentrate them geographically. A tendency in this direction can be noticed in *Domesday Book*. When the estates of a baron in a shire were few and small, he was inclined to grant them all as fiefs. When he kept a small estate in demesne, it was usually near a larger one. This policy was continued as sub-infeudation progressed. By the twelfth century baronial demesnes were in general as well concentrated as other considerations would permit. The considerations that prevented complete geographical consolidation of demesnes were both administrative and military. If a baron had fairly important properties in a region, he wanted an administrative seat there and a fortress to watch over his interests. Thus the great post-Domesday barony of the Mowbrays had large groups of estates—in the Vale of York, in the West Riding, in the Isle of Axholme in Lincolnshire, and in the Midlands. Each of these groups centered in a demesne manor adorned with a motte and bailley castle. It seems probable that strategic considerations dealing with desirable locations for castles had much to do with a baron's decision as to which estates should be held in demesne.[2]

The next extensive mass of information about the English baronies and their sub-infeudation is found in the returns to the inquest of knights' fees of 1166.[3] While the returns are not complete, the documents available give the names of the vassals of the majority of the barons of England and the number of knights each owed his lord. Unfortunately the names of the estates held are rarely mentioned. Thus only the names of the barons and their vassals enable us to connect the information found in *Domesday* with that supplied by the returns of 1166. If the baronies of England had remained stable during the interval between these two inquests, it would not be difficult to fit the two sources together, but such was not the case. The vast baronies of the count of Mortain, Earl Roger de Montgomery, and the bishops of Bayeux and Coutance had been forfeited or escheated to the crown and had lost their identities. Some of their estates and fees had gone into new baronies created for the favorites and illegitimate sons of King Henry I, and many of their vassals had become tenants-in-chief and were rated as barons in 1166.[4] Smaller baronies such as those of Walscin de Douay and Ernulf de Hesding had been split into parcels.[5]

While many of the Domesday baronies were being split up, new ones were being formed out of the debris and from the royal demesne. Two of King Henry I's illegitimate sons were cared for in this way. Reginald de Dunstanville received the count of Mortain's Cornish lands and most of his Devonshire estates. Robert of Caen was provided with an heiress, daughter

---

[2] Sidney Painter "English castles in the middle ages," *Speculum*, X (1935), 324-327.

[3] *Red book of the exchequer* (ed Hubert Hall, *Rolls series*), I, 186-445.

[4] Thus the baronies held by Richard fitz William, Drogo de Montaigu, and William Fossard had been mesne fiefs of the count of Mortain. *Ibid.*, pp. 220, 228, 407.

[5] In 1166 William fitz John of Harptree held some thirteen knights' fees which had belonged to Walscin de Douay's barony. (*Ibid.*, p. 219.) Walscin's seat and chief demesne manors with some fees formed the new honor of Bampton. Earl Patrick of Salisbury, William fitz Alan, and Payn de Montdoubleau shared the lands of Ernulf de Hesding. (*Ibid.*, pp. 241, 274, 297-298.)

of Robert fitz Hamon, lord of Glamorgan, and in addition was richly endowed with manors from the royal demesne and the lands of the bishop of Coutance. He was also given the services of several of the bishop's vassals and of some minor tenants-in-chief. One of King Henry's favorite knights, Baldwin de Redvers, received large blocks of royal manors in Devonshire and Hampshire, Earl Roger de Montgomery's lands in the Isle of Wight, and the services of at least one tenant-in-chief of some importance, Robert d'Aumale. Another of Henry's favorites, Alan fitz Flaad, was given a fief in Norfolk, a part of the lands of Ernulf de Hesding, and a slice of Earl Roger's Shropshire estates.[6] There is no point in multiplying examples. It is clear that a fair percentage of the baronies of 1166 bore little or no relation to those described in *Domesday Book*.

In the inquest of 1166 King Henry II asked each baron three questions. How many knights' fees had been created on the barony before the death of King Henry I and who held them? How many had been granted since then and to whom? How many knights did the baron have to support on his demesne in order to fill his quota for the royal host?[7] It is important to notice that the barons were not asked to state what their quotas were. Those who were obliged to answer the third question—that is those who had enfeoffed fewer knights than they owed—gave this information indirectly. A few barons voluntarily mentioned the size of their traditional quotas.[8] Henry's purpose in makng this investigation will be discussed later.[9] Here we are concerned only with the information furnished about the means used by the barons to furnish their contingents to the host.

As we are primarily trying to discover how the barons made provision for the service they owed the crown, we must confine ourselves to baronies for which the old *servitium debitum* can be established. Information on this subject can be ob-

---

[6] *Ibid.*, pp. 271-274.

[7] See the *carta* of the archbishop of York, *ibid.*, p. 412.

[8] *Ibid.*, pp. 299, 347, 348, 351, 418.

[9] For a full discussion of this inquest see J. H. Round, *Feudal England* (London, 1895), pp. 236-246.

tained in several ways.   As I have shown above, the old quota can be calculated from the *carta* of barons who had enfeoffed fewer knights than they owed.   Then there are the barons who voluntarily mentioned the size of their quotas.   Finally we have the pipe roll accounts for the scutages levied on the basis of the old *servitium debitum*.[10]

Using these sources Mr. Round compiled a list of baronies for which he felt able to establish the quotas of knights due the crown.[11]   I have been obliged to amend this list.   Baronies for which no *carta* supplying information about sub-infeuda-tion have survived are of no use for my purpose.[12]   Then I dropped a few baronies where the evidence as to the *servitium debitum* failed to convince me and added a few where such evidence seemed sufficient.[13]   Finally Mr. Round and I differ slightly as to the quotas of three baronies.[14]   Essentially, how-ever, I have used Round's list.

There are 65 lay and 22 ecclesiastical baronies for which the *servitium debitum* and the details about sub-infeudation are known.   Let us glance first at the lay baronies.   By the death of Henry I in the year 1135 the lords of 17 of these baronies had enfeoffed more knights than they owed the crown.   Eight barons had created exactly enough fees.   Forty baronies had fewer knights enfeoffed than they were obliged to supply to the host.   By 1166 the number of baronies with more knights than necessary had risen to 24 reducing the number with too few to 33.   The ecclesiastical fiefs furnish a different picture. Eighteen of the 22 baronies had more knights than their quotas demanded before the death of Henry I.   One had just enough

---

[10] *Ibid.*, pp. 262-285.   "Pipe rolls 5, 7, 8, 11 Henry II," *Pipe roll society*, I, IV, V, VIII.

[11] *Feudal England*, pp. 253-256.

[12] This excluded seven baronies on Round's list—Tickhill, the Earl Warren, St. Valery, Balliol, Limesi, Holderness, and Bruce.

[13] On this ground I omitted eight fiefs—Totness, Mowbray, Richmond, Mont-doubleau, Roumar, Fitz Robert, Traci, and Waleran.   I added Bigod, Chandos, Robert de Ghent, Ely Giffard, Kington, Percy, Ros (Kent), and Wormgay.

[14] The baronies of Arsic, Dover, and Fitz Alan.   In the first case Round clearly was in error.   The Arsic barony certainly owed twenty knights, not ten. It paid twenty marcs in 1161, but Round himself admits that a number of baronies paid at one marc per fee that year.   ("Pipe roll 7 Henry II," *Pipe roll society*, IV, 26; *Feudal England*, p. 281.)   The other two are debatable.

while only 3 had too few. By 1166 one of the 3 with too few had exactly enough.

The statistics given above for the lay baronies require some explanation. Numerically the sample seems sufficient. Counting as a barony any tenure in chief of 5 or more knights' fees there were some 133 baronies in 1166. Although the list of 65 used lacks a fair proportion of the large fiefs, this was counterbalanced by the omission of a number of very small ones.[15] But one of the methods used to obtain the old *servitium debitum* seems to warp the results. The presence on the list of 10 or 12 baronies was made possible by the fact that they had enfeoffed too few knights and hence it was possible to calculate their old quotas from the returns to the inquest. The omission of these fiefs would leave 17 baronies with too many fees against about 30 with too few. When one considers that Miss Chew who has done important work on this subject states that " the majority (of tenants-in-chief) enfeoffed more than the number of *milites* for which they were responsible " even this reduced proportion seems interesting.[16]

The contrast between baronies in respect to sub-enfeoffment becomes more striking when one examines the percentages by which they exceeded or failed to fill their quotas. Of the 17 lay baronies which had more knights than were needed 9 exceeded their quotas by less than 20 per cent, 2 by 20-50 per cent, 2 by 50-100 per cent, and 4 had over twice as many knights as they owed. Of the 40 baronies containing too few fees 15 had a deficiency of less than 20 per cent, 19 of 20-50 per cent, and 6 had less than half the necessary knights. William de Beauchamp of Worcestershire owed 7 knights to the royal host and had enfeoffed 16. Hugh Bigod owed 60 and had enfeoffed 125. At the other extreme Roger de Buron owed 10 and had enfeoffed only 5. Ralph Halselin owed 25 and had enfeoffed 12½.

These variations in the extent of sub-infeudation can be in

---

[15] I omitted about a score of baronies of ten fees or less.

[16] *Ecclesiastical tenants-in-chief*, p. 17. It is only fair to add that as the over-enfeoffment on some baronies was enormous, Miss Chew's statement that the total of knights enfeoffed was greater than the total service due the crown is probably correct.

large measure explained by inequalities in the assessment of the *servitium debitum*.   As Mr. Corbett has pointed out that there was little relation between the comparative values of baronies and their comparative quotas of knights, a few examples will suffice.[17]   The Domesday valuation of the Aincurt barony was some three times as great as that of the Arcy fief, yet the former owed forty knights to the latter's twenty.   The barony of Cainhoe had a total value of £86, that of Odell of £98, and the Mandeville fee was worth over £700, but their respective quotas were fifteen, thirty, and sixty.   The Conqueror could have had little accurate information about the lands he was granting, and the quotas must have been assigned in a most casual manner.   Undoubtedly royal favor also played a part especially in the case of great lords like the Mandevilles.   Two at least of the grants made by Henry I seem to be cases of favoritism.   Baldwin de Redvers owed only fifteen knights for his vast barony of Plympton which contained in the twelfth century eighty-nine knights' fees.   He appears to have owed no service for the baronies of Christchurch and the Isle of Wight.   Alan fitz Flaad owed six knights although there were twenty-seven enfeoffed on his lands.

It is extremely difficult to illustrate the practical results of these discrepancies in assessment.   We know how many knights had been enfeoffed on a barony before the death of Henry I, but we have no information as to what proportion of the barony had been used to endow them.   I have, however, been able to obtain very rough figures for eight baronies.[18]   To do this I have taken the manors known to have been held in demesne in the twelfth and early thirteenth centuries, found their total Domesday values, and subtracted the result from the total Domesday valuation of the barony.[19]   Waving aside the

---

[17] *Cambridge medieval history*, V, 512.

[18] Aincurt, Arcy, Bolbec, Chokes, Fitz Hamon, Odell, Mandeville (Essex), and Beauchamp (Somerset).

[19] The names of the estates held in demesne in the twelfth and thirteenth centuries were obtained from the following sources: Aincurt barony: Nottingham and Derby demesnes, *Inquest of 1242* in *Book of fees*; Lincolnshire demesnes, *Rotuli de dominibus et pueris et puellis* (ed. J. H. Round, *Pipe roll society*, XXXV), pp. 18-19.   Arcy barony: *Ibid.*, pp. 2, 16.   Bolbec barony: *Ibid.*, pp. 34, 40.   Chokes barony, "Pipe roll 1 John," *Pipe roll society*,

innumerable possibilites of error, this gives us the proportion of the barony granted out in fiefs. On this basis five of the eight baronies had about 70 per cent of their resources in the hands of mesne lords. The proportion of the *servitium debitum* provided for by these sub-enfeoffments varied from 80 per cent to 100 per cent. Thus the Arcy barony produced 100 per cent of its quota from 68 per cent of its resources while the barony held *in capite* by Hugh de Bolbec used 72 per cent of its revenues to support 80 per cent of its quota. The results of low assessments are shown in the barony of Cainhoe and the Mandeville fee. The lord of Cainhoe used 35 per cent of his barony to supply 95 per cent of his quota. The Mandevilles had granted about half their barony in fiefs, but this supplied 173 per cent of their *servitium debitum*. If these figures are valid, the Mandevilles could have filled their quota by granting out 29 per cent of their barony, the lord of Cainhoe by granting 37 per cent, while the Bolbecs would have had to grant 90 per cent of their revenues.

In general then it seems probable that the barons who had not enfeoffed enough knights to fill their quotas were hindered by a lack of resources. Hugh de Bolbec apparently kept but one manor of his barony in demesne.[20] Even a petty baron needed a manor as his seat and as a support for his family and household. A greater one required, as I have suggested above, demesne manors to use as administrative centers and as sites for his residential or strategic castles. In short a baron was obliged to keep a reasonable portion of his fief in demesne. If the remainder would not support enough fees to fill his quota, he had to supply the deficiency with household knights. But there is evidence that policy as well as economic capacity entered into the question. On the basis of the figures used above the Aincurt and Chokes baronies were equally assessed —each could fill its quota by granting about 77 per cent of its

XLVIII, 9. Fitz Hamon barony: *Rotuli de dominibus*, pp. 26, 38-40, 44. Odell barony: *Bracton's note book* (ed. F. W. Maitland, London, 1887), III, 196. Mandeville barony: *Curia regis rolls*, VII, 110-111. Beauchamp barony: *Pipe roll 8 John* in Public Record Office.

[20] In speaking of the Bolbec barony I am considering only the lands held *in capite* of the crown, not the fief held from the Earls Giffard.

resources in knights' fees. Yet on the Aincurt barony 50 per cent of the revenue had been used to provide 72 per cent of the quota while on the Chokes fee 73 per cent of the revenues had been granted to enough knights to supply 95 per cent of the *servitium debitum*. In short the Aincurts had apparently deliberately conserved their demesne and continued to fill their quota with household knights.

It would be idle to speculate about the motives that might have moved barons like the Aincurts to preserve a large portion of their demesne. The question is interesting chiefly because of later developments. In the Angevin period when it became possible to turn the produce of demesnes into money income and the possession of knightly vassals grew less important, these barons had a decided advantage over their fellows. But it would be reckless to suggest that they foresaw this. One can merely state that some barons used restraint in granting knights' fees during the Norman period and that their successors profited from this policy.

The reasons which persuaded barons to enfeoff more knights than they owed the crown can be surmised with little difficulty. Traditional feudal ideas tended to measure a man's importance by the number of his vassals. In contemporary literature one of the most common methods of indicating a lord's position was to mention the number and quality of the noblemen who attended his court or rode in his train. Long after knightly vassals had lost much of their practical value to their lord they continued to serve as supports to his prestige. But in the Norman period there were more mundane reasons for extensive granting of fiefs. The barons wanted soldiers, and they had relatives and servants to furnish with the means of livelihood.

The pressure continually exerted on a baron to grant fiefs to his relatives and household knights needs no extensive discussion. Obviously a younger brother preferred a fief of his own to being supported in his brother's household. All household knights looked forward to the day when they would be rewarded with fiefs. Some of these demands could be met by the grant of heiresses, but they were not always available when needed. An examination of the returns of 1166 shows clearly the importance of fiefs granted to relatives. Hugh de Bolbec had about a quarter of all the fees granted by the Giffards, earls of Buckingham.[21] Robert de Albini held half the fees of his brother's barony of Belvoir.[22] These were unusual. More common were fiefs of one or two fees. Thus in the Arcy barony one relative had five fees, another three, and another one-quarter of a fee.[23] As the names give no clue to the fiefs granted to household knights, they cannot be distinguished in the inquest returns, but numerous charters attest the practice. Sometimes barons went to exceptional lengths to reward their men. Edward of Salisbury wished to reward a knight, but had no fief he was willing to bestow on him. He asked the bishop of Salisbury to grant the knight a fief. The bishop refused, but said he was willing to grant it to the baron so he could bestow it on the knight.[24] This whole matter was neatly stated by the archbishop of York in his return to the inquest of 1166—he owed twenty knights but had enfeoffed many more to care for relatives and men.[25]

In summary one can say that feudal tradition and his own needs tended to make a baron enfeoff as many knights as his resources would permit. The amazing fact is that so many lords enfeoffed fewer knights than they owed the crown. In most cases this was probably the result of a lack of sufficient resources to supply the necessary fiefs without reducing the demesne too greatly. But in some cases at least it seems to have sprung from a definite policy of preserving the baronial demesne and filling the quota by using household knights.

So far in this discussion of the military service owed by the baronies to the royal host we have assumed that each baron sent his quota of knights and that each of his mesne tenants contributed his proportionate share. But by the time of King Henry I this was not always the case. There is clear evidence that Henry sometimes permitted ecclesiastical barons to commute their service for a money payment.[26] Mr. Stenton asserts

[21] *Red book of the exchequer*, I, 312.   [22] *Ibid.*, p. 328.   [23] *Ibid.*, p. 386.
[24] *Bracton's note book*, III, 542.
[25] *Red book of the exchequer*, I, 412-413.
[26] Round, *Feudal England*, pp. 268-270; Chew, *Ecclesiastical tenants-in-chief*, pp. 38-39; Stenton, *English feudalism*, pp. 178-183.

that the same practice was followed in respect to lay baronies, but here the evidence is not quite conclusive. He cites a number of charters issued by lay barons which mention scutage as an obligation owed them by their tenants. The most definite of these is a charter by which Gilbert, earl of Pembroke, confirmed certain lands to Southwark Priory "free from all service except scutage, so that when it shall happen that a knight gives twenty shillings, that land shall give two shillings, and if a knight gives one marc, it shall give sixteen pence." [27] This certainly suggests that an authority superior to Earl Gilbert was fixing the rate, but it does not prove it conclusively. Mr. Stenton also points out that the returns to the inquest of 1166 show that by the death of Henry I a fair number of mesne fiefs had been created which owed the service of small fractions of a knight. He argues, and one can only agree with him, that the service of a twentieth part of a knight's fee must have been performed through a money payment.[28] In short the evidence presented by Mr. Stenton shows beyond a doubt that lay barons were accustomed to permit their tenants to commute their service by paying scutage. It does not, however, absolutely prove that the king granted this privilege to the barons themselves.

While I cannot find any conclusive evidence that Henry I took scutage in lieu of service from his lay barons, he may well have done so. The forces that eventually moved the crown to allow extensive commutation of the knight service owed it were already at work in his reign. The military problems facing the English king had changed greatly since the days of the Conqueror. William had organized the English military system to protect his new realm from Saxon revolt and invasions by Welsh, Scots, and Vikings. The latter were a particularly serious menace, and William doubted the ability of England to withstand them. Several times when he feared Viking invasion he reinforced his English levies with continental troops. The deaths of several English earls in Viking raids show that his fears were not groundless. On the other hand William felt no need for English military assistance on

[27] *Ibid.*, pp. 182-183. A marc was worth 13s 4d.
[28] *Ibid.*, pp. 185-187.

the continent. The Capetian monarchy was weak and its great vassals disunited. If the Norman duke had sufficient skill in feudal politics to keep his neighbors from combining against him, the military resources of his duchy were adequate for his needs. As the counts of Flanders and Blois were his firm allies, William never faced very serious military problems.

By the time of Henry I the situation had begun to change. There was no longer any danger of a Saxon rising. The Viking raids had ceased, and no invasion by them had materialized. The king of Scotland was Henry's relative by marriage and close ally. While the Welsh were troublesome at times, they could usually be controlled by the marcher lords. In short except in the case of baronial revolts Henry had no need for large forces of knights in England. But in France the Capetian monarchy was growing stronger under the vigorous hand of Louis VI, and the counts of Flanders and Anjou were usually Henry's foes. Hence it was on the continent that Henry I had the greatest need for military might.

This was even more true of his grandson Henry II. As the lord of a large continental empire his responsibilities were much greater than those of Henry I. He was duke of Normandy and count of Anjou and Maine in his own right. By his marriage to Eleanor of Aquitaine he was lord of that vast duchy. This great fief was a serious military liability. Its barons were strong, turbulent, and given to revolt. Moreover its traditional enemy was the powerful count of Toulouse. Then in the north the Capetian kings had grown far more dangerous. They had established their authority firmly in their duchy of France and had extended its borders. The marriage of Louis VII to Adele of Champagne secured for him the support of her potent brothers, Henry the Liberal, count of Champagne, Thibaut, count of Blois and Chartres, and Stephen, count of Sançerre. No longer was the Capetian domain surrounded by allies of the Norman duke. Thus Henry faced a dangerous foe along long frontiers and needed all the military resources he could muster. When he thought of the English military system, it was to consider how he could use it to further his aims on the continent.

The English feudal levy can have been of little value for

campaigns in France. It was difficult to transport it over the channel and get it to the scene of action before its term of service expired.[29] Moreover it was too large for effective use. The baronies that owed service to the crown contained over 6,500 knights' fees.[30] While the *servitium debitum* was lower, Round's figure of 5,000 is probably about right, the English feudal host would have formed an immense army by the standards of the twelfth century.[31] Then too it would have been unwise to denude England of knights by taking the entire levy to the continent. Moreover it seems likely that tactical considerations affected Henry's policy. Heavily armed knights were necessary to meet other knights in pitched battle in the open field, but such contests were a small part of the soldier's work. Henry needed troops to garrison his castles, besiege those of his foes, and ravage the enemy's lands. For these purposes knights were uneconomical—they cost too much in relation to their value. This was especially true when the introduction of the cross-bow gave the infantry an effective missile weapon.

As I have suggested, Henry I may well have found the English feudal levy unsatisfactory for continental service and turned to scutage as a solution to the problem. It seems fairly certain that this was the motive of Henry II. When he needed troops for service in his continental lands, he could permit a large part of the English baronage to pay scutage. With this money he could hire the soldiers he wanted, knights, Welsh spearmen, or Flemish cross-bowmen, for as long as he needed them and

[29] I can find no direct evidence as to the length of the term of service in England. Round points out that the ordinary pay of a knight in the twelfth century was eight pence per day and that a scutage of two marcs per fee would hire a knight for forty days. This is suggestive, but hardly conclusive. (*Feudal England*, pp. 271-272.) Professor Mitchell demonstrates that John and Henry III did not recognize the forty-day limit, but as his evidence comes from the period of reduced quotas, it seems dangerous to apply it to the earlier era. (S. K. Mitchell, *Studies in taxation under John and Henry III* [New Haven, 1914], pp. 309-311.) It would be perfectly conceivable that the forty-day limit had been recognized under the old *servitium debitum* and was abandoned when the quotas were reduced in the thirteenth century.

[30] This is my estimate based on the aid to marry the king's daughter of 1168. ("Pipe roll 14 Henry II," *Pipe roll society*, XII.) I have added the most nearly contemporary figures I can find for baronies missing in these accounts.

[31] *Feudal England*, p. 292.

could pay them. If for any reason he wished a large body of knights for a short time, he could demand the service owed him. The payment of scutage in place of serving in the host was a favor granted by the crown, not a baronial privilege.

During the first eleven years of his reign Henry II took five scutages. The first of these levies was confined to the ecclesiastical baronies, but the others covered the lay fiefs as well.[32] Hence one can say that from the very beginning of his reign Henry adopted the policy of allowing commutation of the service owed him. This practice was bound to change the king's attitude toward the quotas established by his predecessors. As long as the crown sought actual knights from the barons, it mattered little how many knights the barons had enfeoffed. The traditional quotas supplied more knights than the king could use. But he could use any amount of money. It must have annoyed Henry to be able to collect scutage on only sixty knights from the Mandeville barony when he felt certain that the Mandevilles had granted many more knights' fees. There is some evidence that this had occurred to Henry I when he took scutage from his ecclesiastical barons. The bishop of Ely paid a heavy fine to be freed from paying scutage on the fees he held in excess of his quota.[33] As Henry II was collecting from lay fiefs as well, the question interested him still more deeply. Moreover it is important to note that not only scutage was involved. The feudal aids were also levied on the basis of the number of knights owed to the crown. In short Henry had sound reasons for being dissatisfied with the old *servitium debitum*.

This dissatisfaction was probably Henry's chief motive in making the inquest of 1166. Let me repeat his questions. How many knights were enfeoffed on your barony before Henry I died? How many have been granted fiefs since? How many knights do you owe from your demesne? In the assessments for the aid to marry the king's daughter in 1168 the first and third items were added together as so many knights held *de veteri*. Then the second appeared as knights held *de novo*. Thus Walter de Aincurt had 24 knights enfeoffed before the death

---

[32] For a detailed discussion of these levies see *ibid.*, pp. 273-285.
[33] *Ibid.*, p. 268; *Pipe roll 31 Henry I (Record commission)*, p. 44.

of Henry I, had enfeoffed 5 since, and owed 11 from his demesne. His assessment appeared as 35 *de veteri* and 5 *de novo* or exactly the same as his old *servitium debitum* of 40.[34] Hugh Bigod, earl of Norfolk, had enfeoffed 125 knights before the death of Henry I and 37½ since although he owed but 60. His assessment appeared as 125 *de veteri* and 37½ *de novo*.[35] In short a baron who had enfeoffed more knights than he owed was asked to pay scutage on the whole number. The baron who had enfeoffed too few to fill his quota paid on the old *servitium debitum*.

I have never been able to formulate a satisfactory explanation for the distinction between old and new fees. The historian is always tempted to notice how an innovation worked out eventually and accept the result as the intention of the innovator. The use of this very dubious method furnishes the following explanation. Henry never really expected to get all he demanded and realized that he would have to come to a compromise with his barons. Hence he arranged the assessments so that the natural compromise would be reasonably satisfactory to the crown. This seems possible but not probable. It is more likely that the distinction grew out of the feeling that Stephen's reign had been a sort of interregnum. It had been a "time of war." Under Henry II's possessory assize of *ultima praesentatione* appointments to benefices made in Stephen's time could not be used as evidence of the possession of the right of presentation. It is quite possible that in the stress of civil war enfeoffments had been made under duress. At any rate it is clear that in the early years of Henry II's reign both king and barons considered the time of King Henry I as the most recent normal period. I suspect that the barons objected to paying scutage on fees granted during Stephen's reign, and that while Henry refused to accept the protest, he recognized it by making the distinction between old and new fees.

Whatever the reasons may have been for the form of assessment, the crown soon accepted a compromise. The aid to

---

[34] *Red book of the exchequer*, I, 380-381; "Pipe roll 14 Henry II," *Pipe roll society*, XII, 64.
[35] *Ibid.*, p. 22; *Red book of the exchequer*, I, 395-397.

marry the king's daughter of 1168 and the scutage of Ireland of 1172 were assessed on the full numbers of fees established by the inquest of 1166, but the barons showed a strong disinclination to pay on their new fees.[36]   By 1175 the sums owed on the old fees under these two levies were in general paid up, but many barons were still in arrears in respect to the fees held *de novo*.[37]   I am inclined to believe that about this time a formal compromise was reached.   The crown offered to relax its demands for scutage from the new fees if the barons would clear up the arrears.   Certainly most of these were paid off during 1176, and when the scutage of Wales was assessed in 1187, nothing was said about new fees except when a barony was in the king's hands.[38]   In short by 1187 a compromise *servitium debitum* had been established—the number of fees held *de veteri*.

On the whole this was a most equitable arrangement.   As the fees granted *de novo* were comparatively few in number, the crown obtained scutage payments from a large proportion of the knights enfeoffed in excess of the old *servitium debitum*. At the same time the inequalities of assessment among the baronies were reduced.   Let us look first at the effect on two fiefs which had been under-assessed.   The Bigod earls of Norfolk who had owed 60 knights were assessed in 1167 for 125 fees *de veteri* and 37½ *de novo*.   By the compromise their quota was doubled, but they retained the profits from their 37½ new fees.[39]   The Mandeville earls of Essex had also owed 60 knights.   They had enfeoffed 98 *de veteri* and 7 *de novo*.[40] A number of over-assessed fiefs gained by the new system.   The Aincurts had owed 40 knights.   They had created 24 fees before the death of Henry I, owed 11 knights from their demesne, and had granted 5 new fees.   Thus their compromise quota was 35.[41]   The Bayeux barony had owed 20 knights.   In 1167 it was assessed for 16½ fees *de veteri* and 4 *de novo* giving it a

[36] " Pipe rolls 14 and 18 Henry II," *Pipe roll society*, XII, XVIII.
[37] " Pipe roll 21 Henry II," *ibid.*, XXII.
[38] " Pipe rolls 22 and 33 Henry II," *ibid.*, XXV, XXXVII.
[39] " Pipe roll 2 Richard I," *ibid.*, XXXIX, 103.
[40] *Ibid.*, p. 109.
[41] " Pipe roll 33 Henry II," *ibid.*, XXXVII, 75.

new quota of 16½.[42]   Let me illustrate this change further by using the figures with which I have previously illustrated the inequality of the old assessments.   The Aincurts had used 56 per cent of their Domesday barony to provide 72 per cent of their old quota.   Under the compromise their fees furnished 83 per cent of the quota.   The Mandevilles had used 51 per cent of their fief to supply 173 per cent of their old *servitium debitum*.   Their fees under the new system came to 106 per cent of their quota.   In short the new basis of assessment did not remove the inequalities among the baronies, but it lessened them considerably.   The broad results of this change can best be seen by examining its effect on the quotas of the sixty-five baronies used as illustrations in a previous chapter.   Sixteen of these baronies had their quotas increased, fourteen had them decreased, while thirty-five continued to pay on the same number of knights.

This is not the place to attempt a history of scutage.   For our purpose it is sufficient to state that in general the compromise assessments established in 1187 remained in force as long as scutage continued to be collected.[43]   There were a number of reasons for this stability.   As we shall see below, the crown soon devised a new method of extracting money from barons who were unwilling to serve in the host—a method that did not supplant scutage but supplemented it.   Moreover while I cannot prove it statistically, I am inclined to doubt that the barons of England granted many knights' fees out of their demesne after 1166.   Feudalism continued to develop, but the process was vertical rather than horizontal—an increase in the complexity of the feudal hierarchy rather than an actual increase in the lands held by mesne tenants.   Finally by the end of John's reign the quotas on which scutage was based had become, as we shall see, purely fiscal figures with little or no

[42] " Pipe roll 2 Richard I," *ibid.*, XXXIX, 90.

[43] There were, of course, variations in a few individual cases, but a comparison between the assessments for the scutage of Wales in 1190 and those for the scutage of Brittany in 1230 will demonstrate the general stability of the quotas. (" Pipe rolls 2 Richard I and 14 Henry III," *Pipe roll society*, XXXIX, XLII.) Mr. John E. Morris has pointed out that the assessments under Edward I were the same as under Henry III. (*The Welsh wars of Edward I* [Oxford, 1901], p. 38.)

connection with the size of the contingent the king expected the baron to lead to the host.

It is impossible to determine exactly when a baron's quota of knights for actual service in the host began to differ radically from that on which he paid scutage. Presumably the Conqueror expected his barons to produce the knights called for by their *servitia debita.* By the middle of the thirteenth century it is clear that the crown recognized new service quotas much smaller than the old ones.[44] But the transition between these two sets of quotas is extremely difficult to trace. As I have suggested above, I doubt that the full feudal levy of England on the basis of the old *servitium debitum* was ever summoned for a campaign on the continent. It was too large, its term of service was too short, and its absence would have left England at the mercy of the Scots and Welsh. There were several courses open to the king. He could accept scutage and hire soldiers. He could summon a part of the levy for a longer period. He could accept a reduced contingent as the full service owed by the baron, allow it to serve its term at the baron's cost, and then keep it longer at the expense of the crown. Henry I accepted scutage. Henry II took scutage regularly, and at least once called for a fraction of the feudal levy.[45] But there is no evidence that either of these kings permitted a baron to perform his service by serving the proper period with a reduced contingent.

The history of the relations between crown and barons in respect to military service during the reigns of Richard I, John, and Henry III has been dealt with in detail by Mr. Mitchell.[46] I shall simply summarize his conclusions. Both Richard and John followed the practice of calling parts of the feudal levy. Both took scutage frequently. But they also developed new devices. As a rule they were unwilling to permit a tenant-in-chief to avoid service by simply paying scutage—they demanded a fine in addition to or in place of scutage. Finally it seems clear that when a baron chose to perform his obligations by serving in the host, these two kings frequently permitted

---

[44] Mitchell, *Studies in taxation*, pp. 247-248, 304.
[45] *Ibid.*, p. 302.
[46] *Ibid.* See entries in index under knights' service.

him to lead a contingent far smaller than his *servitium debitum*. While the total amount of evidence on this practice is impressive, it is difficult to find clear cases. To be certain one must know how many knights a baron led on an expedition and that the king recognized that this contingent was satisfactory by releasing the baron from any obligation to pay scutage or a fine. Both of these facts can be ascertained in very few cases, but they seem numerous enough to prove the existence of the practice. On the other hand there is no evidence that new service quotas had been established. In all probability a baron who wished to serve made a bargain with the crown in regard to the size of the contingent to be required from him.

In the Middle Ages when man's memory was not extensively aided by written documents the transition between practice and custom was usually brief. The fact that Richard and John had accepted the service of reduced contingents made it almost certain that before long the crown would be obliged to recognize new and smaller service quotas. While it is impossible to say precisely when this change began, it seems to have taken place between 1230 and 1250. In 1231 King Henry III made generous grants to his younger brother, Richard. He gave him the earldom of Cornwall for the service of 5 knights and the honor of Wallingford for the service of 3.[47] The earldom of Cornwall was assessed for scutage at 215 knights' fees and the honor of Wallingford at about 100. Hence it is clear that the royal government was thinking in terms of greatly reduced service quotas. Mr. Mitchell shows that by 1246 many barons considered that new *servitia debita* had been established for their fiefs, but it is not quite certain that the crown recognized them.[48] It is only in 1277 that it becomes apparent that both crown and barons have fully accepted the new quotas.[49]

One can only speculate as to why the crown was willing to accept the service of reduced contingents. Mr. Mitchell has shown conclusively that King John wanted more knights than his levy yielded, yet he allowed his barons to perform their service with small, sometimes very small, parts of their quotas.[50]

[47] *Calendar of charter rolls* (*Rolls series*), I, 139.
[48] *Studies in taxation*, pp. 244-248.
[49] *Parliamentary writs* (ed. F. Palgrave, *Record commission*), I, 197-213.
[50] *Studies in taxation*, pp. 308-312.

Mr. Mitchell points out that prices were rising during this period and that the equipment of a knight was growing more elaborate. Early in the reign of Henry II a knight could be hired for eight pence a day, but by John's time a knight's daily wage was about two shillings. While this rise in the cost of knights fully explains the crown's insistence on larger payments from barons who wished to commute their service, it does not demonstrate the necessity for a reduction in the quotas. Theoretically, rising prices should have meant larger money incomes for the feudal class, and as we shall see in a later chapter, such was the actual result. Only if the cost of knightly equipment rose faster than the general price level would the ability of the barons to produce their full quotas have been impaired. As a matter of fact I suspect this took place and is part of the explanation for the reduction in the quotas.

It seems probable, however, that another reason for the change in quotas was the difficulty of extracting heavier service from the mesne tenants. When the cost of knights rose, the barons were caught in a trap. In the early twelfth century a summons to the host was no serious problem for a baron. If he chose to serve, he led his contingent of vassals to the army. If he had enfeoffed more knights than he owed, he could collect scutage from the extra ones. In case a knight was unwilling to follow him, the knight's scutage would pay for a substitute. If the king permitted the baron to avoid service by paying scutage, he collected it at the same rate from his tenants. If he had more fees than he owed, he made a profit. The establishment of the new quotas after the inquest of 1166 reduced the profit the baron could make from the knights enfeoffed in excess of his old *servitium debitum*, but it did not alter the essential fact that the scutage he received equalled his own costs. As a result it made little difference to a baron whether a tenant served or paid scutage, and bit by bit the mesne tenants began to feel that paying scutage fulfilled their obligations to the baron. Then came the rise in the cost of knights. The crown demanded service or a fine far in excess of the scutage due from the barony. The only solution for the baron was to insist on having his tenants serve in the more costly equipment of the day or pay higher commutation. While we have no information about the details of the contest, it is clear that the barons were unable to do either. They could collect the customary scutage and nothing more. Hence any additional cost involved in satisfying the crown had to come from the revenues of their demesnes.

The inability of the barons to force their tenants to serve with adequate equipment or to pay commutation at a rate high enough to enable them to hire substitutes was in part at least the result of the crown's policy. By the time of King John and probably before, the king was limiting the power of the barons to distrain their tenants. The establishment of withername as a plea of the crown gave the sheriff control over feudal discipline. But I doubt that this royal policy was the basic difficulty. The growth of feudalism vertically, the extension of sub-infeudation, was of great importance. While the feudal hierarchy consisted of king, barons, and mesne tenants, it was comparatively easy for the baron to distrain his vassals by seizing their chattels. But when one or two lords stood between the baron and the actual holder of the land it was far more difficult—each lord had to be able to distrain his vassal effectively.[51] Finally I suspect that the fundamental barrier to any increase in the service due from the baron's vassals was the inequality in value of the knights' fees. It is clear that even when the original grants were made there was little uniformity. Then as time went on some estates rose in value far more than others and hence exaggerated the inequalities. Presumably the scutage of the twelfth century, ten shillings, one marc, twenty shillings, or two marcs per fee, was light enough so that all the fees except the recognized small fees of Mortain could pay it. But as we have seen the daily wage of a knight rose from eight pence to two shillings between the middle of the twelfth century and the time of John. If the scutage payments were to be sufficient, they would have had to be tripled. I am sure that it would have been impossible to collect scutages of three pounds or six marcs. Some rich fees could have borne the burden, but others would have found it ruinous.

To summarize the situation one can say that the cost of

[51] A case of 1214 illustrates this situation very well. *Curia regis rolls*, VII, 184.

knightly equipment had risen faster than the income from land. This in itself would probably have forced the crown to make some reduction in service quotas. But the situation was aggravated by other circumstances. Royal policy and the development of sub-enfeoffment made it difficult for the barons to exert effective pressure on their tenants. Moreover the basic unit of the feudal system, the knight's fee, had lost all economic reality. Once it had been some lord's estimate of the income required to support a knight, but it had become a mere unit of assessment. The crown had no choice but to collect what service or commutation it could from its direct vassals, the barons, and raise in other ways the money required to hire additional troops. Hidages, carucages, and income and property taxes could be used to avoid the obsolete assessment by knights' fees.

Unfortunately these reasons for reducing the baronial service quotas are entirely inadequate to explain the extent to which the process was carried. The total service owed the crown was reduced from some 6,500 knights to about 375.[52] Under the new system most baronies had quotas of two or three knights. Only a few very great lords were expected to furnish larger contingents. The bishop of Durham appears to have been the only baron who had a quota of ten knights for a single barony. Gilbert de Clare owed ten knights but he held a number of fiefs, the honors of Gloucester and Clare, one-half the honor of Giffard, and a share of the Marshal estates. The Earl Warren owed seven knights for his ancient barony, Lewes, Reigate, Castle Acre, and Connisborough, and four more for Stamford and Graham. But these were rare exceptions. The earldom of Warwick had a quota of three and one-half—the half knight being provided by furnishing a light-armed horseman. The baronies of Okehampton and Mandeville of Essex owed three knights each. Even the earldom of Cornwall had been reduced from the quota of five knights provided in the grant of 1231 to one of two.[53]

A few examples will suffice to show the essential absence of any connection between the old quotas and the new. The lands of Gilbert de Clare must have had a scutage assessment of well

[52] Morris, *Welsh wars of Edward I*, p. 45.
[53] *Parliamentary writs*, I, 197-213.

over 450 knights.   Thus he owed one knight for forty-five.
The earl of Cornwall owed one for over a hundred.   On the
other hand the Balon barony and Peter de la Mare each owed
one knight for fiefs assessed at one fee.   The Berkeley barony
which paid scutage on five fees, the barony of Dunster paying
on forty-one, and the honor of Okehampton paying on ninety-
two each had a quota of three knights.

In short the crown abandoned entirely the feudal military
system set up by the Conqueror and established a new one.   In
doing so it seems to have gone back to the most elemental feature of feudalism—the personal service owed by a vassal to his
lord.   The king demanded the personal service of all who held
lands from him directly whether as barons, as minor tenants-
in-chief, or as mesne tenants of escheated baronies.   The richer
barons were expected to bring additional knights.   Hence the
minor tenants-in-chief and tenants *de honore* whose scutage
assessments had been one or two fees received little reduction
in their service.   The great lords were granted very large
ones.   The new quotas were essentially as arbitrary and un-
equal as the old, but as far as the barons were concerned they
were so small that it made little difference.   Thus the baronies
of Pleshy and Odell which had been assessed at 98 and 27
fees respectively each owed 3 knights.   But the lord of Odell
could collect £27 from his tenants when the scutage rate was
twenty shillings and hence had £9 to support each of his
knights.   This was more than twice the amount required to
hire a knight at four shillings a day for forty days.   Even if
the baron found it difficult to collect his scutage, if he were
reasonably prosperous he could support his quota from his
demesne.   Only very poverty-stricken barons who could not
collect from their tenants were unable to meet their obligations.

In connection with this question of the ability of the barons
to furnish their contingents to the host it is interesting to notice
that an examination of the annual value of the baronies seems
to explain some of the apparent inequalities in the new quotas.
I have pointed out that the baronies of Berkeley and Okehampton, which had been assessed at five and ninety-two fees respectively, each had quotas of three knights.   The lords of these

fiefs each enjoyed an annual income of about £500.[54] The earl of Cornwall held the honor of Wallingford for the service of three knights and the honor of Knaresborough for that of two. Wallingford had been assessed at one hundred fees and Knaresborough at three, but the latter was worth about £500 while Wallingford yielded less than £300.[55] I do not wish to suggest that the new quotas bore a direct relation to the annual revenues of the baronies. The barony of Odell, which was worth about £100, also owed three knights.[56] I simply believe that annual value may have been one of the things taken into account in setting the quotas.

Let us attempt to sum up the results of our discussion of this highly intriguing subject. Political and economic conditions obliged the English kings to make some reduction in the number of knights they demanded from their barons. The cost of a knight had increased threefold. While the returns from land had been rising as well, the barons benefited only in respect to their demesne as they were unable to exact heavier service from their tenants. Thus a reduction of service quotas by two-thirds may have been necessary. But as Morris points out the service owed in Edward I's day was only one-eighteenth of that due to his great-grandfather Henry II.[57] The only explanation that I can offer for this is that it represented a magnificent baronial victory in a struggle the details of which have been lost to us. The barons obtained the reduction of their military obligations to the crown to a point where they entailed some personal inconvenience but no financial burden. As the king still obtained his heavy cavalry through the feudal levy, the barons retained their control over his military policy. The money which would supply him with an adequate army had to be raised through other means. The fact that types of soldiers other than heavy cavalry were becoming increasingly important does not lessen the triumph of the barons in sliding

---

[54] *Calendar of inquisitions post mortem* (*Rolls series*), XII, 195; *Calendar of close rolls, 1288-1296* (*Rolls series*), p. 236.

[55] *Calendar of patent rolls, 1317-1321* (*Rolls series*), p. 115; *ibid.*, 1327-1330, p. 68.

[56] *Bracton's note book*, III, 196.

[57] *Welsh wars of Edward I*, p. 45.

out of their obligations. It may, however, be part of the explanation of their success.

It is important to notice the effect of these developments on fundamental feudal relationships. In the eleventh century the baron as the king's vassal was bound to follow his lord to war, and the resources of his fief were primarily devoted to furnishing the contingent of knights that he led to the host. As long as the feudal levy was used, that is until 1327, the personal obligation of the baron remained intact, but the reduction in service quotas that marked the late twelfth and early thirteenth century meant that the cost of furnishing his contingent would be a comparatively light tax on his barony. Once the feudal levy had lapsed, the obligation of the barons to perform feudal military service to the crown was at an end. As military service was the fundamental element of feudalism, it seems to me that after its disappearance the relationship between king and barons cannot be called feudal.

Before leaving the subject of the military obligations of the barons toward the crown, something must be said about the guard duty owed at the king's castles.[58] The system of castle-guard established at the time of the Conquest became obsolete even sooner than did the feudal host. Once the danger of Viking invasions and Anglo-Saxon revolts had passed, the strong permanent garrisons provided for such fortresses as Norwich, Windsor, Rockingham, and Northampton became unnecessary. Henry I released the bishop of Ely from the castle-guard duty owed to Norwich.[59] Stephen granted a similar favor to Bury St. Edmunds, but this was apparently revoked by his successor.[60] If the crown could collect money in place of the service for which it had no real need, it was only too glad to do so. A charter of Richard I for the abbey of Peterborough suggests that Henry I had allowed the abbey's knights

[58] For general discussions of this subject see J. H. Round, "Castle-guard," *Archaeological journal*, LIX (1902), pp. 144-159; Stenton, *English feudalism*, pp. 190-215; Painter, "Castle-guard," *American historical review*, XL (1935), pp. 450-459.

[59] *Monasticon Anglicanum* (ed. William Dugdale, London, 1846), I, 482; *Pipe roll 31 Henry I*, p. 44.

[60] *Feudal documents from the abbey of Bury St. Edmunds* (ed. D. C. Douglas, London, 1932), pp. 83-84, 99.

to commute their castle-guard service in time of peace.[61] Certainly by the time of Henry II such commutation was common. Apparently for a time the crown accepted money in time of peace, but demanded service in time of war. But with the appearance of mercenary soldiers, especially cross-bowmen, the need for knights even in time of war grew less. The cross-bowman was far more effective for garrison duty than the knight. Then too the need for garrisons in English castles outside the Welsh and Scots marches usually resulted from civil war, and in such a contest the loyalty of the feudal garrisons was often dubious. King John entrusted his castles to mercenary troops led by such captains as Faulkes de Bréauté, Philip Marc, and Peter de Maulay. A passage in *Magna Carta* suggests that he tried to force the commutation of castle-guard service—" no constable shall distrain any knight to give money for castle-guard if he wishes to perform his tour of duty." [62]

It is easy to understand why the barons and their tenants often preferred to perform their castle-guard service. In time of peace a tour of duty in a royal castle must have been a sociable and pleasant affair. Unless the commutation rate was extremely low, it was cheaper to serve. The rates were apparently set by individual bargains between the barons and the crown. They varied from castle to castle and even between different baronies serving at the same castle. The rate at Dover and Windsor was twenty shillings a year per fee. At Rochester it was twelve shillings. At Rockingham the barony of Wardon paid at five shillings a fee, that of Odell at six shillings, and the tenants of the abbey of Peterborough at four shillings. The rates at Norwich are obscure, but they apparently varied between six and seven shillings per fee.[63] If one takes the very high figure of £20 a year as the value of a fee, the Dover and Windsor commutation rates would be a 5 per cent tax. As the average value of a fee was probably closer to £10, it is easy to see why the knights preferred to serve. Nevertheless while there is evidence that castle-guard service in these royal castles was occasionally performed during the reign of Henry

[61] *Calendar of charter rolls,* IV, 277.
[62] *Magna carta,* c. 29.
[63] Painter, " Castle-guard," pp. 455-457.

III, it is clear that it soon became unusual.[64]   By the second
half of the thirteenth century the services seem to have been
generally commuted, and the castle-guard payments were considered as a rent pertaining to the castle.[65]   They continued as a
burden on the manors which had owed service long after
scutage had passed into oblivion.[66]

Although military service was the basic element of feudalism,
it was not the only obligation owed by a vassal to his lord.
Court service, relief, aids, and the lord's rights of custody and
marriage were important in every feudal state.   Court service
is peculiarly important to our study.   It provides the temporal
bridge which connects the tenurial barons of the early Middle
Ages with the Parliamentary barons of later days.   Unfortunately little or nothing is known about the court service owed
to the English kings by their vassals during the eleventh and
twelfth centuries.   The Norman and early Angevin monarchs
held meetings of the full *curia regis*, but we know little about
the composition of this body.   It was always described in
vague terms.   Thus the Constitutions of Clarendon are stated to
have been published before " archbishops, bishops, clerks, earls,
barons, and magnates."   Further on in the same document
reference is made to " archbishops, bishops, earls, barons, and
the more noble and ancient men of the realm." [67]   In short the
full *curia regis* or great council clearly included the ecclesiastical and lay potentates, archbishops, bishops, earls, and barons.
Then some vague phrase left the king a free hand in choosing
the rest of the assembly.   The names given in the Constitutions

[64] For instance the abbot of Abingdon forced his knights to perform their
service in Windsor under the Montfortian captain John fitz John.   E. F. Jacob,
Studies in the period of baronial reform and rebellion, 1258-1267 (Oxford,
1925), pp. 295-296.

[65] As early as 1230 it seems to have been assumed that the service due.at
Windsor would be in the form of money.   " Pipe roll 14 Henry III," *Pipe roll
society*, XLII, 5.

[66] In 1347 the chief manor of the Louvain fief owed £10 a year to Windsor—
castle-guard originally due from the whole barony. (*Calendar of inquisitions
post mortem*, IX, 10.) There are many similar entries in the *Calendar of inquisitions post mortem*.   Round mentions a late seventeeth-century list of ward
rents due at Windsor. (" Castle-guard," pp. 157-158.)

[67] William Stubbs, *Select charters and other illustrations of English constitutional history* (Oxford, 1895), p. 137.

of Clarendon indicate that the additions were royal officials like Alan de Neville and John Marshal.

The fourteenth chapter of *Magna Carta* provides for an assembly that was to be consulted before a scutage or extraordinary aid could be levied. Two distinct methods were to be used to summon this body. Archbishops, bishops, abbots, earls, and "major barons" were to receive individual writs of summons. Then the sheriffs were to summon, presumably by reading the writs in the shire courts, "all those who hold of us in chief." Apparently this would include tenants by serjeantry and cornage. The status of tenants-in-chief *de honore* is left in doubt. Although this chapter makes no distinction between them and those holding *de corone*, the forty-third chapter of the charter seems to exempt the former from court service to the crown.

It is extremely difficult to estimate the number of tenants-in-chief of the crown. The index of tenants *in capite* in the Record Commission's edition of *Domesday Book* contains some seven hundred. But this does not include the king's thanes and ministers. The index compiled by Ellis has about thirteen hundred names. Unfortunately for my purpose it includes men holding in the boroughs. Perhaps one thousand would be about right for the number of tenants-in-chief in 1086. The inquests of John's reign show about five hundred tenants by knight service and about three hundred by serjeantry and cornage. In 1215 the king's tenants *de honore* numbered about four hundred.[68] In short it appears that the assembly provided for by this charter would have numbered about eight hundred if tenants *de honore* were excluded and about twelve hundred if they were included. Either figure would make a body too large and unwieldy for great usefulness. Moreover it would be based on an essentially artificial foundation—tenure in chief of the king. Many tenants-in-chief were insignificant persons, far inferior in social and political status to the great mesne lords who had no place in this assembly.

It is extremely difficult to determine what this conception of

[68] *Domesday book*, III, 519-541; Henry Ellis, *A general introduction to Domesday Book* (*Record commission*), I, 363-515; *Red book of the exchequer*, II, 451-624.

an assembly represented. Was it the traditional full *curia regis* or Great Council of the Norman and early Angevin kings or an innovation invented by the rebellious barons? The fact that it was based on a sound feudal principle, the right and duty of a vassal to attend his lord's court, tempts one to believe that this was a traditional assembly. But in general feudal theory began to grow logical and orderly in the late twelfth and early thirteenth centuries. The Norman and early Angevin kings were far more likely to consider political reality than feudal theory. To call an important mesne tenant to their councils under some such vague term as "one of the more noble men of the realm" was far more to the point than summoning a crowd of petty tenants-in-chief. As there is no evidence that an assembly like the one described in *Magna Carta* was ever summoned either before or after 1215 and the chapter providing for it did not appear in later issues of the charter, I am forced to the conclusion that this body was an abortive innovation.

One can only speculate as to the reasons for this attempt at innovation. The rebel barons may have wished to deprive the king of all discretion as to who should be summoned by establishing a clear tenurial basis for membership. An obvious solution would have been to make it an assembly of tenants by barony, but this would have ruled out some important royal officials and many of the barons' most ardent supporters. At least two of the twenty-five "barons" chosen to enforce *Magna Carta* were not tenants by barony.[69] But it was difficult to find a middle ground between tenants by barony and all tenants-in-chief. Hence the barons, who probably had little idea how many there were, included all tenants-in-chief. The result was an assembly of all the direct vassals of the king—an enlarged replica of a baronial *curia*.

Although the assembly provided for by the fourteenth chapter of *Magna Carta* fell into the oblivion it deserved, the basic idea that the king should consult a Great Council on certain matters grew stronger as time went on. John promised not to

---

[69] Roger de Montbegon's only tenure in chief *de corone* was some land in Cumberland held by cornage. William de Huntingfield was not a tenant-in-chief *de corone*.

4

levy scutages or extraordinary aids without the consent of this
body. While the twelfth chapter which contains this promise
was excluded from the reissues of the charter, the crown in
general seems to have adhered to it in practice. This is not
the place to examine the origins of Parliamentary authority.
We are interested in the assembly rather than in its powers.
Henry III and the first three Edwards held assemblies of their
vassals either as Great Councils or as part of Parliaments. Our
concern is to attempt to discover the relationship in respect to
composition between these bodies and the one described in
Magna Carta.

Our knowledge of the composition of Great Councils and
Parliaments is obtained from the lists of men summoned to
the meetings. A few such lists have been preserved from the
reign of Henry III, but they become numerous only after the
accession of Edward I.[70] Many scholars have studied these
lists and compared them with the system mentioned in *Magna
Carta*. The accepted view seems to be that if the general summons of all tenants-in-chief by the sheriffs was ever practiced,
it ceased before our series of lists begins. The non-baronial
tenants-in-chief eventually formed part of the electorate that
chose the knights of the shire. Those who held by barony,
that is the "-major barons" of *Magna Carta*, were liable to be
summoned. From their ranks the crown selected the men to
be called to a particular meeting.[71]

The belief that the " major barons " of *Magna Carta* can be
identified with tenants by barony rests on a passage in the
Dialogue of the exchequer. There all tenants holding in chief
de corone are described as major and minor barons.[72] As we
know that many tenants-in-chief *de corone* did not hold by
barony, one might argue that they must be the minor barons.
But it seems difficult to understand why the *Dialogue* should
describe as " minor barons " men who were not barons at all.
I can find no other text that calls all tenants-in-chief barons.

[70] *Reports from the lords' committee touching the dignity of a peer of the
realm*, III, IV.

[71] L. O. Pike, *A constitutional history of the house of lords* (London, 1894),
pp. 93-94.

[72] *Dialogus de scaccario*, p. 134.

Henry I in his charter of liberties speaks of " anyone of my earls, barons, or others who hold of me." I suspect that the author of the *Dialogue* was simply trying to justify the demanding of arbitrary relief from all tenants-in-chief *de corone* and to confine the privilege of paying relief at 100s a fee to tenants *de honore*. Certainly I can see no justification for using this passage to prove that the " major barons " of *Magna Carta* meant all tenants by barony.

There seems to be no sound reason for refusing to give the term " major barons " as used in *Magna Carta* its natural meaning—the more important barons. Men of comparatively modest position held by baronial tenure. The Kilpeks had only one knight's fee *in capite* while the Sudleys had but three. Presumably men like this would not receive individual summonses but would be included in the general summons by the sheriffs. In short the term " major barons " had no tenurial meaning. This leads to the conclusion that under the system provided for by *Magna Carta* tenure by barony had no connection with the obligation or right to attend the Great Council except in so far as all tenants by barony were tenants-in-chief of the king.

Let us now turn to the lists of men summoned during the reigns of Henry III and the three Edwards. If the accepted theory is correct, all of these men should be tenants by barony. Hence it is necessary to obtain a list of tenurial barons and compare it with the lists of men summoned. For the reign of Henry III a fairly good list of tenurial barons can be made by taking those entered on the rolls as paying baronial relief. For the later reigns I have used the *Inquisitions post mortem* to learn whether or not a man held a barony or a fragment of one divided among heiresses. The resulting list cannot be entirely accurate. As we shall see in detail when considering relief, the crown itself was none too certain as to who were its barons by tenure. In 1166 there were two Scalariis baronies each representing half of the family's Domesday fief. Under Henry III we find the lord of one of these paying relief as a baron while the other paid as a tenant by knight service.[73] Again we find

---

[73] *Red book of the exchequer*, I, 367-370; *Excerpta ex rotulis finium in turri Londinensi asservatis Henrico tertio rege* (ed. Charles Roberts, *Record commission*), I, 69, 93.

the Kimes, insignificant tenants-in-chief but very great mesne lords, paying relief as barons while some of the holders of impoverished small baronies were treated as tenants by knight service.[74]   In short there was a wide border where the nature of tenure is hard to determine.   But beyond this border region were many tenants-in-chief who could not by any stretch of the imagination be called tenurial barons.   If men of this sort were summoned, the accepted theory must fall.

The first list that I wish to examine is that of the men summoned to the Montfortian Parliament of 1265.[75]   There we find the names of Ralph Basset of Drayton, Geoffrey de Lucy, and Walter de Coleville.   Ralph Basset held a small estate from the crown by serjeantry, another by a money rent, and perhaps a manor by knight service as of the honor of Chokes. The rest of his extensive lands were held of various baronies.[76] Ralph Basset was a man of importance, but he was certainly not a baron by tenure.   Geoffrey de Lucy held a Kentish manor of the crown by gavelkind.   The rest of his lands were mesne tenancies.[77]   It would be most difficult to argue that he was a baron by tenure.   Walter de Coleville does not seem to have been a tenant-in-chief.   His most important estate, Castle Bytham, was held of the count of Aumale.[78]

Let us turn to those summoned to the Model Parliament of 1295.[79]   We find the names of Brian fitz Alan, Nicholas de Meynil, Ely de Albini, and Henry Hose.   Brian fitz Alan was an important tenant of the honor of Richmond.[80]   Nicholas de Meynil held a fief of the archbishop of Canterbury.[81]   Ely de

---

[74] The Kimes held some 15 fees of the earls of Chester and about 13 from other barons. They held 1½ or 2 fees in chief of the crown. Under Henry III they paid relief as barons. (*Ibid.*, pp. 43, 382. For the family fiefs see William Farrer, *Honors and knights' fees,* [London, 1924], II, 118-126.) The baronies of Roger de Beauchamp of Eaton, Mathew de Louvain, and the two Chauncy lines paid relief as ordinary tenures by knight service. (*Excerpta ex rotulis finium,* I, 76, 141, 173, 182, 207, 321.)

[75] *Reports touching the dignity of a peer,* III, 33-34.

[76] *Calendar of inquisitions post mortem,* VIII, 326-330.

[77] *Ibid.*, II, 312-315.

[78] *Ibid.*, II, 136-137.

[79] *Reports touching the dignity of a peer,* III, 64-66.

[80] The inquisitions covering his lands are incomplete, but they contain no indication that he held lands outside Richmondshire.

[81] *Calendar of inquisitions post mortem,* III, 427-430.

Albini held about two fees in chief and some lands of the barony of Belvoir.[82]   Henry Hose had one-half fee held *in capite*. While he possessed several mesne tenancies, he owed his position to his fief of Herting held of the honor of Arundel.[83]   It seems to me completely fantastic to argue that any of these men were barons by tenure.

In addition to these men who were called to the parliaments of 1265 and 1295 let me cite a few more who were summoned fairly regularly during the reigns of Edward I and Edward II. Henry Tyeis was not even a tenant-in-chief except through the fee he held of the escheated honor of Aumale.[84]   William de Cantilupe does not seem to have been even a tenant *in capite de honore*.[85]   John de Thorp held an estate in chief by socage, but the rest of his lands were mesne fiefs.[86]   Ralph Pipard, John Lovel of Tichmersh, and John ap Adam each held about one knight's fee in chief, but they cannot by any stretch of the imagination be called barons by tenure.[87]

In his *A constitutional history of the house of Lords* Mr. Pike states: " It would be very difficult to show that any of the laymen beneath the rank of Earl who were called to advise the King in the reign either of Henry III or of Edward I did not hold a barony or part of a barony." [88]   Now *Inquisitions post mortem* are often not complete. It is possible that some of the men mentioned above may have held a fraction of a barony, but I am certain that most of them did not.   In short the accepted theory as advanced by Mr. Pike seems to me untenable.

I am convinced that there was no connection between tenure by barony and being summoned to the Great Council or to Parliament.   There is some additional evidence to support this view.   In the year 1300 the magnates of a Parliament held by Edward I at Lincoln sent a letter to the pope.   In this letter each man's name is given in a formal style with the name of his chief seat.[89]   Thus we have Henry of Lancaster, lord of Monmouth, and Edmund de Mortimer, lord of Wigmore.   It is

---

[82] *Ibid.*, IV, 221-222.
[83] *Ibid.*, VII, 332-333.
[84] *Ibid.*, V, 26-27.
[85] *Ibid.*, V, 52-54.
[86] *Ibid.*, VI, 295-297.
[87] *Ibid.*, V, 97-98, 141-142, 208-209.
[88] Pike, *A constitutional history of the house of lords*, p. 94.
[89] *Reports touching the dignity of a peer*, III, 125-127.

interesting to notice that many of these men took their designations from estates that were not held *in capite*. Let me cite William de Cantilupe, lord of Ravensthorp, Brian fitz Alan, lord of Bedale, Henry Tyeis, lord of Chilton, Henry Tresgoz, lord of Goring, and Ralph Pipard, lord of Linford.[90] All these estates were mesne fiefs and, with the possible exception of Bedale, were not even held of baronies in the hands of the crown. This seems to me to indicate a complete lack of any pretense that these men were tenurial barons.

Finally Mr. Pike himself cites evidence to show that as late as the reign of Edward III the fact that a man was summoned to Parliament did not prove his right to the legal privileges of a baron. To obtain these he had to demonstrate that he was a baron by tenure.[91] The famous Furnival case supports this point. Thomas de Furnival, who was regularly summoned to Parliament, denied that he was a baron by tenure, and an inquisition found his contention correct. Both Thomas and the inquisition were wrong—as the heir of one of the Lovetot lines he was a tenurial baron even though his chief seat, Sheffield, may not have been held by barony.[92] Still the fact that he could make such a claim and have an inquisition support it seems to show that there was no connection between barony by tenure and summons to Parliament.

The only testimony I can find that seems to contradict this view is in the *Modus tenendi parliamenti*.[93] It states that those who hold *per comitatum vel baroniam* should be summoned *ratione huiusmodi tenurae*. Later it says, " All earls and barons and their peers ought to be summoned and ought to attend, that is those who have lands and revenues to the value of an earldom or a whole barony, that is (for the value of an earldom) twenty knights' fees, each one computed at £20, that makes £400 in all, or for the value of a whole barony thirteen and one-third knights' fees, each one computed at £20, that

---

[90] Ravensthorp was held of the Wakes as of the old Stutville barony. Bedale was a fief of the honor of Richmond. Chilton was held of the honor of Wallingford and Goring of the honor of Arundel. Linford was held of the De Vere earls of Oxford as of the barony of Bolebec.

[91] *Constitutional history of the house of lords*, p. 95.

[92] *Reports touching the dignity of a peer*, II, 235.

[93] Stubbs, *Select charters*, pp. 502-513.

makes in all 400 marcs; and no lesser laymen ought to be summoned nor come to parliament *ratione tenurae suae. . . .*"

This passage is, of course, completely unrealistic. Tenure by barony was not based on the possession of a certain number of knights' fees nor yet on yearly income. A man could have twenty fees held of him and derive little income from them. Few indeed were the earls who had twenty fees in demesne. The author was an antiquarian and not a very able one. He wished to connect tenure by barony with summons to Parliament, yet he knew that men who were not tenurial barons were summoned. Hence the phrase "and their peers." He also knew that tenurial barony had been connected in some way with the possession of knights' fees. But in his day a man's power depended largely on his money income. The result is fascinating. He took the relief for a knight's fee and divided it into those for earldoms and baronies. This gave him twenty fees for an earl and thirteen and one-third for a baron. Then he assigned each fee the £20 of annual revenue that made its holder obliged to become a knight. In short the statements of the author have no value as evidence, but his frame of reference does. Tenurial barony was to him ancient and vague. In his world political position depended on money income.

Let me now advance my account of the transition from the assembly of *Magna Carta* to those held by Henry III and the three Edwards. The general summons of tenants-in-chief through the sheriffs was never used. It would have produced a hopelessly large and unwieldy body. The Great Council consisted of men summoned by individual writs—the great men, the prelates, earls, and *majores barones*. But in selecting these men the crown was not limited by tenurial considerations. Probably in theory the king could call only tenants-in-chief, but even this restriction seems to have been little observed in practice. In theory he could summon individuals from all the classes mentioned in *Magna Carta*, and in practice he called whomever he pleased.

As we shall see when we examine the subject of baronial resources, tenure by barony had lost much of its importance by the time of *Magna Carta* and declined steadily in significance thereafter. The baron had primarily owed his importance to his knightly vassals, to the number of knights' fees held of him. But as the services owed by the mesne tenants became more and more a matter of fixed money payments and the comparative value of those payments became less as incomes and prices rose, the importance of holding knights' fees declined. A man who held in demesne five rich manors from five different lords was richer than the baron who had one manor in demesne and the service of a score of fees. The king chose his advisers among the rich and powerful. As barony by tenure had ceased to be closely connected with wealth and power, it was ignored.

To sum up, the weight of evidence shows that a baron owed no court service beyond that expected from any tenant-in-chief of the crown. Tenure by barony implied no special obligations or rights in this respect. This does not mean that tenurial barons did not throughout our period form the major part of the Great Council. They were the magnates, the lords of castles and knightly vassals, the men of political importance. When money income began to replace castles and vassals as the basis of power, the tenurial barons as a class held their place. Money came from franchises, towns, and manors, and they possessed these sources of wealth. As long as a tenurial barony of any importance remained intact, its lord was likely to be a Parliamentary baron. As time went on the old baronies escheated and were regranted in parcels, became minutely sub-divided among heiresses, or were alienated by their lords. By the time the hereditary Parliamentary baronage was well established, few tenurial baronies remained intact or even in portions large enough to be of much significance. In fact barony by tenure seems to have been forgotten between the late fourteenth century and its revival by Tudor and Stuart antiquarians.

The obligation of a baron to pay relief to the crown when he inherited his fief has received far too little attention from historians. Military service as the basis of the feudal system has been of prime interest to the student of feudalism. The duty or right to attend Great Councils and Parliaments attracts the attention of the constitutional historian. But one who wishes to understand the political history of the early Angevin period must not neglect relief. It was, I believe, one of the chief instruments by which the crown controlled the barons.

Even when relief came at normal intervals it was a serious drain on the resources of a barony. When a rapid succession of deaths occurred, it could be ruinous. *Magna Carta* fixed the relief due from a barony at £100.[94] I have made a list of forty-one baronies for which I can establish with some certainty the revenue during the late twelfth and early thirteenth centuries. Three of these gave their lords incomes of over £500, three between £300 and £400, five between £200 and £300, fourteen between £100 and £200, and sixteen less than £100. Thus thirty of these forty-one baronies would have required a whole year's income at least to pay relief on the scale established by *Magna Carta*.

The sum of £100 set by *Magna Carta* as the relief due from a barony represented simply a baronial attempt to define the " reasonable relief " required by feudal custom. It was an episode in a long struggle between the English kings and their vassals. The interests of the crown demanded that relief should be arbitrary. On the financial side this enabled the king to adjust the amount to the value of the barony—in short to charge all the traffic would bear. Moreover it permitted him to reward the loyal with low reliefs and punish the disaffected with high ones. The barons, on the other hand, naturally wanted fixed relief at the lowest possible rate.

The *Leis Willelmi* state the reliefs due from earls, barons, and rear-vassals in terms of horses and arms. In the case of the last it provides as an alternative the payment of 100 shillings in money.[95] While the payment of relief in military equipment may have been the practice in the Conqueror's day, it seems more likely that this was an antiquarian relic of a distant feudal past. Certainly William II did not accept fixed relief in horses and arms. The second paragraph of the charter of liberties of Henry I states: " If any one of my earls, barons, or other tenants-in-chief die, his heir will not ransom his land as he did in the time of my brother but shall pay a just and legitimate relief." [96] Clearly William Rufus had been collecting arbitrary reliefs which the barons considered too high. Un-

---

[94] *Magna carta*, c. 2.

[95] Liebermann, *Gesetze der Angelsachsen*, I, 507.

[96] *Charter of liberties*, c. 2.

fortunately we do not know what either Henry I or his barons meant by "reasonable." The evidence we have as to Henry's practice indicates that the question worried him very little and that he continued to exact arbitrary reliefs. The pipe roll of 1135 shows Ralph Halselin paying 200 marcs, the two halves of the Reimes barony £50 each, and Ely Giffard and Odo de Damartin 100 marcs apiece.[97] Geoffrey de Mandeville owed £866 13s 4d which may have been his actual relief or may have been what was left after some had been paid.[98] At any rate it was a heavy charge.

The legal treatises of the late twelfth century insisted on this right of the king's to exact relief from his barons as he saw fit.[99] In general Henry II and Richard I seem to have used the privilege with moderation. As a rule the sum demanded was between 100 and 200 marcs with £100 and 100 marcs the most common figures. But there were striking variations from this norm. In 1166 the constable of Chester paid 1,000 marcs for the lands his mother had held in the honor of Tickhill.[100] In 1185 Robert de Ghent offered the same amount for his ancestral barony.[101] The year 1190 saw some extremely high reliefs—Richard needed money for his crusade. Maurice de Berkeley promised 1,000 marcs, Eustace de Vesci 1,300 marcs, and the earl of Norfolk 1,000 marcs.[102] At least two of these cases were unusual. The house of Berkeley had obtained its rich fief through the favor of Henry II, and Maurice's payment covered confirmation of this grant. The earl of Norfolk's father had been a rebel against Henry II, and while the king had restored his hereditary estates, he had kept a number of valuable manors which previous monarchs had granted the earls from the royal demesne. These manors were returned by Richard. The crown was also willing to use its arbitrary authority to avoid obvious hardship. In 1195 John de Kilpek was pardoned £77 10s of the £100 charged him for relief of

[97] *Pipe roll 31 Henry I*, pp. 9, 54, 78, 98.
[98] *Ibid.*, p. 55.
[99] *Dialogus de scaccario*, p. 135; Glanville, *De legibus* (ed. George E. Woodbine, 1932), p. 128.
[100] " Pipe roll 12 Henry II," *Pipe roll society*, IX, 51.
[101] " Pipe roll 31 Henry II," *ibid.*, XXXIV, 90.
[102] " Pipe roll 2 Richard I," *ibid.*, XXXIX, 21, 58, 101.

his barony " because of the poverty of the tenement and because he has only one knight's fee." [103]

The cases of Maurice de Berkeley and the earl of Norfolk show the extreme difficulty of comparing custom with practice in respect to relief. It seems clear that in Richard's reign there was a distinct belief that £100 was a normal reasonable relief for a barony. In 1198 William de Newmarket offered a fine of 100 marcs if the king would accept a reasonable relief of £100.[104] During Richard's reign this sum was assessed against the tiny barony of John de Kilpek, the comparatively small fiefs of Richard Lovel and Gilbert de Tany, the moderate sized baronies of Ralph Musard, Robert de Albini, and Aubrey de Vere, and the great honors of William de Ferrars and William de Mowbray.[105] Perhaps the most instructive case is that of the earl of Arundel. In 1194 he was charged £100 for relief by the justiciar, Hubert Walter. Later in the same year he was forced, presumably by Richard himself, to promise 760 marcs for the lands held by his father at his death—the barony of Castle Rising.[106] Here it seems obvious that the justiciar considered £100 the normal relief, but the king refused to accept it. In short the crown might agree in theory that £100 was the normal relief due from a barony and still find very few normal cases. A baron's right to his fief might not be quite clear, he might lack the protection accorded by tenure for several generations, or his father might have offended the crown. All such cases called for special bargains—a fine in place of or in addition to relief.

As long as the king had the right to demand arbitrary reliefs, he could use it as a political weapon. Both Henry II and Richard I rewarded their friends and punished their enemies by this means. John not only employed this weapon more freely than his predecessors but he also made it far more potent. His policy seems to have been to keep his barons

[103] " Pipe roll 7 Richard I," *ibid.*, XLIV, 111.
[104] " Pipe roll 10 Richard I," *ibid.*, XLVII, 222.
[105] " Pipe rolls 3 and 4 Richard I," *ibid.*, XL, 97, 111, 254; " Pipe roll 5 Richard I," *ibid.*, XLI, 8, 90; " Pipe roll 6 Richard I," *ibid.*, XLIII, 160, 193; " Pipe roll 7 Richard I," *ibid.*, XLIV, 226.
[106] " Pipe roll 6 Richard I," *ibid.*, XLIII, 63, 66.

perpetually in debt to the crown. This enabled him to favor some by pardoning part of their debts and to harass those he distrusted. A strange quirk in the law of the day made the harassing particularly easy. The king could not legally seize the person or fief of a baron except in accordance with a judgment solemnly delivered by the baron's peers. Feudal law protected a vassal from arbitrary punishment by his lord. But English law supplied a loophole. When a baron owed the crown more money than he could pay at once, he or his seneschal appeared before the exchequer, agreed on a system of installments, and swore to make the payments on time. The *Dialogue of the exchequer* makes clear that if these payments were not made, the seneschal who had taken the oath could be imprisoned. If the lord had taken the oath in person, he was to be confined on parole to the vicinity of the prison. Apparently the lord whose seneschal had sworn was safe, but his chattels were to be seized as soon as the payment was defaulted.[107]

This feature of exchequer practice quickly attracted John's attention. Early in his reign he issued a decree reaffirming and strengthening the rule.[108] To the provision that when a payment was in default, the lord's chattels were to be seized, he made a significant addition—when the debt was for relief, the land for which it was due was to be seized. Then the *Dialogue* states that in the opinion of some people a lord whose seneschal had made default could not himself take oath to pay that debt. John made this provision positive. While the exact effect of this is not quite clear, it would seem to place the lord at the king's mercy. Certainly John used this method against his enemies. With this weapon he crushed the De Briouses and disciplined Thomas de Multon.[109] It was a perpetual threat hanging over the heads of all barons who were deeply in debt to the crown. Now relief was not only a privileged debt under John's decree, but it was also one that every baron

[107] *Dialogus de scaccario*, pp. 151-153.
[108] Roger of Hovedon, *Chronica* (ed. W. Stubbs, *Rolls series*), IV, 152.
[109] Goddard Henry Orpen, *Ireland under the Normans* (Oxford, 1911), II, 237-241; *Rotuli litterarum patentium* (ed. T. D. Hardy, *Record commission*), p. 85b.

had to incur. Hence exorbitant reliefs suited John's policy. John de Lacy, constable of Chester, promised to pay 7,000 marcs for his father's lands. This represented about six years' income from the fief. Then in 1214, in the hope of weaning the young constable from the rebel party, the king forgave about half the sum and in the following year wiped the debt out entirely.[110] In 1214 William fitz Alan promised 10,000 marcs for his fief. As this was equal to about thirty years' revenue of the barony, it was an utterly fantastic sum.[111] One can easily see why the barons who dictated the terms of *Magna Carta* felt strongly about relief.

The provision of *Magna Carta* setting the relief for a barony at £100 was observed reasonably well in practice. The cases in which greater sums were demanded became few. In 1220 Richard de Harcourt paid £500, and in 1224 Nigel de Mowbray was charged the same amount.[112] In the latter year John de Birkin paid 300 marcs relief for the barony of Matilda de Caus, but three years later his heir paid only 200 marcs.[113] In 1227 Robert fitz Meldred paid 200 marcs for the barony of Henry de Neville of Raby.[114] In 1244 John fitz Alan was charged £1,000.[115] In 1247 Roger de Mortimer of Wigmore paid a relief of 2,000 marcs and John de Verdun one of 300 marcs.[116] The small number of these cases inclines one to believe that each was governed by exceptional circumstances, but I can find no evidence as to what those circumstances may have been. Perhaps it is significant that the two who were charged very large sums were great marcher lords.

The question as to whether the government of Henry III accepted especially low reliefs from poor baronies is complicated by the fact that there was no clear rule as to what fiefs were baronies. On several occasions inquisitions were ordered

---

[110] *Rotuli de oblatis et finibus* (ed. T. D. Hardy, *Record commission*), p. 494; *Pipe roll 16 John*, Public Record Office, E 372-60; *Rot. pat.*, p. 129b. The value of the De Lacy lands comes from *Pipe roll 14 John*, Public Record Office, E 372-58.

[111] *Pipe roll 16 John*, Public Record Office, E 372-60. The value comes from "Pipe roll 13 Henry II," *Pipe roll society*, XI, 72.

[112] *Excerpta ex rotulis finium*, I, 58, 113.

[113] *Ibid.*, pp. 116, 162.   [115] *Ibid.*, p. 417.

[114] *Ibid.*, p. 156.   [116] *Ibid.*, II, 7, 11.

to determine whether or not a fief was held by barony.[117] This confusion becomes obvious when one examines the reliefs demanded. I have already cited the case of the two Scalariis baronies one of which paid as a barony and the other as a tenure by knight service. Each consisted of fifteen fees, but one was charged £100 and the other £75.[118] In 1226 Mathew de Louvain paid £50 for the ten fees he held. In 1261 his son was charged 100 marcs.[119] In 1234 the heiresses of the barony of Cainhoe paid as tenants by knight service instead of as holders of a divided barony.[120] Most peculiar of all is the case of John de Balliol. At first he was charged £150 for his thirty fees. Apparently he protested, for it was later reduced to the standard £100.[121]

It seems clear that Henry III's government had no definite list of baronies. In the case of fiefs that were both small and poor, such as those held by the Beauchamps of Eaton Socon, the Scropes, and the two Chauncy families, reliefs were collected at the rate of 100 shillings per fee even though the Beauchamp fief at least was at times called a barony.[122] Somewhat larger fiefs like that held by Mathew de Louvain could be given relief by either charging 100 shillings a fee or a lump sum smaller than the standard £100.[123] In one case the holder of a very poor barony was charged a lump sum smaller than the total of his fees at 100 shillings each.[124] But this practice of tempering the cost of relief for small, poor baronies was not always followed—the Sudley barony of three fees paid £100 in 1222.[125] In short even though baronial relief had become fixed the crown could still use its rights for political purposes in the border region between tenure by barony and by simple knight service.

The last important development in the history of relief dur-

---

[117] *Ibid.*, I, 92; II, 266, 405.
[118] *Ibid.*, I, 69, 93. The roll reads £65, but this seems clearly an error.
[119] *Ibid.*, I, 141; II, 362-363.
[120] *Ibid.*, I, 259-260.
[121] *Ibid.*, pp. 183, 212.
[122] *Ibid.*, I, 76, 173, 182, 207, 321; *Book of fees*, II, 888.
[123] *Excerpta ex rotulis finium*, I, 141; II, 362-363.
[124] *Ibid.*, I, 69.
[125] *Ibid.*, p. 82.

ing our period was the reduction of the sum due for a barony
from £100 to 100 marcs. As prices and money revenues were
rising, this reduction of one-third in the standard relief represented at least a minor victory for the barons. It is difficult to
fix exactly the date of this change. The fine rolls of Henry III
show that £100 was charged the heirs of four baronies in
1263.[126] In 1265 Geoffrey Luterel was assessed 100 marcs.[127]
From then until the death of Henry III no definite sum was
mentioned—the escheator was simply ordered to take security
for the payment of " reasonable relief." This evidence seems
to indicate that the change took place in 1264. The fact that
Bracton writing before 1268 gives 100 marcs as the relief due
from a barony serves to support this date.[128] Unfortunately
Bémont cites evidence to show that Edward I collected relief
at the £100 rate until his reissue of the charter in 1297. This
document finally set the relief for a barony at 100 marcs.[129]
On the basis of the evidence available one can merely suggest
that the barons forced Henry III to grant the reduction, but
that it was later repudiated by Edward. He in turn was forced
to give way in 1297.[130]

To summarize, the Norman and early Angevin kings found
relief a valuable political and economic weapon in their relations with the barons. They could charge their friends less
than their foes, the poor less than the rich. Theoretically any
gain in the annual value of a barony could be drained off by
the crown through high relief. John used relief peculiarly
effectively as a political weapon, and it is very possible that he
was also governed by economic motives. The barons, who had
long contended that a fixed sum should be set as a " reasonable
relief," succeeded in placing such a provision in *Magna Carta*.
This ended the use of relief as an instrument of policy except
perhaps in the case of very poor baronies. But relief remained
for some time a serious burden on all except the richest fiefs

[126] *Ibid.*, II, 390, 396, 398.

[127] *Ibid.*, p. 425.

[128] *De legibus*, II, 244. The date 1268 was supplied by Professor Woodbine.

[129] Charles Bémont, *Chartes des libertés anglaises* (*Collection de textes pour
servir à l'étude et à l'enseignement de l'histoire*, Paris, 1892), p. 48, note 6.

[130] This question could probably be settled by an examination of the pipe
rolls. They are at present unavailable.

held by barony. This led to the long struggle, eventually successful, to reduce baronial relief from £100 to 100 marcs. During the same period the money return from most baronies was rising steadily. Hence by the early fourteenth century relief must have been a far less serious burden than in the early thirteenth.

Another financial obligation of the English tenants-in-chief to the crown was the feudal aid. It was assessed and collected in the same manner as a scutage. *Magna Carta* recognized three occasions on which the king had the right to demand an aid—the knighting of his eldest son, the marriage of his eldest daughter, and the raising of ransom if the king was captured. If he wished an aid for any other purpose, he must obtain the consent of the assembly provided for by the charter.[131] In so far as feudal aids were concerned the practice of the early Angevin kings furnished no justification for this provision.[132] John never made a levy of this sort. In all probability this clause was aimed at non-feudal taxes such as carucages and levies on movables. Feudal aids were taken by Henry III, Edward I, and Edward III on some seven occasions between 1217 and 1348.[133] The first two were levied at a rate of two marcs per fee, the next at twenty shillings. and the others at £2. A statute of 1350 fixed the rate for the future at £1 per fee.[134] The lateness of the date at which the rate became fixed seems to indicate that the feudal aid was of little concern to the barons. As this tax was based on the scutage assessments, it became obsolete with them. The crown raised the revenue it needed by non-feudal levies and simply used the feudal aid as a source of occasional small windfalls. After the twelfth century it cannot have been a serious burden on any barony.

From the point of view of the crown the most important of all feudal incidents were its rights of wardship and marriage. They were valuable both financially and politically. When a

---

[131] *Magna carta*, c. 12, 14.

[132] Henry II levied an aid to marry his daughter in 1168. In 1194 an aid was taken to ransom King Richard. " Pipe rolls 14 Henry II and 6 Richard I," *Pipe roll society*, XII, XLIII.

[133] See index under aids in Ramsay, *Revenues of the kings of England*, and under aids on knights' fees in Mitchell, *Studies in taxation*.

[134] *The statutes of the realm* (*Record commission*), I, 322.

baron died leaving a minor heir, the crown could enjoy the revenues of the fief until the heir came of age, sell the custody, or use it to reward a faithful servant. As the custody of the lands of minors was a magnificent source of revenue and patronage, the king was inclined to press his rights as far as possible. Under the doctrine of prerogative wardship he had the custody of all the lands of a minor tenant-in-chief. This was often a serious hardship for a baron from whom the minor held a mesne fief. For instance the Fitz Johns of Harptree in Somerset held only one-half a fee in chief, but they held 10 fees of the earldom of Gloucester. If the Fitz John fief fell to a minor heir, the king had the custody of the lands held of the earl. A list of the fees held of the earl of Gloucester and Hertford in 1263 show that 96 out of a total of 243 were held by tenants-in-chief of the crown and hence were subject to prerogative wardship.[135] About a quarter of the fees of the Mowbray barony were held by tenants-in-chief of the crown.[136]

Naturally the barons were anxious to limit prerogative wardship as much as possible. They sought to do this by defining strictly the tenures which could give justification for its exercise. *Magna Carta* provided that the fact that a man held *in capite* by non-military tenure—socage, burgage, fee farm, or petty serjeantry—did not give the king the custody of lands he might hold from others by knight service.[137] Chapter 43 of the charter suggests but does not actually state that the king could not claim prerogative wardship in the case of a tenant-in-chief *de honore*. The second reissue of the charter made this prohibition definite, and this was accepted by Bracton as the established law.[138] Prerogative wardship remained as it was defined by *Magna Carta*. The petition of the barons at the Parliament of Oxford in 1257 seems to demand its abolition, but nothing came of this request.[139] Edward I was inclined to press his rights up to if not slightly beyond their limits. At the death of Geoffrey de Lucy, a tenant of the earl of Gloucester, the

---

[135] *Close rolls, 1261-4* (*Rolls series*), pp. 284-293.
[136] *Red book of the exchequer*, II, 735-737.
[137] *Magna carta*, c. 37.
[138] *Charter of 1217*, c. 38; Bracton, *De legibus*, II, 253.
[139] *Petition of the barons*, c. 3, Stubbs, *Select charters*, pp. 382-387.

crown and the earl disputed the custody of his lands. Geoffrey's grandfather had held *iure iuxoris* half of a royal serjeantry. As he had had no issue by the heiress to the serjeantry, it had passed to others, and neither Geoffrey nor his father had held it. Nevertheless the exchequer decided that because Geoffrey's grandfather had done homage to the king, his lands should be in the custody of the crown.[140] To say the least this seems a strained interpretation of prerogative wardship even if it be granted that the serjeantry was grand rather than petty. A statute reaffirmed the king's right of prerogative wardship and listed the baronies that were exempt from it. The palatine lords, the bishop of Durham and the lords marchers, and the archbishop of Canterbury had custody of all fees held of them even when the tenant held elsewhere of the king *de corone*.[141]

The barons disliked prerogative wardship because it deprived them of part of their feudal revenues from their vassals. They also objected to having the crown waste the lands of a minor, and *Magna Carta* forbade this abuse.[142] The king was entitled to the income from the fief, but he was expected to leave the capital intact. For the rest there seems to have been little dispute over the crown's right of wardship. Not only was it a basic feudal privilege deeply imbedded in traditional custom, but it bothered the barons very little. A living baron was not likely to worry much about who enjoyed the revenue of his lands after his death, and the minor who was in custody was in no position to contest the crown's right. In short wardship was never a burden on an adult, active baron. At the same time it was the most valuable of the king's rights. Scutage, relief, and aid could not be increased as prices and the revenues from land rose, but wardship was inflation-proof. Its annual value was the value of the fief less the cost of supporting the heir. It remained an important part of the king's income until its abolition in the seventeenth century.

The king's right of marriage was important from both the political and financial point of view. Unfortunately its exact extent is not clear. No tenant-in-chief could marry his daughter

---

[140] *Red book of the exchequer*, III, 1013-1014.
[141] *Statutes of the realm*, I, 126.
[142] *Magna carta*, c. 4.

without the king's consent.   If a tenant-in-chief died leaving unmarried daughters, the king could marry them to whom he pleased.   The widow of a tenant-in-chief could not remarry without the king's leave.   This much was generally recognized. The question as to whether or not the king could force a widow to remarry was long an issue between crown and baronage.   Henry I in his charter of liberties promised that he would not marry a widow against her will.[143]   *Magna Carta* states, "No widow shall be forced to marry if she wishes to live unmarried."[144]   Evidence as to the crown's practice is difficult to find.   The pipe roll of 1135 shows Henry I obliging Lucy, countess of Chester, to pay 500 marcs for the privilege of staying unwed for five years.[145]   Two other ladies paid fines to have their dowers, and this may have been a less direct way of collecting money for allowing them to stay single.[146]   The rolls for most of the reign of Henry II contain very few entries relating to the king's right of marriage—in fact one is led to wonder if payments in connection with it were not made direct to his chamber without passing through the exchequer.   But in 1180 a widow pays to be allowed to remain single, and there are a few similar cases in the rest of Henry's reign.[147]   Under Richard and John such entries become very common.[148]   In John's reign there are a few clear cases of widows forced to marry men chosen by the king.[149]   The crown's inclination to insist that a widow marry or at least pay a round sum for the right to remain single is easily explained.   A widow was entitled to one-third of her late husband's estate as a dowry, and she usually had a marriage portion as well.   By forcing her to marry the king could use her lands for political patronage or sell her hand at a good price.   Like most of the provisions of *Magna Carta* the prohibition against forcing widows to remarry was not entirely efficacious—the pipe roll of 1230 shows two ladies paying fines to remain single.[150]

---

[143] *Charter of liberties*, c. 4.   [145] *Pipe roll 31 Henry I*, p. 110.

[144] *Magna carta*, c. 8.   [146] *Ibid.*, pp. 67, 95.

[147] " Pipe roll 26 Henry II," *Pipe roll society*, XXIX, 140; " Pipe roll 28 Henry II," *ibid.*, XXXI, 100.

[148] See indices to published pipe rolls under " Fines et Oblata."

[149] *Rot. claus.*, I, 12b; *Curia regis rolls*, III, 257.

[150] " Pipe roll 14 Henry III," *Pipe roll society*, XLII, 255, 259.

The other doubtful question concerns the king's rights over the marriage of males in his custody. The charter of liberties of Henry I and Glanville's treatise speak only of the marriage of females.[151] *Magna Carta* uses the term *haeredes* with no specification as to sex.[152] Bracton states positively that a lord has the right to marry a minor male in his custody.[153] Here again the practice is difficult to determine. The pipe roll of 1135 shows that Henry I received fines from males for leave to wed which seems to imply that he had the right to marry them.[154] In 1188 Henry II sold the marriage of a male heir.[155] The practice became common during the reigns of Richard and John.

Although the argument for it rests largely on the dubious ground of lack of evidence against it, there is an interesting possibility that should be mentioned. We have seen that in respect to taking fines from widows for leave to remain single and from male heirs for permission to marry the practice of Henry I resembles that of Richard and John. Only after 1180 do we find any examples of such payments in the reign of Henry II. In fact the pipe rolls of Henry II show astonishingly few cases of the sale of widows and female wards of the crown. As I have suggested above, this may mean that such payments were made into the chamber and so are not found on the pipe rolls. But there is another possible interpretation. The charter of Henry I and *Magna Carta* show that the crown's right of marriage was a cause of friction between it and the barons. Perhaps Henry II in the early years of his reign refrained from raising this issue. Only after the suppression of the baronial revolt did he feel free to return to the practices of his grandfather's day.

The political aspects of the right of marriage were extremely significant. It enabled the crown to control the family alliances formed among the barons. Then every marriage involved the transfer of a marriage portion, and many governed the

---

[151] *Charter of liberties*, c. 3; Glanville, *De legibus*, p. 109.
[152] *Magna carta*, c. 6.
[153] Bracton, *De legibus*, II, 256-257.
[154] *Pipe roll 31 Henry I*, pp. 8, 26.
[155] " Pipe roll 34 Henry II," *Pipe roll society*, XXXVIII, 100.

future possession of a barony or part of one. It was extremely important that the crown should control the passing of lands, castles, and fees from one family to another. Most vital of all was the king's right to marry an heiress after her father's death. This privilege enabled him to choose the next lord of the fief. There is some evidence that during the twelfth century the king claimed a special prerogative. If a baron who had several daughters married all but one before he died, the king could marry the one left and give her the entire fief.[156] The crown could make the fortune of a feudal house by permitting it to make good marriages. The Bohuns emerged from obscurity by marrying a daughter of Edward of Salisbury, rose another step by wedding a daughter of Miles of Gloucester, and reached the height of their power through a Mandeville heiress. On the other hand great baronies could be broken into insignificant fragments by marrying heiresses to men of little position. In short through its right of marriage the crown could to a great extent control the accumulation and dispersion of great feudal estates.

The right of marriage benefited the crown financially in two ways—a marriage was a marketable commodity which could be sold for cash, and a lady and her lands could be used to support someone for whom the king felt obliged to provide. It is extremely difficult to make any general statement about the value of the marriages in the king's gift for the circumstances varied with each case. Presumably the basic consideration was the political and financial importance of the estates involved. A widow with her dowry was more valuable than her unmarried sister. A sole heiress was worth more than one of several. But obviously other considerations could be involved. The king in all probability shaded prices for his friends.[157] If the beauty and charm of the lady and his affection for her had moved a man to offer a high price, we should have no knowledge of the motive. The numerous couples who paid fines for wedding without the king's consent would seem to indicate that love played its part. As far as the actual evidence goes,

[156] Sir Frederick Pollock and Frederic William Maitland, *History of English law* (Cambridge, 1895), II, 273.

[157] For a case in point see *Rot. claus.*, I, 168

one can only say that there was clearly no fixed ratio between the value of a lady's hand and the annual income from her lands. The few cases in which the value of the lands involved can be ascertained suggest that a lady was worth from two to four times her annual income. In general the prices for the widows and heiresses of barons ranged from 200 to 500 marcs. The oft-cited 20,000 marcs which Geoffrey de Mandeville offered in 1214 for the person and estate of Isabel of Gloucester is clearly a case of King John's strange schemes like the 10,000 marcs charged William fitz Alan for relief.[158] As the honor of Gloucester was certainly not worth more than £600 and probably not more than £400, this sum of 20,000 marcs was obviously based on political not financial considerations.[159]

Although at normal rates the king's right of marriage brought a considerable return to the exchequer, it was not as a rule a burden the barons could object to. It is true that occasionally a baron had to pay for the king's leave to marry his daughter, but this does not seem to have been usual. Ordinarily the king exercised his right over widows and children in his custody. For the buyer the purchase of one of the crown's wards was a pure speculation. A man considered the value of the lady's estates, guessed at the number of years he might hope to enjoy them, perhaps glanced at the charms of the lady herself, and then decided how much he was willing to pay for her. Often he could obtain terms of payment so favorable that he could take the money required out of the income of the estates and so required no initial capital for his speculation. His profits depended on the quality of the bargain he made with the crown and on pure chance. Suppose a man offered £500 for a lady whose lands were worth £150 a year. If she died childless in four years, he came out about even. If she lived longer, he gained. If she died after bearing him a child, he could enjoy her estates for life and make another similar speculation. In short while the right of marriage was a source of revenue to the king, it also offered exciting opportunities for profit to his vassals.

---

[158] *Rotuli de oblatis et finibus*, p. 520.
[159] In 1188 it yielded just under £600. " Pipe roll 34 Henry II," *Pipe roll*

The second aspect of the financial value of the right of marriage to the crown requires little discussion. A king felt obliged to provide for his children, both legitimate and illegitimate, and his loyal servants. Henry I gave the heiress of the Fitz Hamons to his eldest bastard, Robert. Later another of Henry's illegitimate sons, also named Robert, received the heiress of the great barony of Okehampton. Stephen gave the heiress of the vast Warren estates to his second son, William, and the same lady was used by Henry II to provide for his bastard brother, Hamelin. Henry II cared for his third and fourth sons, Geoffrey and John, by giving them respectively Constance, duchess of Brittany and countess of Richmond, and Isabel, daughter of Earl William of Gloucester. Richard I presented his bastard brother William Longsword with the heiress to the earldom of Salisbury. Thus ladies in the king's gift provided an economical means of providing for the royal progeny.

The practice of rewarding faithful royal servants with valuable ladies was common under the early Angevin kings. The most striking case was the gift by Henry II and Richard of Isabel de Clare, lady of Striguil, Pembroke, and Leinster to William Marshal. Geoffrey fitz Peter obtained a lady who soon became the heiress to the great Mandeville barony. Saher de Quency received one of the heiresses of Earl Robert of Leicester. Hubert de Burgh enjoyed at various times the lady of Wormgay and Isabel of Gloucester. Robert de Turnham, Robert de Tresgoz, and Geoffrey Luterel received heiresses of baronial rank. These favored ones were all Englishmen, but John at least had no objection to giving ladies in his care to foreigners. Faulkes de Bréauté was married to the widow of the earl of Devon. Peter de Maulay was given the heiress of the Fossards. Other foreign soldiers in John's pay received less valuable ladies.

The sixth chapter of *Magna Carta* provided that the king should marry heirs in his custody *absque disparagatione*. It is extremely difficult to determine exactly what the barons had in mind when they forced this promise from the king. The general idea is clear enough—an heir should be married to a

society, XXXVIII, 13. In 1199 it brought in only £446. "Pipe roll 1 John," *ibid.*, XLVIII, 35.

worthy partner. It was a generally accepted principle of feudal custom. There seems no doubt that it was considered disparagement to marry the heir of a baron to a villain or burgher though this rule was not definitely expressed until 1235.[160] I suspect that in earlier times there was no need to state this—it was generally assumed. But did the barons mean more than this? Did they intend that the heir of a baron should be married to the child of a baron? As a class the barons of England might well have wished to keep the baronies of the realm in their own hands. There is no evidence that any such idea lay behind this provision. William Marshal was an almost landless knight when he married Isabel de Clare, yet we find no suggestion that the union disparaged the lady. As far as one can discover any English freeholder was a fit partner for the heir of a baron.

Are we then forced to conclude that the barons were simply repeating a traditional feudal formula or that John had been marrying noble heiresses to villains or burghers? Neither of these alternatives seems likely. It is more probable that the clause was aimed at John's foreign soldiers. This frame of mind appears clearly in the petition of the barons at the Parliament of Oxford. Chapter six of this petition reads: " Likewise they beg in regard to marriages in the king's gift that they be not married where they are disparaged, that is to men who are not of the nationality of the English realm." [161] The barons of England were not trying to keep the fiefs within their own ranks, but they did want to limit the competition to Englishmen. Even though serious violence is done to the belief in the internationalism of the feudal class, it seems necessary to conclude that John's barons considered a foreigner unworthy of their children. In short disparagement of heirs by the king was essentially a political issue. There was little likelihood that its social implications would be involved through the king's attempting to give the heir of a tenant-in-chief to one of villain or burgher rank. The statute of Merton which definitely calls such a marriage disparagement seems aimed at mesne lords rather than at the king.

[160] *Statutes of the realm*, I, 3.
[161] *Petition of the barons*, c. 6.

CHAPTER III

NON-FEUDAL OBLIGATIONS

Having discussed at some length the feudal obligations owed by the barons to the crown let us turn to the non-feudal public burdens imposed on them. Here an important distinction must be made. We have seen that in regard to all feudal obligations the baron was responsible to the crown for the service owed by his entire barony. Although the king might assist him to force his vassals to perform their share of the service due from the barony, there was no direct relationship between the crown and the baron's men. But this was not the case in respect to non-feudal public burdens. There the king looked directly to each freeholder, and once a baron had granted land as a fief, it ceased to be his responsibility.[1] Hence when the baron sought exemption from public burdens, his interest was usually confined to the lands he had retained in his own hands. There were, however, some advantages to be gained by the baron if he could obtain exemptions for his vassals. It added to one's prestige to have one's men enjoy a privileged position. Moreover when the vassals' lands were in the baron's custody, he was directly interested in the burdens borne by them. In short a baron liked to see his vassals freed from all obligations that did not benefit him, but his primary care was to obtain freedom for his own lands, for his demesne.

As this term "demesne" will be used very frequently in subsequent pages, it is extremely important that it be clearly defined. It had two distinct meanings in mediaeval English usage. In *Domesday Book* demesne means the land that a member of the feudal class cultivated himself with the labor services owed by his tenants. The charter of liberties of Henry I refers to this land as "demesne plowlands," and this became the ordinary usage whenever there seemed danger of confusion between the narrow and broad meanings of "demesne." When I wish to refer to this land, I shall use the term "manorial demesne." In its broader and more com-

[1] Bracton, *De legibus*, II, 116-117.

mon meaning demesne covers both the manorial demesne and the land held by unfree tenants. This is the land held " in demesne as of fee " so prominent in Henry II's possessory assizes and hence in English common law. The author of the *Dialogue of the exchequer* used demesne in this sense, but felt called on to defend himself against those who held to the narrower meaning of the word.[2] When I speak of demesne without qualification, I intend to use the term in its broad sense. In fact I cannot usually be certain that I am staying within the limits I have marked. In strict theory the tenements of small free tenants did not form part of the demesne, but it is clear that contemporary usage often included them in it. In short the only positive statement one can make is that the demesne of a baron could not include lands held by knight service.

The most important public burden of the Norman period was the tax known as danegeld. Unfortunately comparatively little is known about how often it was taken and the rate at which it was levied. In the winter of 1083-4 the Conqueror collected danegeld at the rate of six shillings per hide.[3] About 1096 William II levied it at four shillings on each hide.[4] Mr. Round has shown conclusively that other danegelds were collected by the first two Norman kings, but we are ignorant of their number and the rate at which they were levied.[5] Henry I seems to have turned danegeld into an annual tax of two shillings on every hide.[6] His grandson Henry II took it twice at the same rate—in the second and eighth years of his reign.[7] If one accepts Mr. Maitland's conclusion that at the time of the Domesday inquest the average hide was worth £1 a year, the six shillings collected in 1083-4 represented a 30 per cent tax on landed incomes.[8] As it seems certain that Domesday valua-

[2] *Dialogus de scaccario*, p. 102.

[3] J. H. Round, "Danegeld and the finance of Domesday," *Domesday studies* (ed. P. E. Dove, London, 1888), I, 82-83.

[4] *Ibid.*, pp. 83-84.   [5] *Ibid.*, pp. 87-88.

[6] Henry of Huntingdon, *Historia Anglorum* (ed. T. Arnold, *Rolls series*), p. 258. See accounts of previous danegelds in *Pipe roll 31 Henry I*.

[7] "Pipe roll 2 Henry II," *The great rolls of the pipe for the second, third, and fourth years of the reign of king Henry II* (ed. Joseph Hunter, *Record commission*), pp. 1-68; "Pipe roll 8 Henry II," *Pipe roll society*, V.

[8] F. W. Maitand, *Domesday book and beyond* (Cambridge, 1907), pp. 462 466.

tions included revenue in kind, a cash tax at this rate must have been crushing. The references cited by Round in connection with the four-shilling geld of 1096 supports this conclusion. While it is likely that the revenue from land had increased and that money was more plentiful by the time of Henry I, his annual tax of two shillings on a hide must have been a serious burden well worth avoiding.

There were two obvious ways by which a baron could mitigate or avoid the cost of paying danegeld—he could get his assessment lowered or obtain a partial or complete exemption from the tax. As the hide was a unit of assessment, the crown could reduce the number of hides. Sometimes the king granted a reduction in the assessment of a particular estate. Then there were wholesale reductions such as those granted in the counties of Sussex, Surrey, Hampshire, and Berkshire between the Conquest and the Domesday inquest.[9] The isolated reductions were clearly marks of royal favor, and there are distinct indications that favoritism played a part in the wholesale ones. Thus in Sussex the assessments of the demesne manors of the lords of the rapes—the counts of Mortain and Eu, Earl Roger de Montgomery, William de Warren, and William de Briouse—were reduced on an average well over 50 per cent while very few of the estates held by their vassals received any reduction. In Surrey the fiefs of Richard fitz Gilbert de Clare and the bishop of Bayeux fared far better than average, though here there was no striking difference between the treatment accorded to them and their tenants. In short it seems clear that those who were in the royal favor could obtain reductions in danegeld assessments.

If a baron succeeded in having the assessments on some of his manors reduced, he lessened, presumably forever, the tax burden on those lands. An exemption from danegeld did not change the obligations due from the land but simply freed the privileged holder from paying. Lower assessments reduced the danegeld totals on the king's books—exemptions simply cut the actual receipts. Exemptions from danegeld were of three types. A class or group of landholders might be exempt be-

---

[9] Round, "Danegeld and the finance of Domesday," pp. 110-111; F. H. Baring, *Domesday tables* (London, 1909).

cause of its position.   A baron might obtain permanent exemption for himself and his successors.   The third and apparently most common type was arbitrary relief from paying on a particular occasion granted as a special favor from the crown.

In 1083-4 the barons were not obliged to pay danegeld on their manorial demesnes.[10]   Round suggests that this concession was made because the rate of the levy was very high.   In Wiltshire it resulted in the exemption of about 30 per cent of the hides.   The decided favor shown to the barons as against their vassals indicated the great influence of the former.   A passage in the *Leges Edwardi Confessoris* states that the demesnes of the church were exempt until the levy of 1096.[11] As this compilation dates from the middle of the twelfth century, it is of doubtful authority.   A writ of William I granting freedom from geld to the demesnes of the abbey of Bury St. Edmunds casts doubt on the existence of any such general exemption.[12]   It is, of course, possible that the passage in the *Leges* referred to manorial demesnes and that William's writ used the word in its broader sense.   Henry I in his coronation charter promised that all who held by knight's service would be freed from paying geld on their manorial demesnes.[13]   This great extension of the scheme followed in 1083-4 would have exempted some 50 per cent of the hidage of England.   If Henry paid any attention to this promise, he did so only for a time.   Although the total hidage shown on the pipe roll of 1135 is below that of *Domesday Book*, the difference is not enough to cover any such sweeping exemption.   The writs of quittance entered on this roll do not cover all the barons, to say nothing of all tenants by knight service.   Finally a few of these writs specifically exempt the manorial demesnes of individuals and hence show that no general exemption for these lands was recognized.[14]

While there is no valid evidence that general class exemptions from the payment of danegeld were granted on other

[10] *Exon. Domesday, Domesday book*, IV, 1-493.
[11] Liebermann, *Gesetze der Angelsachsen*, I, 636.
[12] *Feudal documents from the abbey of Bury St. Edmunds*, p. 49.
[13] *Charter of liberties*, c. 11.
[14] *Pipe roll 31 Henry I*, pp. 34, 67, 99, 108.

occasions than the levy of 1083-4, certain landholders were exempt by charter or custom. Royal charters wholly or partially freeing ecclesiastical estates from this burden do not concern us except to note that they were fairly common. Our interest lies in the exemptions granted to laymen. The earliest charter I can find that specifically frees a lay fief from the payment of danegeld belongs to the middle years of Henry I.[15] But there is evidence that other grants were made by the Norman kings. In the pipe roll of 1135 Brian fitz Count, lord of the barony of Wallingford, is given quittance from geld on all his lands, both demesnes and fees. Under Henry II this exemption was allowed to the "barons of Wallingford."[16] The only possible explanation would seem to be that some lord of Wallingford had obtained a grant of exemption for himself, his vassals, and their successors. On the roll of 1135 the Earl Warren and the earl of Gloucester received quittances for all their lands.[17] In 1155 the so-called *nova terra* of Earl Warren in Norfolk was apparently exempted without question, but the crown tried to collect the geld due from his other lands. The earl protested, and the collection was postponed. Next year he had writs giving full exemption to his lands in East Anglia and Surrey and to his demesne in his barony of Lewes.[18] In 1155 the earl of Gloucester refused to pay geld on his demesne and the following year had writs of quittance.[19] Now it seems clear that both these earls believed that they were entitled to at least partial exemption from geld, and Henry II appears to have recognized the justice of their claims. I believe both had some sort of grant of exemption from one of the Norman kings.

The lord and tenants of the Wallingford barony and the two earls mentioned above probably had charters freeing them from geld, but some lay lords were exempt by custom. The *Dialogue of the exchequer* tells us that the barons of the

---

[15] *Calendar of charter rolls*, III, 360.

[16] *Pipe roll 31 Henry I*, pp. 5, 22, 62, 102, 125; *Pipe roll 2 Henry II*, pp. 20, 23, 34, 37.

[17] *Pipe roll 31 Henry I*, pp. 6, 16, 23, 34, 41, 46-7, 49, 51, 60, 62, 68, 72, 80, 86, 95, 98, 102, 104, 108, 126.

[18] *Pipe roll 2 Henry II*, pp. 7, 10, 61; *Pipe roll 3 Henry II*, pp. 79, 94.

[19] *Pipe roll 2 Henry II*, pp. 9, 33, 67; *Pipe roll 3 Henry II*, p. 100.

exchequer were quit of geld on their demesnes and fees and the sheriffs on their demesnes.[20]   The writs of quittance on the pipe rolls indicate that this privilege was recognized in practice.   As a matter of fact the *Dialogue* informs us that in the case of the barons of the exchequer the writs were never actually issued and the statement of their existence was a pure matter of form.   In short the barons were capable of seeing to the enforcement of their own financial immunities.

It would be pleasant to be able to draw up a list of those exempt from danegeld by charter or custom for comparison with the lists of quittances granted by the crown.   Unfortunately this is impossible.   Our evidence is far too scanty to enable us to assert that no laymen except those mentioned above were permanently exempt.   In fact I suspect very strongly that the earls of Leicester and the kings of Scotland, earls of Huntingdon, enjoyed at least partial exemption.   It is rarely possible to be certain as to who was a baron of the exchequer. Nevertheless it is clear that many quittances were granted as a momentary mark of royal favor.   The kings gave few charters of exemption, but they were fairly generous in freeing important men from a particular levy.   When used in this way writs of quittance were a valuable political tool—a means of rewarding the faithful and winning over the doubtful.

The last danegeld was levied by Henry II in the year 1162. There has been much scholarly speculation as to why the king abandoned this fairly lucrative tax.   In 1162 the geld yielded £3,132 as against £2,408 for the most profitable feudal aid of Henry's reign.   It amounted to slightly less than a third as much as the total of the county farms.[21]   Hence I cannot accept the argument that the exemptions had grown so numerous that danegeld was not worth collecting.   I suspect that we have here an unrecorded baronial victory over the crown.   Stephen had promised to abolish danegeld.   Henry II collected it but twice in his first eight years and then gave it up.   The only reasonable answer is fierce baronial opposition to the levy.   I do not believe that Henry abandoned it formally—he simply stopped levying it.   The *Dialogue of the exchequer* in its dis-

---

[20] *Dialogus de scaccario*, pp. 95, 102.
[21] Ramsay, *Revenues of the kings of England*, I, 192-195.

cussion of danegeld does not suggest that it was obsolete or that the king could no longer levy it if he saw fit.

From 1162 to the end of his reign Henry II made no attempt to levy a land tax, but his sons and grandson used this source of revenue under new names—carucage or hidage. In 1194 Richard I demanded two shillings from every carucate. As there is no evidence that a special assessment was made, one must presume that this was simply a danegeld under a new name. In 1198 he asked for five shillings a carucate, but this time apparently it was a tax on actual plowlands and was not based on the old danegeld assessment. Similar taxes were levied by King John in 1200, by William Marshal as regent in 1217, and by Hubert de Burgh in the name of Henry III in 1220.[22] As these levies do not appear on the pipe rolls, little is known about them. A few charters to laymen grant exemption from hidage, but all the clear cases are later than 1220 when this tax was last collected.[23] A charter of John dated 1206 seems to free John de Hastings and four of his vassals from hidage, but doubt is thrown on its meaning by the same king's charter freeing Robert de Braybrook from " the hidage called sheriff's aid." [24] While the crown occasionally released an individual from a particular levy, there is no evidence that any lay barons enjoyed exemption by custom. In 1220 some great lords were allowed to collect the tax in their lands and pay it in to the royal coffers. A few others like the earl Marshal and the earl of Chester seem to have avoided the tax by simply refusing to pay it.[25] This levy of 1220 met strong opposition from the barons.[26] Perhaps it is for this reason that we hear no more of hidage and carucage.

Next in importance to danegeld among the public burdens of the Norman period stood murder fines and common penalties assessed against counties and hundreds. The murder fine was

---

[22] On these taxes see under carucage in the indices of Ramsay, *Revenues of the kings of England* and Mitchell, *Studies in taxation.*

[23] *Close rolls, 1256-9*, p. 62; *Calendar of charter rolls*, I, 54, II, 61.

[24] *Rot. chart.*, p. 146b; *Facsimiles of early charters from Northamptonshire collections* (ed. F. M. Stenton, *Northamptonshire record society*), no. XVII.

[25] *Book of fees*, I, 298, 312, 326.

[26] Mitchell, *Studies in taxation*, pp. 129-136.

apparently originally a means devised by the Conqueror to protect his followers. If a man was found slain and the people of
the neighborhood could neither produce the culprit nor prove
that the victim was an Englishman, a heavy financial penalty
was laid on them. According to the *Leges Henrici* if the body
was found in a house, court, or enclosed area, the manor paid
to the extent of its resources, and any deficiency was made up
by the rest of the hundred. If the body was found in the
open, the whole hundred shared equally in the payment.[27] The
earliest surviving records indicate that in practice murder fines
were assessed against the whole hundred. The *Dialogue of the
exchequer* does not mention the possibility that a single manor
might bear most of the burden. The *Dialogue* also points out
that by the time it was written there was little chance of prov-
ing any freeman to be a pure Englishman Hence the murder
fine was levied in the case of all unsolved homicides except
when the victim was a local villain.[28] Common penalties were
exactions levied against counties and hundreds for such offences
as improper procedure in their courts. As murder fines and
common penalties were distributed by laying a share on each
hide, they were in reality a sort of punitive taxation.

The *Leges Henrici* state that forty-six marcs was the standard
murder fine. ·The *Dialogue of the exchequer* says that it varied
between £36 and £44 according to circumstances. Taking the
theoretical hundred of 100 hides, a forty-six marc fine would
amount to roughly six shillings a hide. If sums as large as
this were ever actually exacted, exemption from participation
in murder fines was indeed a valuable privilege. The pipe roll
of 1135 shows these penalties varying from one marc to twenty
with most of them between ten and twenty. Early in the reign
of Henry II the variation was almost as wide, from one marc
to £10, but the average was lower, from two marcs to £5. By
1203 the rates range from one marc to £5 with two marcs, £1,
and three marcs the most usual penalties. In short if the large
sums mentioned in the laws were actually collected in the
eleventh century, murder fines were then a heavy burden. They
were serious and well worth avoiding at the rate used by

---

[27] *Leges Henrici*, c. 91.   [28] *Dialogus de scaccario*, pp. 99-100.

Henry I. By John's time they were not of any great importance, and freedom from them must have been sought as a matter of prestige rather than of money.

Exemption from participation in murder fines and common penalties was a very common, in fact almost a universal ecclesiastical privilege, but it was rarely accorded to lay barons. The earliest charter I have found specifically granting this exemption to a layman dates from the reign of Henry I, and indirect evidence indicates that a few great barons enjoyed it during the Norman period. In 1251 Henry III announced that an inquest had decided that all the " new land " of Earl Warren and his demesnes as a whole were exempt from common penalties and participated in murder fines only when the murder had been committed in them.[29] This late evidence is supported by an entry in the pipe roll of 1196 pardoning to the Earl Warren his share of a murder fine *per libertatem quam habet in nova terra*.[30] As this " new land " consisted of the manors described in *Domesday Book* as given " for the exchange of Lewes," it seems probable that its special privileges dated from the Conqueror's time.[31] The pipe rolls indicate that this exemption was regularly accorded in practice. In July 1199 King John granted to Robert, earl of Leicester, all the privileges enjoyed by his ancestor, Robert, count of Meulan. Freedom from murder fines was specifically mentioned.[32] The pipe rolls show that quittances were regularly issued to the earls of Leicester. Then a charter of Henry III which I cannot find but which was continually mentioned in the thirteenth century granted to John, earl of Chester and Huntingdon, all the rights enjoyed by his ancestors who were earls of Huntingdon including freedom from murder fines.[33] This is supported by entries in the pipe rolls of Richard's reign which acquit David, earl of Huntingdon, *per libertatem cartam*.[34] Finally a charter of John granting the manor of Ailsbury to Geoffrey fitz Peter, earl of

---

[29] *Close rolls, 1247-1251*, p. 474.
[30] " Pipe roll 8 Richard I," *Pipe roll society*, XLV, 133.
[31] Farrer, *Honors and knights' fees*, III, 297-298.
[32] *Calendar of charter rolls*, I, 180; *Rot. chart.*, p. 5.
[33] *Placita de quo warranto* (ed. W. Illingworth, *Record commission*), pp. 304, 547.
[34] " Pipe rolls 3 and 8 Richard I," *Pipe roll society*, XL, 115; XLV, 228.

Essex, confers extensive privileges including exemption from murder fines and mentions that Geoffrey already enjoyed these rights in the lands of the Mandeville barony.[35]

I do not wish to suggest that no other great lords of the Norman period enjoyed freedom from murder fines—in fact I suspect very strongly that men like the count of Mortain, the bishop of Bayeux, and Earl Roger de Montgomery had it. But I believe it was a rare and cherished privilege. The Angevin kings granted it very sparingly. I can find only about a dozen specific concessions of exemption from murder fines in charters issued by Richard, John, and Henry III. All these grants were to men like Hugh de Neville, Hugh de Welles, Hubert de Burgh, and Roger de Mortimer who stood high in the royal favor.[36] A number of charters of the Angevin kings which granted very extensive privileges specifically excluded exemption from murder fines.[37] Long after these penalties had lost their importance as financial exactions, the prestige involved in being exempt from them made them a source of dispute between king and barons.[38]

Quittances from murder fines and common penalties were used as were quittances from danegeld to reward the king's friends. The barons of the exchequer were exempt by custom, but many other men received writs releasing them from particular payments. In the Norman period, when murder fines were comparatively heavy, this must have been a most useful political weapon in the hands of the crown. If you were in the king's favor you paid a low relief, were partially or wholly exempt from danegeld, and did not participate in murder fines or common penalties. Under the Angevin kings the low rate at which these fines were levied made freedom from particular penalties less avidly sought for. The formula often found in the pipe rolls—such a hundred owes so much with the liberties excepted—suggests that the exemptions had become stable and arbitrary writs of quittance rare.

[35] *Rot. chart.*, pp. 127-128.
[36] *Ibid.*, pp. 128b, 129b; *Calendar of charter rolls*, I, 54, II, 61.
[37] *Rot. chart.*, pp. 31-32; *Calendar of charter rolls*, III, 305.
[38] *Close rolls, 1234-7*, p. 79; *ibid., 1247-1251*, pp. 253, 274, 474; *Memoranda roll, 1230-1* (ed. Chalfant Robinson, *Pipe roll society*), pp. 35, 73.

From the purely financial point of view the heaviest of the public burdens borne by the manors of England was the levy called sheriff's aid. Mr. Morris has shown that this tax was certainly collected in the reign of Henry I and probably in that of William II.[39] By 1163 it was an annual levy made at the rate of two shillings on the hide or carucate.[40] It was collected by the sheriff and formed part of the farm of the county—that is part of the revenues which enabled the sheriff to pay the lump sum demanded from him annually at the exchequer.[41] As the charter of John to Robert de Braybrook mentions " hidages called sheriff's aids," it seems safe to assume that many of the references to hidage in thirteenth-century documents are to this tax.[42] This would answer the difficult question as to why hidage should so often appear in the statements of the annual obligations borne by manors in the hundred rolls. Certainly the hidage listed among the perquisites of the shrievalty of Bedford and Buckinghamshire in a document in the *Red book of the exchequer* must be the sheriff's aid.[43] As an annual levy at a high rate, this tax was well worth avoiding if possible.

Unfortunately for the historian the fact that the sheriff's aid was not a direct obligation to the crown but formed part of the farm of the county prevented it from appearing in the pipe rolls. Hence our only source of knowledge as to exemptions from it comes from charters granting this privilege. As a result it is impossible to make any statement about the exemptions enjoyed by lay barons during the Norman period. John's charter to Robert of Leicester granting him all the rights

[39] W. A. Morris, *The mediaeval English sheriff* (Manchester, 1927), p. 99.

[40] *Materials for the history of archbishop Thomas Becket* (ed. J. C. Robertson, *Rolls series*), II, 373-374; Round, *Feudal England*, pp. 497-502.

[41] Mr. Morris believes that sheriff's aid was removed from the farm and made a direct source of royal revenue in 1163. In this I believe he is mistaken. Sheriff's aid was never accounted for on the pipe roll. In three documents showing how county farms were made up it is included among the sheriff's revenues. (*Red book of the exchequer*, II, 774-777.) The document chiefly relied on by Mr. Morris to support his view simply states that when a barony which had been exempt from sheriff's aid fell into the king's hands, the sheriff could not collect the aid and add it to his income. As the amount of the farm had been set with this exemption in mind, the aid from the tenants of the barony when it was an escheat belonged to the crown. (*Ibid.*, pp. 768-769.)

[42] *Facsimiles of early charters from Northamptonshire collections*, no. XVII.

[43] *Red book of the exchequer*, II, 777.

enjoyed by Robert, count of Meulan, mentions sheriff's aid.[44]
I am inclined to believe that barons who were exempt from
participating in murder fines were probably also released from
paying sheriff's aid, but I can present no evidence to support
this belief. In fact our only knowledge of the extent of exemptions from this levy comes from three late twelfth- or early
thirteenth-century documents in the *Red book of the exchequer*.
They show the total sheriff's aid from Essex as £11 5s 5d, from
Hertfordshire as £20 3s 6d, from Warwick and Leicestershire
as £62 2s 9d, and from Buckinghamshire and Bedfordshire as
£102 2s 4d.[45] A levy of two shillings a hide should have
yielded £213 in Essex, £98 in Hertfordshire, £218 in Warwick
and Leicestershire, and £262 in Buckinghamshire and Bedfordshire.[46] From this it seems clear that there were extensive
exemptions from the levy in these counties.

Exemption from sheriff's aid was granted fairly freely by the
Angevin kings. Some dozen charters of King John confer this
privilege, and Henry III was equally generous with it.[47] Although most of these grants were to royal favorites who were
not among the greatest landholders, they included confirma-
tions to the earls of Leicester and Huntingdon and apparently
a new concession to the earl of Richmond.[48] While there is
little evidence of the usurpation of this privilege, sheriff's aid
was the type of obligation which could be avoided by this
means. Danegeld and murder fines were paid directly into the
exchequer and accounted for on the rolls. They could only
be avoided through a royal charter or writ shown to the
barons of the exchequer. But the sheriff collected his aid to
help him pay the farm. The crown occasionally granted exemption from the aid without giving relief to the sheriff, and it had
no direct interest in helping him collect it.[49] There is evidence

---

[44] *Calendar of charter rolls*, I, 180; *Rot. chart*, p. 5.

[45] *Red book of the exchequer*, II, 774-777.

[46] I have taken the figures for the yield at two shillings a hide from the table
of the danegeld of 1162 in Ramsay, *Revenues of the kings of England*, I, 194.

[47] As examples see *Rot. chart.*, pp. 31-32, 61, 106b, 128, 128b, 129b, 146b;
Calendar of charter rolls, I, 54, 181, II, 61.

[48] *Ibid.*, I, 180; *Placita de quo warranto*, p. 547; *Close rolls, 1256-9*, p. 62;
Rotuli parliamentorum (*Record commission*), I, 165.

[49] No credits to sheriffs appear for the grants made by John to Ralph Musard
and Baldwin de Bethune. The credits allowed for the grant to the earl of

that barons quarrelled with sheriffs over the liability of their manors for sheriff's aid.[50]   In one case at least tenants of a barony in one shire paid the aid while those in other counties were exempt.[51]   Clearly it was possible for a powerful lord, especially in time of civil commotion, to refuse to pay the aid and defy the sheriff to collect it.   As we shall see such usurpation was common in the case of other privileges.   The lack of positive evidence for it does not convince me that usurpation did not play its part in building up the total exemptions from sheriff's aid.

A highly interesting question arises in connection with sheriff's aid.   Some of the royal charters giving exemption from this levy confined the privilege to the demesnes of the grantee, but others extended it to cover knights' fees as well.   The charters to the earls of Leicester and Huntingdon freed both their demesnes and their fees.   One is naturally led to wonder whether this meant that the tenants did not pay aid or paid it to their lord instead of to the sheriff.   The *Dialogue of the exchequer* states that it was a serious offence for one who had obtained release from an obligation to collect it from his men.[52] But in one case at least John specifically authorized a lord to collect sheriff's aid for his own use.[53]   In the absence of any clear evidence that barons who had obtained exemption for their demesnes and fees collected sheriff's aid from their tenants, one must assume that it was not generally done, but I should not be surprised to find someday an indication that such a levy swelled the coffers of some great lord.   The money paid for view of frankpledge, which was also a source of the sheriff's official revenue, was collected by certain franchise holders such as the earls of Gloucester and Leicester and the lord of Wallingford.   Perhaps this was considered a payment for a service and hence was in a different category than was the sheriff's aid.

Leicester ceased in 1203.   For proof that sheriffs were sometimes forced to make up in other ways the aid they lost by grants of exemption see *Red book of the exchequer*, II, 768-769.

[50] *Calendar of inquisitions miscellaneous* (*Rolls series*), I, 60.

[51] *Memoranda roll, 1230-1*, pp. 73-74.

[52] *Dialogus de scaccario*, p. 95.

[53] *Rot. chart.*, p. 204.

So far we have been discussing public burdens that were from the beginning purely financial. Now we must turn to an obligation that was primarily a public service—the duty of doing suit at the shire and hundred courts. In the thirteenth century this service was valued in terms of money, but it is not clear on what basis the valuation was made. It may have been an estimate of the value of the penalties to be collected from the suitors. Perhaps those who attended the courts were expected to make a payment to the sheriff. We find sheriffs receiving credit on their farms for estates which had been granted exemption from this obligation, and in the hundred rolls the removal of a suit from the shire and hundred courts was considered a diminution of the royal revenue.[54]

The judicial functions of these courts will be considered in connection with the discussion of baronial franchises. Here we are simply interested in the obligation to attend their meetings. The *Leges Henrici* state that if a baron or his steward was present, all his demesnes were considered to have performed their obligation.[55] A decree of Henry I commanded all men whose predecessors had owed suit in the time of King Edward to attend the shire and hundred courts even if they had received a royal charter of exemption.[56] While it is difficult to obtain positive evidence, it seems fairly clear that Henry continued to grant such exemptions, and the presumption is that they were effective.

Exemption from doing suit at the shire and hundred courts was one of the most common privileges granted by the Angevin kings. Practically everyone who was freed from paying sheriff's aid was acquitted of these suits, and a number of lords received the latter privilege without the former. During the reign of Henry II all the lands of the earls of Leicester, Huntingdon, Essex, and Warren were apparently free from this burden.[57] Henry III granted exemption to Hubert de Burgh, Warin de

---

[54] "Pipe rolls 4 and 5 John," *Pipe roll society*, LIII, 144, LIV, 199; *Pipe rolls 6 and 7 John*, Public Record Office. These revenues were part of the sheriff's farm. *Red book of exchequer*, II, 777.

[55] *Leges Henrici*, c. 7, 7.

[56] Liebermann, *Die Gesetze des Angelsachsen*, I, 524.

[57] *Rot. chart.*, pp. 5, 128; *Placita de quo warranto*, p. 547; *Close rolls, 1242-7*, p. 219; *ibid.*, *1251-3*, p. 189.

Montchenesi, and Peter of Savoy, earl of Richmond.[58] Besides these great lords the kings granted it freely to their favorites of lesser importance.[59]

The most interesting feature of this privilege was the ease with which it could be usurped especially in a period when the royal government was weak. One could simply stop doing suit. In times of peace it was difficult enough for a sheriff to distrain a great baron, and in times of civil commotion it was practically impossible. The earliest example I can find of such usurpation in time of war was in the honor of Giffard. In 1222 twelve knights appeared before the king's justices to say what revenues King John had enjoyed from the Giffard lands before the war between him and his barons. The jurors stated that the holders of the honor, William Marshal, earl of Pembroke, and Gilbert de Clare, earl of Hertford, had been exempt from suit to shire and hundred on their demesnes but not on their fees.[60] Obviously the two magnates had withdrawn the suit due from their fees during the civil war. What is more they seem to have won the debate despite the testimony of the jurors. An entry in the hundred rolls states that Fawley in Buckinghamshire did suit to shire and hundred paying fees of ten shillings until William Marshal the elder obtained exemption.[61] The hundred rolls make clear that the fees of this honor were exempt in the later thirteenth century.[62]

The great period for usurpation of exemption from suit at shire and hundred courts was the time of civil commotion in the reign of Henry III. The most prominent offenders in regard to the extent of their operations were Richard and Gilbert de Clare, successively earls of Gloucester and Hertford. Throughout the hundred rolls and the *quo warranto* pleas we read with tiresome regularity the statement that a suit had been removed by Earl Richard or his son.[63] Apparently their object

[58] *Ibid.*, *1256-9*, p. 62; *Calendar of charter rolls*, I, 54; *Rotuli hundredorum* (*Record commission*), I, 468.

[59] As examples see *Rot. chart*, pp. 31-32, 106b, 126, 128b, 129b, 146b, 181; *Close rolls, 1227-1231*, p. 338; *ibid., 1231-4*, p. 196; *ibid., 1234-7*, p. 238; *Calendar of charter rolls*, I, 253.

[60] *Bracton's note book*, III, 450.

[61] *Rot. hund.*, I, 22.

[62] For examples see *ibid.*, pp. 25, 31.

[63] *Rot. hund.*, I, 2, 50, 201, II, 8, 10; *Placita de quo warranto*, pp. 183, 703.

was bit by bit to usurp exemption for all their fees and demesnes. As they were holders of many private hundreds, they,
often managed to transfer the suit to one of their own courts.[64]
The extent of this usurpation can be judged from the fact that
at one point in the *quo warranto* proceedings the king's attorney
claimed that the earl had withdrawn suits to the value of
£100.[65] Close behind the earls of Gloucester in this activity
was the king's brother Richard of Cornwall.[66] Naturally other
barons followed their example. In 1266 Roger de Mortimer
obtained a charter acquitting his demesne manor of Cleobury
Mortimer from suit at shire and hundred courts. Then he
coolly withdrew the suit owed by the fees attached to this
manor and those held of his chief barony of Wigmore.[67] The
Corbet seat of Cause was over the border of Wales and hence
owed no suit, but many of its fees were in Shropshire. The
Corbets withdrew their suits and transferred them to Cause.[68]
There were, in fact, few barons who did not withdraw some
suits owed. The jurors of the wapentake of Bingham in
Nottinghamshire reported that the baronies of Tutbury, Aincurt, Basset of Weldon, Lovetot, Biset, and Ghent had all
removed their fees.[69]

It is, of course, not always possible to be certain whether
the suits which the jurors state to have been withdrawn had
been removed legally or illegally. Thus the earl of Richmond
is charged with many usurpations, but his demesnes and fees
had been acquitted by a charter from Henry III. On the
other hand the earl of Gloucester admitted his usurpations
and eventually made reparation. There may have been many
border-line cases like that of Roger de Mowbray. Roger was
summoned to show by what authority he did no suit to the
shire court of Lincolnshire. He answered that neither he nor
his ancestors ever had. The jurors disagreed. They stated

[64] *Rot. hund.*, II, 14, 126, 131, 133.
[65] *Placita de quo warranto*, p. 183. This apparently included some sheriff's
aid and fees for view of frankpledge as well as the value of the suits.
[66] *Rot. hund.*, I, 27; II, 30, 46.
[67] *Calendar of charter rolls*, II, 61; *Rot. hund.*, II, 108; *Placita de quo
warranto*, p. 675.
[68] *Rot. hund.*, II, 60.
[69] *Ibid.*, p. 27.

that the suit had been performed until the reign of Henry III. Then Roger and the sheriff made an agreement. Roger paid the sheriff five marcs to be quit of suit and view of frankpledge. Roger or his seneschal were to attend one meeting of the shire court each year and to be quit of the rest unless they were needed for a serious case.[70] This clearly shows one of the conditions that served to make usurpation of exemption from suits easy. The popular courts had little business and hence little real need for suitors. Like so many other services, suit of court had become largely a financial matter. A sheriff could be persuaded or forced to accept a cash compromise. Such an arrangement was illegal—exemption could be granted by the crown alone, but it was hardly pure usurpation.

It is extremely difficult to get a clear idea of the value to a baron of exemption from suit at the popular courts. The earl of Gloucester was charged with removing suits worth £100, but this figure is too round and too vague to inspire much confidence. The eagerness of the barons to obtain or usurp the privilege indicates that it was valuable. I can find no regular basis for the sums paid for suit by individual estates—they seem to have no connection with the number of hides but to be purely arbitrary. Thus one fee held of the barony of Cainhoe was assessed for hidage at five hides and paid 6s 8d for suit. Another fee of the same barony had seven and one-half hides, but paid only two shillings for suit.[71] In general the payments for suit varied between two and ten shillings for a manor. For a great barony like that of the earls of Gloucester containing hundreds of estates—they must have held well over 450 knights' fees—the total of such sums could be very large.

Obviously one of the chief purposes of the hundred and *quo warranto* inquests was to check illegal withdrawals of suits due to the shire and hundred courts and recover the revenue lost to the crown. As far as the first of these purposes was concerned they seem to have been successful. The baron who had once failed to establish his claim to exemption had not much chance to usurp it later. The record was easily available to the royal judges. Unfortunately it is impossible to discover how many

[70] *Placita de quo warranto*, p. 429.   [71] *Rot. hund.*, I, 4; II, 326.

usurped suits were regained. The earl of Gloucester made reparation. Probably others did as well, but clear evidence is lacking.

To sum up, a few great lords like the earls of Leicester and Huntingdon held this privilege at least as early as the reign of Henry II. Richard and John granted it to a few favorites none of whom were really great landholders. Henry III gave it to some great fiefs like the earldom of Richmond. Naturally barons who lacked this privilege desired it. William Marshal and Gilbert de Clare usurped it during the revolt against John for their fees of the honor of Giffard. There was probably a steady series of scattered usurpations throughout the reign of Henry III. But the great opportunity came with the civil wars and was used most profitably by such immensely powerful magnates as the earls of Gloucester and Richard of Cornwall. In fact one can say that there appears to have been a concerted attempt on the part of the English barons to usurp this privilege during the civil commotions.

On the whole it seems safe to say that in general the lay barons of England did not succeed in their efforts to avoid the public burdens imposed on their lands. Their closest approach to it came in the widespread usurpation of exemption from suit of court during the civil wars of Henry III's reign. But the recognized freedom from hidage, murder and common fines, sheriff's aid, and suit at shire and hundred courts that was enjoyed by most important ecclesiastics was possessed by few lay lords. A small number of fortunate and powerful magnates like the earls of Leicester and Huntingdon, a few relatives of the king such as Richard of Cornwall and Peter of Savoy, and a larger but still not very large group of royal favorites were the only laymen to approach the ecclesiastical privileges in this respect. As for the new types of taxes which stemmed from the Saladin tithe, I can find no evidence that hereditary exemptions were ever granted. Favored barons might receive exemption on their demesnes in the case of an individual levy, but even such cases seem rare. In the reign of Henry III certain great lords like the earl Marshal, the earl of Richmond, and the earl of Leicester seem to have been allowed to assess and collect these taxes in their baronies, but this does not imply exemption but merely freedom from royal agents.

CHAPTER IV

FRANCHISAL RESOURCES

In the preceding chapter we have discussed the public obligations, both feudal and non-feudal, which burdened the English baronies. Now we must turn to an examination of the barons' resources. I am using resources in the broadest possible sense—as meaning anything that contributed to the satisfaction of their desires. Resources that furnished prestige and power directly are fully as important as those that did so indirectly by increasing baronial wealth. For convenience in discussion I have divided the resources of English barons into five more or less logical classes—franchisal, feudal, manorial, natural, and commercial. Franchisal resources consist of the prestige, power, and money income derived from the performance of essentially public functions by the baron. Feudal resources comprise the services and financial dues owed by the baron's vassals. Manorial resources include all the benefits drawn directly or indirectly from agriculture such as the profits from the cultivation of the manorial demesne and the rents paid by villains and free tenants. The fourth class consists of the income obtained from the exploitation of natural resources like woods, mines, and fisheries. Finally most barons had some resources that were essentially commercial—profits from fairs and markets and rents of burgage tenants.

The term franchise as used in mediaeval England meant any privilege that could in theory be derived from no source except a royal grant. The exemptions from public burdens discussed in the preceding chapter were called franchises and so were authorizations to make parks and warrens and to hold fairs and markets. I am using the word in a more limited sense to include only the privilege of performing public functions. These functions might be executive or military, but they were more commonly simply police and judicial. As the performance of public function involved the enjoyment of its perquisites, franchises were a source of money revenue. The man who exercises judicial and police authority obtains power over those subject to his jurisdiction. Finally the enjoyment of high prerogatives which were essentially a part of the public authority enhanced one's position in feudal society. In short franchises were highly desirable possessions from the baron's point of view.

Before embarking on the history of English baronial franchises, it seems necessary to glance at the background of the subject. When William of Normandy conquered England, he found a land with a well-developed system of government. There were two distinct types of institution—royal and popular. The king and his officers, the earls and the sheriffs, exercised a certain amount of authority. They were the military leaders of the nation. The sheriffs under the king's direction administered the royal estates and collected the royal revenues. The king, presumably with the advice of his Witan, could legislate. Men convicted of certain major crimes were at his mercy. The earl and the sheriff presided over the popular courts. The profits from these courts were divided among king, earl, and sheriff. But the king neither prosecuted nor tried men charged with the crimes which placed them at his mercy. The earls and sheriffs were moderators rather than judges in the popular courts. Men charged with crime were prosecuted, tried, and convicted or acquitted in accord with customary law and royal legislation as interpreted by the suitors of the court. The accused who refused to appear was outlawed. In short the sphere of government occupied by the king and his officers was extremely limited. By far the chief part of government as far as ordinary men were concerned was carried on by the shire and hundred courts.

Private jurisdiction was not unknown in Anglo-Saxon England. *Sac* and *soc* in all probability implied rights of jurisdiction over minor offences. Privileged landholders had *infangentheof* and *utfangentheof*. While the exact content of these franchises is far from clear even in the thirteenth century to say nothing of the eleventh, in general they gave the right to hang thieves caught with stolen property. These seem to have been real rights of jurisdiction. Other private interests in the administration of justice were probably purely financial. The king at times granted hundred courts to private individuals. A few great ecclesiastics shared the royal interest in some of the more serious offences. But as the crown's connection with the popular courts was confined largely to collecting the profits, it seems likely that the same was true of its grantees. In short the landholder who possessed a hundred court simply received the proceeds.

The knights who followed Duke William to England represented most of the provinces of northwestern France. They came from Normandy, Brittany, Flanders, Maine, Anjou, and the duchy of France. So diverse were the political conditions and feudal customs in these regions that it is extremely difficult to generalize about the ideas of government brought by the conquerors to England. One can say that with the exception of part of Brittany these regions had all been included in the Frankish state—in other words in the ninth century their political institutions had differed but little from those of Anglo-Saxon England. But the development of feudalism had wrought great changes. To an extent that varied from fief to fief the feudal lords had absorbed the authority of the central government. In Brittany the baron enjoyed full powers of justice in his lands. In Normandy the "justice of the sword" was in general reserved by the duke. But however the power might be divided, the connection between feudal lordship and rights of jurisdiction was firmly established in French custom and practice. The men who received fiefs from the Conqueror expected such privileges.

The influence of French custom on English baronial ideas did not end with the conquest. Many barons held lands in both England and Normandy. English barons and knights followed the Norman kings on their continental campaigns. Henry I granted English baronies to Breton and Angevin newcomers. The crusades introduced the barons of England to their peers from all over Europe. Certainly until the thirteenth century and probably later still the English baronage was French in language and to a great extent in ideas. The English barons must have been fully aware of the privileges enjoyed by their French contemporaries. I suspect that this knowledge had much to do with their avidity for franchises of all sorts. Unfortunately I can find only one clear case of this influence. In 1249 Roger Bigod, earl of Norfolk, claimed certain privileges on the ground that the count of Gisnes had them and that he was an earl holding as freely from the English king as the count did from the king of France.[1]

It seems clear that the Conqueror's barons and their successors were unlikely to be content with the limited privileges enjoyed by their Anglo-Saxon predecessors. They would continually strive to increase their power and revenue. If English institutions had remained static, they could only have done this by encroaching on the authority of the popular courts. But the Norman and Angevin kings were determined innovators who steadily increased the scope of royal authority. Their legislation created new police and judicial functions. The barons struggled zealously to obtain for themselves as many as possible of these new powers. Thus while royal legislation to some extent regulated and even decreased baronial authority, it also created new franchises for them to seek.

Let us now turn to the examination of the various franchises in detail. I shall start with the most common and consider them in the approximate order of their importance judged by the prestige involved in their possession. This order is in general the exact reverse of that in which the franchises appear in the thirteenth century hundred and *quo warranto* inquests. The allied but slightly different subject of hereditary possession of public offices will be treated at the end of the chapter.

The most widely held of all franchises was that known as *sac* and *soc*. According to Pollock and Maitland the earliest authentic appearance of the term is in a writ issued by King Cnut in favor of the archbishop of Canterbury.[2] It appears regularly in the few surviving charters of the Conqueror and his sons. By the time of Henry I this franchise was apparently enjoyed by all tenants by knight service.[3] The general meaning of *sac* and *soc* is clear—it meant the right to hold a court, try cases, and receive the profits. Unfortunately it is not certain what cases the possessor of this franchise could try. Bracton

---

[1] Matthew Paris, *Chronica maiora* (ed. H. R. Luard, *Rolls series*), V, 85-86.
[2] *History of English law*, I, 20.
[3] *Leges Henrici*, c. 20, 2; c. 27.

states that the lord with *sac* and *soc* had jurisdiction over the inhabitants of his demesne manors in cases of minor affrays in which men were beaten or wounded and in which no charge was made that the peace of the king or sheriff had been broken. He could also hear cases involving the wounding of animals and debts sued for without a royal writ.[4] A brief reference to the subject in Glanville indicates that the same situation existed at the end of the twelfth century.[5] In short in Glanville and Bracton the holder of *sac* and *soc* enjoyed over his own men jurisdiction equivalent to that of the hundred court except that he lacked the right to hang thieves.

There is no clear evidence as to the extent of the jurisdiction given by this franchise under the Norman kings. The *Leges Henrici* state carefully what men the holder had jurisdiction over. In case both accuser and accused were the men of the same lord who had *sac* and *soc*, the plea would be heard in his court. If they were men of different lords who had this franchise, the case would go to the court of the accused's lord.[6] Presumably if the lord of the accused lacked *sac* and *soc*, the case would go to the hundred court. But the *Leges* are far from specific as to what cases could be heard by these lords with *sac* and *soc*. There is a long list of royal pleas which certainly were not in their jurisdiction. Reference is made to pleas belonging to the sheriff, but they are not specified.[7]

Pollock and Maitland seem to have believed that in the eleventh century *sac* and *soc* was an extensive franchise covering all pleas except those reserved to the crown.[8] They also believed that the pleas of the crown were far fewer under the Conqueror than under Henry I.[9] I am inclined to believe that the latter statement is true, but I have grave doubts about the former. In the eleventh century *soc* was occasionally used in a broad sense to mean simply jurisdiction. In this use it could cover the wide franchises enjoyed by the great ecclesiastical lords. But I am convinced that the ordinary grant of *sac* and

[4] Bracton, *De legibus*, II, 436.
[5] Glanville, *De legibus*, p. 42.
[6] *Leges Henrici*, c. 25; c. 57, 1.
[7] *Leges Henrici*, c. 9, 11; c. 10, 1; c. 20, 2-3.
[8] *History of English law*, I, 563-565.
[9] *Ibid.*, p. 564.

soc conveyed no such powers. My reason for this belief is as follows. The usual grant in the Norman period gave *sac, soc, thol, theam,* and *infangentheof. Infangentheof* was the right to hang a thief caught with the stolen goods after a hot pursuit. It seems incredible to me that if *sac* and *soc* conveyed a wide franchise, it should be necessary to add to it to enable a lord to hang a hand-having thief. In short, I believe that *sac* and *soc* in the Norman period conveyed much the same jurisdiction that it did in the time of Glanville and Bracton.

The franchise of *sac* and *soc* is of no great interest to the historian of the English barony because it was too widely held to be called a baronial privilege. There is in fact some doubt whether it should be called a franchise. Pollock and Maitland consider it a mere attribute of landholding.[10] Yet the *Leges Henrici* make clear that the king could grant land and retain the *soc,* and it speaks of *domini* who lack this privilege.[11] But such men must have been far below baronial rank and are of no interest to us.

Next above *sac* and *soc* in importance comes a group of franchises that were enjoyed by most lords of any importance—the right to enforce the assize of bread and ale, view of frankpledge, and *infangentheof.* All barons and honorial barons possessed these privileges in their demesne manors. The first two were also enjoyed by many mesne tenants whom it would be difficult to classify as honorial barons. Mr. Stenton believes that this general level of privilege marked baronial status in the days before there was any clear distinction between royal and honorial barons.[12]

The assize of bread and ale was apparently created by the legislation of Henry II. In the 1170's we begin to find on the pipe rolls records of amercements for its infraction.[13] We hear practically nothing of the right to enforce this assize as a franchise before the great inquests of the thirteenth century where it appears as a privilege long enjoyed. Basing his statement on an inquest of 1234 Bracton calls this a plea belonging

[10] *Ibid.,* p. 567.
[11] *Leges Henrici,* c. 19, 2-3; c. 57, 8.
[12] *English feudalism,* pp. 99-101.
[13] "Pipe roll 23 Henry II," *Pipe roll society,* XXVI, 29-30.

to the sheriff and so outside the jurisdiction of the ordinary holder of *sac* and *soc*.[14] The hundred and *quo warranto* inquests show that it was held by all lords of any importance. I suspect that Henry II made no serious attempt to monopolize for the crown the profits from enforcing this assize and allowed it to be exercised freely by men of position.

For the first century after the creation of the assize of bread and ale infractions of it were apparently always punished by amercement. But a statute of Henry III prescribed corporal punishment for flagrant offences.[15] This seems to have been ignored by most franchise holders. As far as I can discover the franchise was at best not very profitable, and the holders were unwilling to give up the money penalties and go to the trouble of erecting the pillories and tumbrils required to administer corporal punishment. But in the *quo warranto* proceedings the king's officers were inclined to insist that lack of this equipment forfeited the franchise. Many lords were obliged to repurchase their privileges by paying a small fine.

The most valuable of all the lesser franchises was that known as " view of frankpledge." The frankpledge system by which ten men were bound together and sworn to produce any of their number sought by the courts had its origin in Anglo-Saxon institutions but took definite form under the Norman kings.[16] The *Leges Henrici* state that a specially full session of the hundred court consisting of all the inhabitants of the hundred both free and unfree should be held twice a year to make sure that everyone was in frankpledge.[17] No specific mention is made of the sheriff, but presumably he presided over such meetings. Certainly by the time of Henry II this official was responsible for supervising the frankpledge system.[18] The legislation of Henry II placed on the sheriff the responsibility for receiving presentments involving major offences, and this business was transacted at these special sessions of the hundred. The sheriff also heard his own pleas on this occasion.[19] The

[14] Bracton, *De legibus*, II, 437; *Bracton's note book*, III, 129.
[15] *Statutes of the realm*, I, 199-200.
[16] W. A. Morris, *The frankpledge system* (New York, 1910), pp. 1-41.
[17] *Leges Henrici*, c. 8, 1-2.
[18] *Assize of Clarendon*, c. 8, Stubbs, *Select charters*, pp. 143-146.
[19] Morris, *The frankpledge system*, p. 117.

result was the bi-annual " sheriff's tourn " mentioned in the second reissue of *Magna Carta*.[20] But in *Magna Carta* only one of these sessions was described as devoted to supervising the frankpledge system while the other was reserved for present-ments and pleas. Hence from 1217 at least the view of frank-pledge was simply one of the functions of the sheriff's tourn.

There is no suggestion in the *Leges Henrici* that any lord had the right to supervise the frankpledge system in his lands or to withhold his tenants from the bi-annual special meetings of the hundred court. As we shall see when discussing the franchise called " return of writ," it seems likely that a few great ecclesiastical and perhaps some lay lords could bar the sheriff from entering their lands. Such men must have super-vised the frankpledge system themselves. Henry II tried to deprive even these lords of this privilege. The ninth article of the Assize of Clarendon decrees: " And let there be no one inside or outside a castle, not even in the honor of Walling-ford, who forbids the sheriff to enter his court or liberty to view frankpledge. . . . " [21] There is no reason to believe that Henry succeeded in this effort to reduce the privileges of these great lords, but the wording of the passage seems to indicate that the men who claimed the right to ban the sheriff were few and highly privileged.

The charter of 1217 provided that the sheriff should in view-ing frankpledge respect all liberties existing in the time of Henry II or acquired since.[22] Richard and John had granted this franchise fairly generously—in fact most charters issued by them which conferred special rights included it. The same was true in the reign of Henry III.[23] But as I have pointed out before, such grants were not actually very numerous. In short the laws and the charters would suggest that the right to hold view of frankpledge was a rather rare franchise possessed by a few highly privileged great lords and some special favorites of the crown. But when one examines the hundred and *quo*

---

[20] *Charter of 1217*, c. 42.

[21] *Assize of Clarendon*, c. 9.

[22] *Charter of 1217*, c. 42.

[23] *Rot. chart.*, pp. 106b, 128b, 129b, 134-135; *Calendar of charter rolls*, I, 181, 253.

warranto inquests of the late thirteenth century, it becomes apparent that view of frankpledge was a very common franchise—almost as common as the right to enforce the assize of bread and ale. Moreover, it is interesting to note that there was no uniformity in respect to the conditions under which this privilege was exercised. One baron would have the right to hold the view on his demesne and take the profits.[24] Another could hold the view but was obliged to pay the sheriff either a fixed sum or part or all of the profits.[25] Then some lords could hold the view only in the presence of the sheriff. In these cases the sheriff might get none of the proceeds, part, or all.[26] This wide variety of arrangements, varying from fief to fief in the same shire and hundred, seems to me to point to individual bargains with the sheriffs. Only in the case of Roger de Mowbray mentioned above can I find definite evidence of such a bargain, but the existence of many more seems clear.[27] What is more, the crown at times recognized the variations. Usually in John's charters the grantee was simply given the franchise, but in one case at least it was limited. Fulk D'Oiry was granted the right to hold the view for his tenants in the manor of Gedney. He was to summon the sheriff to supervise the proceedings, but if that official did not come, he could proceed without him. In any case the profits went to the lord.[28] Under these circumstances I doubt that the sheriff came very often.

The profits gained by the sheriff from viewing frankpledge formed a part of his farm and hence were only of indirect interest to the crown. Exposed to the pressure of the barons to permit them to exercise this function, he made the best bargain he could. Undoubtedly there was some pure usurpation especially in time of civil war. The sheriff on his side was not above taking advantage of such an opportunity as the death of a great lord or the carelessness of a baronial bailli to claim his rights in a formerly exempt manor.[29] There is no way of

---

[24] *Placita de quo warranto*, pp. 3-4, 85, 88-89.

[25] *Ibid.*, pp. 424, 429.

[26] *Ibid.*, p. 483b; *Rot. hund.*, I, 471, II, 746.

[27] *Placita de quo warranto*, p. 429.

[28] *Rot. chart.*, pp. 134-135.

[29] *Close rolls, 1256-9*, p. 316; *Calendar of inquisitions miscellaneous*, I, 120-121.

determining in what period most of the bargains between lords
and sheriffs were made. Mr. Morris is certainly safe in saying
the wide extension of this franchise took place during the first
century after 1166.[30] What evidence we have seems to indicate
that the major part of the process took place in the middle
years of the thirteenth century.

The privilege of holding view of frankpledge usually exempted the holder and the tenants on his demesne from attending the sheriff's tourn and permitted the lord to exercise the
functions performed by the sheriff on these occasions. But
here again there was no uniformity. Some lords with view of
frankpledge were not exempt from the tourn. Others simply
appeared in person or by bailli and claimed their franchise. In
short the bargains made with the sheriffs seem to have included
the tourn as a whole as well as view of frankpledge.

It seems clear that the chief feature of the franchise of view
of frankpledge from the barons' point of view was the police
power it conferred. This is demonstrated by the large numbers
of cases where the lord held the view but gave the profits to
the sheriff. When the franchise included the exercise of the
functions of the sheriff in his tourn, it conferred extremely wide
police power, and even when it was limited to the view, the
authority given was important. Jurisdiction has always been
closely connected with power. The lord who held this franchise had a highly effective means of controlling his tenants.

In discussing the right to enforce the assize of bread and
ale and to hold view of frankpledge I have assumed that these
privileges were limited to the holder's demesne. As a rule this
was the case. The relations between lord and vassal were
purely feudal and had no connection with the non-feudal public
burdens and jurisdictions. But the example of the baronies of
France and the English palatinates where feudal and public
authority were combined was always before the eyes of the
English barons. They strove continually to make the fief the
unit of local government in place of the shire and hundred.[31]
The wording of the Assize of Clarendon suggests that the
whole honor of Wallingford, demesnes and fees, had its own

[30] *The frankpledge system*, p. 135.
[31] For an excellent example see *Placita de quo warranto*, p. 12.

views in 1166.[32] The hundred and *quo warranto* rolls show
that the Earls Warren enjoyed this privilege and make no suggestion that it was a recent usurpation. As these earls had been
very highly privileged from an early date, their possession of
this franchise may have gone back to Norman times. King
John granted Earl Robert of Leicester exemption from " paying
money for view of frankpledge " for his demesnes and fees,
and there is no evidence that would justify us in questioning
the statement in the charter that this privilege had been enjoyed
by Count Robert of Meulan. Whatever the exact intention of
John's charter may have been, in the inquests we find the lords
of the honor of Leicester holding view of frankpledge in their
fees and taking the profits.[33]

While it seems likely that the baronies mentioned above had
the franchise of view of frankpledge for both demesnes and
fees as early as the reign of Henry II, there can be little doubt
that most of those who enjoyed it at the time of the hundred
and *quo warranto* inquests had acquired it comparatively recently. Although parts of the great honor of Richmond seem
to have enjoyed it before Henry III's reign, only that king's
charter to Peter of Savoy freed all its fees from views held by
the sheriffs.[34] About half of the grants conferring view of
frankpledge issued by John and Henry III extended the franchise over both demesnes and fees.[35] In addition to the actual
royal grants there were some usurpations. Apparently when
William Marshal and Gilbert de Clare withdrew their fees of
the honor of Giffard from suit at the shire and hundred courts,
they quietly usurped the privilege of holding view of frankpledge.[36] Among the many usurpations committed by the earls
of Gloucester during the civil wars of Henry III's reign the
withdrawal of their tenants from the sheriff's tourn and view

[32] *Assize of Clarendon*, c. 9.

[33] *Calendar of charter rolls*, I, 180; *Close rolls, 1256-9*, p. 316; *Calendar of
inquisitions post mortem*, II, 248.

[34] *Close rolls, 1234-7*, p. 79; *ibid., 1256-9*, p. 62; *Rot. hund.*, I, 51-53.

[35] *Calendar of charter rolls*, I, 54, 181; *Close rolls, 1231-4*, p. 196; *ibid.,
1234-7*, p. 238; *Facsimiles of early charters from Northamptonshire collections*,
no. XVII.

[36] *Close rolls, 1247-1251*, p. 102; *Rot. hund.*, I, 23b, 29, 31b; *Placita de qu
warranto*, p. 86.

of frankpledge was one of the most common.[37]   While Earl
Richard of Cornwall could probably claim with justice that his
honor of Wallingford had long enjoyed this franchise, he
extended it to other fiefs held by him.[38]

The right to hold view of frankpledge in one's fees was a
very high franchise. It was granted to a few great barons and
some royal favorites. Only the most powerful could usurp it
successfully. It was as valuable as it was difficult to obtain.
The possession of extensive police power over the tenants of his
vassals was of great advantage to a baron. It must have done
much to hold the barony together as the purely feudal bonds
decayed.   Moreover the fees collected from view of frankpledge in the whole of a large barony amounted to a fairly
attractive sum. Exact figures are hard to obtain except for individual manors, but at the death of Edmund of Cornwall in
1300 the views of the honor of Wallingford were worth £16 6s
a year and those of the honor of St. Valery £6 14s 4d.[39]   Although these were not great sums, they were large enough to
interest a thirteenth-century English baron.

The right to enforce the assize of bread and ale was so
widely held that it can have made little difference to the crown
whether it was possessed by the baron or his vassals.   In
general it seems clear that it belonged to the man who held
the land in demesne. But there were some exceptions. Edward
II specifically gave Peter Gaveston this privilege in the whole
honor of Knaresborough—over his own tenants and those of
his vassals.[40]   The inquests indicate that the lords of the rapes
of Sussex held this privilege in all their fees except for the
demesnes of a few honorial barons.[41]   But these seem to have
been exceptions. The franchise conferred little power and
prestige and yielded an insignificant revenue. The barons were
inclined to leave it to their vassals.

The franchise called *infangentheof* was less widely distributed than the right to enforce the assize of bread and ale

[37] *Ibid.*, pp. 95, 183; *Rot. hund.*, I, 2, 50, 201.

[38] For instance to the honor of St. Valery. *Calendar of inquisitions post mortem*, III, 465.

[39] *Ibid.*, pp. 466-468.

[40] *Calendar of charter rolls*, III, 139-140.

[41] *Placita de quo warranto*, p. 751; *Rot. hund.*, II, 201.

and to hold view of frankpledge. With some few exceptions its possession was limited to barons and mesne tenants important enough to be called honorial barons. As defined in the thirteenth century it allowed the holder to hang an inhabitant of his demesne caught on the demesne in possession of freshly stolen property.[42] Since there is no evidence to the contrary, one must assume that its meaning was the same in the Norman period. Mr. Stenton believes that by the thirteenth century the holder of his franchise could not hang a thief without the supervision of a royal official. The case he cites in support of this view does not seem to me conclusive. In 1260 Peter Achard, a minor tenant-in-chief, was presented by a jury for hanging a thief convicted in his court *sine aliquo ballivo domini regis*. The presentment added that the thief was hanged on an oak where as far as the jurors could remember no one had been hanged before. The record states that Peter paid a fine of forty shillings, but does not specify the offence. Mr. Stenton states that the irregularity lay in the absence of a royal officer, but I am not so sure.[43] There is clear evidence that the use of improvised gallows was considered irregular in the thirteenth century.[44] Other evidence shows that men were fined for hanging thieves in the absence of a royal officer, but in all the cases I know of the lord involved was of very minor importance.[45] Bracton in his discussion of *infangentheof* makes no mention of the need for the supervision of a royal officer. In short I suspect that Mr. Stenton has generalized too freely. Local custom may have decreed that certain holders of this franchise were limited to exercising it under supervision, but the paucity of references to this requirement convinces me that it was not a general rule.

As far as I can discover *infangentheof* was always limited to a lord's demesne and was never exercised over his fees. Although the thirteenth-century inquests seem to show some exceptions to this statement, they are apparent rather than real. *Infangentheof* when not exercised by a franchise holder be-

---

[42] Bracton, *De legibus*, II, 436.
[43] *English feudalism*, p. 101 and note 1.
[44] *Rot. hund.*, I, 235.
[45] For an example see " Pipe roll 2 John," *Pipe roll society*, L, 22.

longed to the hundred. When a baron held a hundred, he exercised this right over its entire area both inside and outside his fief. In the case of compact baronies like the rapes of Sussex practically all the land in the hundreds was held by vassals of the lord. Thus the Earl Warren had *infangentheof* throughout his barony of Lewes, but he exercised it as holder of the hundreds contained in the rape of Lewes.[46]

Infangentheof supplies the best illustration of the importance of the possession of franchises to baronial pride and prestige. Practically it must have been of very slight value. If any money profits were made from it, they must have been very small. The occasions for exercising it were few and far apart—once or twice in a generation seems to have been a fair average.[47] The police power involved cannot have amounted to much. Yet this franchise was continually in dispute. The crown and holders of private hundreds questioned the right of lords who claimed the franchise, and the lords defended themselves with vigor.[48] The reason for this concern about a privilege of little actual value seems obvious. In France the gallows was the mark of seignorial authority—of the power over life and member. In England the franchise of *infangentheof* gave a baron his only opportunity to judge a capital offence. It also entitled, in fact required, him to have gallows. From the time of the Conquest its possession had marked baronial status. In short *infangentheof* was the highest franchise most barons and important mesne tenants could hope to possess, and it was valued for that reason.

Although *utfangentheof* was a much rarer franchise than *infangentheof*, it does not seem to have marked a higher level of privilege. According to Bracton it permitted a lord possessing it to hang a thief from outside his demesne caught on the demesne with property stolen there.[49] It seems impossible to

[46] *Placita de quo warranto*, p. 751.
[47] For instance see *Rotuli curiae regis* (ed. F. Palgrave, *Record commission*) II, 10-11; *Rolls of the justices in eyre for Gloucestershire, Warwickshire and Staffordshire* (ed. D. M. Stenton, *Selden society*), pp. 123-126.
[48] In addition to above see *Rot. hund.*, I, 235; *Placita de quo warranto*, pp. 218-219, 531; *Bracton's note book*, II, 629-631; III, 504-5; *Curia regis rolls*, IV, 89.
[49] *De legibus*, II, 436.

make any valid generalization about who enjoyed *utfangentheof*. A charter of 1290 states that all the barons of Kent possessed this franchise, but it seems clear that this was not true of England as a whole.[50] The list of known holders of *utfangentheof* includes great lords like the earls of Richmond, lesser barons like the Aincurts, and important mesne tenants such as the Traillys.[51] Apparently all the tenants of the honors of Chester and Huntingdon enjoyed this franchise.[52] It was granted, though not too freely, to minor lords in royal favor.[53] On the whole one can say that it was of little importance. It gave no great prestige beyond that conferred by *infangentheof* and was of equally slight practical value.

One of the most puzzling of English franchises was the one that permitted its holder to enjoy the profits from wrecks. A wreck was anything cast up on the shore from which no living thing survived. In Normandy and Brittany it was an important and lucrative privilege. The counts of Léon in Brittany drew a large revenue from this source. But it does not seem to have been of great importance in England. It is rarely mentioned in contemporary documents. The earl of Arundel and the bishop of Ely quarrelled over a particular wreck.[54] The crown questioned a mesne tenant's right to the franchise.[55] The inquests of the thirteenth century show that this privilege was enjoyed by a number of great lords. The earls of Gloucester, Richmond, Arundel, Norfolk, and Warren had the franchise in extensive areas. Apparently all tenants of the honor of Chester enjoyed it, and there is some evidence that the same was true of those who held of the honor of Lancaster.[56] Unfortunately the descriptions given of the areas over which various lords exercised this franchise make it impossible to determine what proportion of the whole English coast was covered by them. As the crown seems to have made no great effort to control

[50] *Calendar of charter rolls*, II, 344.
[51] *Placita de quo warranto*, pp. 27, 100, 651.
[52] *Ibid.*, p. 304; *Close rolls, 1256-9*, p. 75.
[53] *Rot. chart.*, pp. 106b, 128b, 129b.
[54] *Curia regis rolls*, VII, 5, 57.
[55] *Bracton's note book*, III, 279.
[56] *Close rolls, 1256-9*, p. 75; *Rot. hund.*, I, 271.

this franchise and disputes about it were few, it seems safe to assume that it was of no great importance.

We have discussed the widely distributed franchises, the right to enforce the assize of bread and ale, view of frank-pledge, and *infangentheof*, and the less usual but little more exalted *utfangentheof* and wreck. Now we must turn to a distinctly higher level of privilege to examine the franchise that gave its possessor the right to hold pleas of withername. Most franchises were delegations of non-feudal public authority, but this one allowed its holder to perform an essentially feudal function that had been taken over by the crown. If the feudal system was to be effective, a lord had to be able to force his vassals to perform the services due him. When a vassal was delinquent, the lord seized his chattels to the estimated value of the service in question. Then the vassal could seek out the lord or his officer and regain his chattels either by performing the service or furnishing pledges that he would dispute the lord's claim to the service in the proper court. If the lord seized a vassal's chattels without due cause or refused to release them on receipt of the service or pledges, the vassal's recourse was the plea of withername. Obviously whoever could hold these pleas could supervise and control feudal distraint.

From at least as early as the reign of Henry I the kings of England had interfered in the feudal jurisdiction of their vassals. The *Leges Henrici* state that pleas of default of justice and false judgment were royal.[57] In France if a vassal complained that his lord refused him justice, he appealed to the court of the next higher lord. In England such cases went to the shire court or before the king's justices. Henry II further restricted the feudal courts by insisting that actions for freehold land could only be commenced on the authority of a royal writ—the writ of right. He also introduced the grand assize which withdrew many such cases from the feudal courts. Apparently this same king began the process of making the control of feudal distraint a royal monopoly. During the last twenty years of his reign a number of entries on the pipe rolls show lords paying fines for improper distraint.[58] Glanville

---

[57] *Leges Henrici*, c. 10, 1.
[58] "Pipe rolls 12, 14, 22, 29, 31, 32 Henry II," *Pipe roll society*, IX, 104; XII, 150; XXII, 37, 214; XXIX, 5; XXXI, 70, 182; XXXII, 46.

gives a writ of replevin—a writ ordering the sheriff to procure the release of chattels held in the course of distraint.[59]   In short it seems likely that before the time of Henry II the supervision and control of feudal distraint was the function of the feudal courts.   Henry attempted to transfer this jurisdiction to the sheriff.

Henry II made it possible for the victim of unlawful distraint to bring his case before the sheriff by going to the chancery and buying a writ of replevin.   He probably also allowed him to complain directly to the sheriff and authorized that officer to act on such a complaint.   But there is no evidence that he attempted to make these the only legal procedures in cases of this sort.   Presumably if the aggrieved vassal wished, he could take his complaint to a superior lord.   The effort to bring all such cases under royal control apparently began in the reign of King John.[60]   Pleas dealing with the taking and detaining of chattels as distraint were given a new name—*vetitum namii*, usually rendered into English as withername—and were made a royal monopoly.[61]   In 1244 Henry III ordered the sheriffs to allow no one to hold pleas of withername unless he could produce a charter granting this franchise or prove that he or his ancestors had held such pleas before 1216.[62]   In 1252 the sheriffs were again reminded that no one could hold pleas of withername without a royal license.[63]   To Bracton withername was a plea of the crown.   Because of the need for deciding such cases speedily, the sheriff could hear them, but he did so as a royal justice, and withername was not one of his own pleas.[64]

This ingenious maneuver of giving a new name to an old

---

[59] *De legibus*, p. 153.

[60] Pollock and Maitland point out that late thirteenth-century lawyers ascribed this development to John's reign. (*History of English law*, II, 576 note 2)   In 1244 Henry III ordered that all lords claiming the right to hold pleas of withername by prescription prove usage before 1216. (*Close rolls, 1242-7*, p. 242.)

[61] The plea of *vetitum namii* is mentioned in a charter dated in the first year of Richard I, but the document looks suspicious and has probably been added to. *Calendar of charter rolls*, II, 305-306.

[62] *Close rolls, 1242-7*, p. 242.

[63] *Ibid.*, *1251-3*, p. 228.

[64] *De legibus*, II, 437.

plea and thus seeking to establish a royal monopoly was not
entirely successful. In the reign of Edward I great barons were
still calmly ignoring the innovation. The baillis of the Earl
Warren in the rape of Lewes heard cases involving chattels
unjustly detained in distraint, but they never called them pleas
of withername.[65] The countess of Aumale, lady of Plympton,
followed the same practice in her great fief. If her court could
not settle a case, she sent it on to the sheriff.[66] In short if a
baron could keep his tenants from taking their complaints to
the chancery or to the sheriff, it was difficult to prevent him
from maintaining his ancient jurisdiction. In the *quo warranto*
proceedings against the earl of Gloucester the king's attorney
came pretty close to admitting that little could be done about a
powerful baron who continued to handle cases of unlawful
distraint as long as he did not venture to hear those instituted
by the authority of a royal writ.[67]

I can find no charter that specifically grants to a layman the
right to hold pleas of withername, but it seems clear that the
royal government considered that the grant of the higher franchise, return of writ, included this privilege. Return of writ
banned the sheriff from the lands of the franchise holder and
hence automatically prevented him from performing his functions in respect to pleas of withername. A few barons claimed
this franchise on the basis of general statements in their charters. The lord of the barony of Ongar maintained that Henry
II had given the hundred of Ongar to his ancestor Richard de
Lucy with all the rights the king enjoyed in it, and hence he
was entitled to hold pleas of withername. The king's attorney
replied that no such plea had existed in Henry II's day.[68] The
earl of Norfolk claimed this franchise on the basis of a grant
by Henry II of a manor with " all liberties." [69] These argu-
ments seem rather weak—withername was clearly not a plea
belonging to hundreds or manors. Those whose charters gave
them the right to hold all the pleas of the sheriff had a fairly
strong case even though Bracton insisted that withername was
not really one of these. Apparently the successors of Baldwin

---

[65] *Placita de quo warranto*, p. 751.
[66] *Ibid.*, p. 177.
[67] *Ibid.*, p. 183.
[68] *Ibid.*, p. 232.
[69] *Rot. hund.*, I, 471.

de Bethune who received a grant of this type from John held pleas of withername, and their right was not questioned.[70] Then there were some usurpations. The earl of Gloucester was not content to ignore the royal monopoly and hear his tenants' complaints of unjust distraint without calling it withername. He held pleas of withername commenced by the king's writ.[71]

On the whole the crown had been successful. An ordinary feudal process had become a plea of the crown. The king through the sheriffs supervised and controlled feudal distraint. The fact that the most privileged group of barons, those holding the franchise of return of writ, and a few others continued to hold pleas of withername did not seriously affect the picture. Two factors go far towards explaining the crown's comparatively easy triumph in so important a matter. The great baronies were in decay, and the barons were losing their hold over their vassals. Furthermore the vassals may well have preferred to have the sheriff control distraint. Hence only the most powerful and favored barons could resist the crown's encroachment on their feudal privileges.

Between the franchises so far discussed and the higher ones to which we must now turn there was a fundamental distinction. While the former did not involve the exclusion of all royal officers, the latter did. The conception of "immunity" as developed in the Merovingian and Carolingian states formed the basis for the dispersion of public judicial and police authority throughout the French feudal hierarchy. No French noble of baronial status was obliged to allow anyone else's officers to meddle with such matters in his fief. Thus feudal tradition made the question as to whether or not your lord's agents could enter your land a fundamental one. If you could exclude them, you occupied an obviously privileged position and enjoyed the prestige associated with it.

The question of the extent to which this privilege was enjoyed by English barons in the Norman period is extremely obscure. In the charters of the Conqueror and his sons one

---

[70] *Rot. chart.*, pp. 31-32; *Placita de quo warranto*, p. 330.
[71] *Ibid.*, p. 183.

occasionally finds the so-called *non-intromittat* clause. Unfortunately there is no evidence as to the precise construction placed on this expression by contemporaries. If the words be taken literally, it would seem to exclude the sheriff and his deputies and hence be the equivalent of immunity. I have never found this clause in a grant made to a layman during the Norman period. Until the extant charters of Henry I have been fully collected and published, it is not safe to make positive statements, but at this time one can only say that such grants seem to have been confined to great ecclesiastical barons.

Despite the lack of absolutely conclusive evidence, it seems clear that during the Norman period the king's officers were excluded from a few lay baronies. The Conqueror's writs concerning Cheshire, Shropshire, and Herefordshire did not include a sheriff among the addressees.[72] A mandate of Henry I dealing with the barony of Holderness was addressed to Count Stephen of Aumale, his sewer, and his ministers.[73] These are the only immunists for whom I can find definite contemporary evidence, but the records for the early years of Henry II suggest that there were others. Cornwall did not appear on the pipe rolls until after the death of Earl Reginald de Dunstanville. There can be little question that royal officers were excluded from it under his rule. Although the eleventh chapter of the Assize of Clarendon which forbids anyone to prevent the sheriff from entering his lands to arrest offenders mentions specifically only the honor of Wallingford, its wording clearly implies that there were other baronies that had privileges that might obstruct the enforcement of the assize. Later evidence gives hints as to the identity of some of these fiefs. In 1170 the men of the Isle of Wight were fined £100 for twice failing to appear before the king's justices.[74] As the Isle had once belonged to Roger de Montgomery, earl of Shrewsbury, its inhabitants may well have been relying on an ancient right.

[72] *Regesta regum Anglo-Normannorum* (ed. H. W. C. Davis, Oxford, 1913), I, XXXI. A letter written by Archbishop Lanfranc to Earl Roger of Hereford indicates that the immunity of these lords from the sheriffs was open to dispute. *Ibid.*, p. 21.

[73] W. Farrer, "An outline itinerary of Henry I," *English historical review*, XXXIV (1919), 370.

[74] "Pipe roll 16 Henry II," *Pipe roll society*, XV, 126.

Then in the years 1175-9 the custodians of the honors of Berkhamsted, Richmond, Tickhill, and Wallingford accounted for
the chattels of felons condemned under the Assize of Northampton.[75] Presumably this meant that had these baronies not
been in the king's hands, these chattels would have gone to the
barons. Now the right to the chattels of felons and fugitives
did not necessarily imply the exclusion of the sheriff, but it
usually did. Certainly Henry II was forced to recognize that
these were highly privileged baronies. I believe that their
rights went back to the Norman period and included immunity
from the sheriffs. It is important to notice that we know of the
special status of these baronies because they were in the king's
hand. Similar privileges in the possession of a baron would
leave no record in our sources.

During the reigns of William I and William II immunity
from the sheriff must have meant in practice the enjoyment of
almost complete judicial and police authority. Perhaps the
king insisted on having the profits from the pleas of the crown.
At times such pleas may have been heard by special royal justices. But there is no evidence that there was any regular
system for handling pleas of the crown by means of itinerant
royal justices before the reign of Henry I. When these officials
appeared, the question must have arisen as to whether immunity
from the sheriffs served to exclude the justices. I suspect that
it did. I base this conclusion largely on the case of the Isle
of Wight mentioned above and on later evidence as to the
privileges of the honor of Berkhamsted.[76]

The comparatively simple system of high franchises based on
the ancient conception of immunity which existed in Norman
England was changed and complicated by the innovations of
Henry II. Consider, for instance, the effect of the introduction
of the original writ. The necessity of executing these writs
vastly increased the business of the sheriff and made immunity
from his visits even more desirable. But in respect to pleas
commenced by these new writs the sheriff was merely an errand

---

[75] " Pipe rolls 21, 22, 23, 25 Henry II," *ibid.*, XXII, 6; XXV, 27; XXVI,
81, 87; XXVIII, 56, 100.
[76] " Pipe roll 16 Henry II," *ibid.*, XV, 126; *Calendar of charter rolls*, II,
325; *Close rolls*, 1234-7, p. 74.

boy. The writs were issued by the chancery and the pleas heard by the king's justices. Hence the exclusion of the sheriff no longer sufficed to assure any great degree of independence from the royal government. As a result the more powerful barons sought special privileges. The bishop of Durham, the earls of Chester and Cornwall, and the lords of the Welsh marches were completely successful. The king's writ did not run in their lands. They were allowed to adopt Henry's innovations, but they administered them through their own chanceries, justices, and sheriffs. These were the palatinates. It was essentially the invention of the original writ that drew the clear and definite line between them and the lesser franchises. Before this innovation all barons who could exclude the sheriffs were in much the same position—after it many gradations appeared among those who enjoyed this immunity. In fact it seems to me futile to use the term palatinate before the reign of Henry II.

The nature of palatine jurisdiction in England is too well known to require discussion here.[77] I simply wish to make a few remarks about the distribution of this exalted franchise in our period and the limitations placed on the independence of the lords who possessed it. The only English palatinates that endured for more than one generation were Durham, Cheshire, the king of Scotland's liberty of Tyndale, and the lordships in the Welsh marches. Cornwall was clearly a palatinate while it was ruled by Reginald de Dunstanville.[78] The thirteenth-century earls, Richard of Cornwall and his son Edmund, enjoyed much less authority. They appointed the sheriff and received the full revenue of the shire.[79] But the king's writ ran in Cornwall, he considered the sheriff to be his officer, and his justices held their eyres. While the earls in practice were given the

[77] The best work on this subject is G. T. Lapsley, *The county palatine of Durham* (New York, 1900).

[78] Earl Reginald could pardon outlaws. (*Selden society*, III, 77-78.) When his illegitimate son, Henry fitz Count, was in control of the county in the early years of Henry III, he assumed the authority of a palatine lord. (*Bracton's note book*, III, 422; *Patent rolls, 1216-1225*, pp. 202-203.) The fact that Cornwall did not appear on the pipe rolls while the earl lived is not conclusive—it was absent when ruled by Richard of Cornwall who did not have palatine authority.

[79] *Rot. hund.*, I, 56; *Reports on the dignity of a peer*, V, 12.

fines and amercements resulting from the eyres, it was done by separate acts of royal grace so that no precedent should be established.[80] Lancaster was a palatinate for a time under its first duke and later under John of Ghent.[81] These two shires joined Dorset, Somerset, Devon, Nottingham, and Derby in the short-lived palatinate created by King Richard I for his brother, John, count of Mortain.[82] Had Richard produced an heir and John remained loyal to his brother, this vast palatinate might have changed the course of English history. Its creation was an indiscretion that was never repeated.

When the palatinates are considered from the point of view of the extent of their independence, they fall into two classes. The palatine counties—Durham, Chester, and Pembroke—were in a far stronger position than the lesser lordships. As vassals of the English crown all the palatine lords were subject to the king and his courts. When the king wished to summon an ordinary marcher lord, he simply ordered the sheriff of the nearest county to do it. To summon a palatine earl was a far more complicated matter—in fact on one occasion an earl of Chester maintained, though unsuccessfully, that it could not be done.[83] If the crown questioned the privileges of a lord, the ordinary marcher baron had only tradition to support his position, but the earls palatine could point to regularly organized shire governments under their control. There is, in fact, some doubt whether the marcher lordships were considered to be in the same legal status as the counties palatine.[84] An earl of Chester in naming his peers mentioned only the bishop of Durham and the earl of Pembroke.[85] I include the marcher lords because they possessed the privileges that marked the palatinates—their own chanceries, justices, and writs.

The palatine franchise conferred great power and prestige on

---

[80] *Close rolls, 1231-4*, p. 286; *ibid., 1237-1242*, p. 58; *ibid., 1242-7*, p. 156; *ibid., 1247-1251*, p. 164.

[81] *Reports on the dignity of a peer*, V, 47; S. Armitage-Smith, *John of Gaunt* (London, 1904), pp. 205-208.

[82] Kate Norgate, *John Lackland* (London, 1902), pp. 27-28.

[83] *Bracton's note book*, III, 146-147.

[84] Lapsley, *County palatine of Durham*, pp. 234, 258.

[85] *Bracton's note book*, III, 146-147. Tout has pointed out that Glamorgan was a county palatine. "The earldoms under Edward I," *Transactions of the royal historical society, new series*, VIII (1894), 149.

its possessor. Within his palatinate a baron enjoyed the dignity of full regal authority and he had complete judicial and police power over its inhabitants. All the profits of government were his free from both feudal and non-feudal public burdens. From the purely economic point of view these advantages were balanced to a great extent by the fact that all the permanent palatinates were exposed to attack by either the Scots or the Welsh, and hence their lords were obliged to make heavy expenditures for their defense. But the costly military establishment required to protect these fiefs greatly increased the military power of the palatine lords. The ordinary English baron in time of peace had no permanent armed force beyond a few household knights and serjeants. His feudal vassals were for the most part unused to war. The marcher lord had to keep a standing army of knights and serjeants, and his vassals were continually exercised in warlike pursuits. Moreover, when he was not fighting the Welsh, he could hire them as mercenaries for campaigns in other regions. Until the Hundred Years War scattered experienced soldiers over England as a whole and the livery system allowed barons to keep them in private militia forces, the marcher lords were the dominant military power in England.

Between the palatine lords and those who could merely exclude the sheriff were various levels of privilege. The Umfranville lords of Redesdale in the Scots marches had their own justices. When the king's justices came into Northumberland, they turned over the articles of the eyre to the lord's officers.[86] Presumably the same system was used in the case of the honor of Knaresborough after it came into the hands of Earl Richard of Cornwall. Richard had his own justices who heard all royal pleas relating to this barony.[87] The honor of Berkhamsted was a shade lower in the scale. The king's justices held a special session at Berkhamsted to hear the pleas concerning the barony, and all the profits went to the lord.[88] At the time of the *quo warranto* proceedings a similar franchise was claimed by the earl of Gloucester in his fief of Tunbridge.[89] There is some

[86] *Placita de quo warranto*, p. 593.
[87] *Ibid.*, p. 200.
[88] *Calendar of charter rolls*, II, 325.
[89] *Placita de quo warranto*, p. 348.

evidence that the king's justices held a special session in the lands of the honor of Richmond in Holland.[90]

In the case of the honor of Berkhamsted these special privileges were probably derived from the ancient rights of the counts of Mortain who had been its lords.[91] As the liberty of Redesdale seems to have been created by Henry II, its franchise can hardly have antedated his reign. The right to have his own justices at Knaresborough was granted to Richard of Cornwall by his brother, King Henry III. The liberties of Tunbridge seem to have been the result of usurpation. Tunbridge was held by the De Clares from the archbishop of Canterbury. The archbishop had long been one of the most highly privileged of ecclesiastical lords, and in the thirteenth century he enjoyed the right to have the royal justices hold a special session in his lands.[92] The De Clares apparently forced the archbishop to grant them similar privileges—a grant that would have had no validity whatever if made to a less powerful baron than the great earl of Gloucester. The actual grant did not cover the whole fief held of the archbishop but simply a *banlieu* around Tunbridge, but the earl soon removed that limitation by further usurpations.[93]

Below the barons who were entitled to have their own justices or a special session of the king's came a group of lords who could exclude another official established by early Angevin legislation, the coroner. This privilege seems to have existed chiefly in the comparatively lawless districts along the borders of England. It was enjoyed by the lords of Cockermouth and Egremont in Cumberland and claimed by the Corbets and Mortimers in their English estates adjoining their marcher fiefs.[94] In the two latter cases the origin of the franchise was probably an extension over the English border of part of the palatine powers enjoyed in the marcher lordships. The only baron in the interior of England who had this privilege without the

---

[90] "Pipe roll 22 Henry II," *Pipe roll society*, XXV, 122.

[91] They can actually be traced only to the time the honor was held by Queen Isabella of Angouleme. *Calendar of charter rolls*, II, 325.

[92] *Bracton's note book*, II, 230.

[93] *Placita de quo warranto*, p. 348.

[94] *Ibid.*, pp. 112-114, 675, 686; *Rot. hund.*, II, 96.

higher ones discussed above was the count of Aumale in Holderness. His bailli served as both coroner and sheriff within the liberty.[95]

Perhaps the most obscure of all the high franchises was the right to enjoy the profits from seizing the chattels of felons and fugitives. This obscurity arises from the fact that the words used to describe the privilege apparently had different meanings in various regions. In England as a whole the possessor of this franchise was entitled to the chattels of all felons and fugitives. While it was a rather common ecclesiastical privilege, the only laymen who enjoyed it were the lords who had their own justices or private assizes of the king's. But along the Scots border every lord of any importance claimed this right. It was enjoyed by all the barons of the palatinate of Durham. The clue to the solution of this problem seems to lie in the *quo warranto* proceedings concerning the barony of Alnwick. Its lord claimed the chattels of all felons condemned in his court, yet the highest other franchise he held was *infangentheof*.[96] In short I suspect that the lord of Alnwick simply enjoyed the chattels of hand-having thieves. As such offenders were numerous in Northumberland, it was a valuable right. But the ordinary English baron who had the franchise of *infangentheof* must have had the same privilege. It simply did not amount to much because of the rarity of its exercise.

Now let us turn to the barons whose immunity simply served to exclude the sheriff from their lands. By 1250 this franchise was known as "return of writ."[97] Although the name does not seem to have been used before the reign of Henry III, the privilege it represented had taken definite form by 1200.[98] When a sheriff received a writ concerning the lands covered by such a franchise, he passed it on to the lord's bailli for execu-

---

[95] *Ibid.*, I, 106.

[96] *Placita de quo warranto*, p. 587.

[97] The term "return of writ" appears in a charter of Richard I, but I feel sure it is a later interpolation. (*Calendar of charter rolls*, II, 305.) It becomes common in 1249-51. (*Close rolls, 1247-1251*, pp. 209, 400, 518.) In a writ of the same year "return of writ" is used in combination with *ne intromittat* in a way that convinces me it was a new term. (*Close rolls, 1251-3*, p. 19.)

[98] *Curia regis rolls*, II, 58, 79, 80.

tion. If that official failed to act, the chancery or the royal justices could issue another writ ordering the sheriff to ignore the franchise. The bailli of the franchise holder also performed the financial functions of the sheriff by collecting debts due the crown and distraining delinquent debtors. Criminals were arrested by him and delivered to the sheriff. In short within the barony the bailli performed all the functions of the sheriff.

Unfortunately before the time of the hundred and *quo warranto* inquests it is extremely difficult to discover what barons possessed this franchise. In John's reign there is clear evidence that it was enjoyed by the lords of Berkeley and by the earls of Arundel and Warren in at least part of their lands.[99] The count of Aumale in Holderness, the constable of Chester in some of his Yorkshire and Lincolnshire estates, and the earl of Devon in the Isle of Wight certainly held this franchise in the early years of Henry III.[100] The house of Berkeley received its lands and presumably its privileges from Henry II. The baronies of Holderness and the Isle of Wight had probably been immunities in Norman times. I am inclined to believe that the privileges of the earls of Arundel and Warren were equally ancient.

The honors in the king's hand present a special problem. It is clear that in John's reign the sheriff was excluded by the custodians of the honors of Lancaster, Peverel of Nottingham, and Richmond.[101] In the reign of Henry III we have evidence that the same was true for the honor of Wallingford.[102] The question naturally arises as to whether this was an ancient privilege which had been possessed by the lords of these baronies or a new one granted the royal baillis. There are good reasons for believing that it was ancient in the cases of Lancaster, Richmond, and Wallingford. The custodians of the honor of Peverel seem to have obtained it from John.[103] It was probably not too difficult for the custodian of an escheated

[99] *Ibid.*, II, 58, 79, 80, 151; III, 22, 50; V, 52.

[100] *Close rolls, 1247-1251*, p. 209; *Memoranda roll, 1230-1*, p. 18.

[101] " Pipe roll 5 John," *Pipe roll society*, LIV, 171; *Rot. pat.*, pp. 53b, 176b; *Selden society*, LVI, 15, 422.

[102] *Bracton's note book*, II, 407-408.

[103] " Pipe roll 5 John," *Pipe roll society*, LIV, 171.

honor to acquire this privilege. He was a royal official, and it
can have made little difference to the crown whether or not he
excluded the sheriff.

The hundred and *quo warranto* inquests make few additions
to our list of baronies which enjoyed the franchise of return of
writs. Perhaps the most puzzling of these is the honor of
Leicester. Under Henry I, Stephen, Henry II, Richard, and
John the earls of Leicester were highly privileged barons, but
I know of no evidence to indicate that they could exclude the
sheriffs from their lands. In the hundred rolls it is clear that
the entire honor of Leicester enjoyed this privilege.[104] I suspect that it was acquired by Simon de Montfort for his half
of the honor, and that after that it was difficult to deny it to
the half in possession of the earls of Winchester. Most of the
other additions can be easily explained. Henry III's brother,
Richard of Cornwall, was given the highly privileged honors of
Berkhamsted and Wallingford. He was specifically granted
high franchises in Knaresborough. Naturally he was inclined
to extend his privileges to his other lands, and no one was
likely to oppose him. The same may be said of Henry's second
son, Edmund of Lancaster. The Lacy earls of Lincoln seem to
have extended to the honor of Bolingbroke privileges already
enjoyed in other baronies.[105] Then here again we find the
earls of Gloucester at work. They claim that return of writs
was an ancient privilege of their honor, but the indications are
that they usurped this privilege for most of the lands of the
honor of Gloucester during the civil wars.[106] In Suffolk they
acquired this franchise for some of their estates by the same
means employed to obtain their high privileges in their Tunbridge fief. The abbot of St. Edmunds enjoyed return of writ.
The earls persuaded the abbot to grant them the same right
in their lands lying within his liberty.[107]

In addition to the barons who could exclude the sheriff from
their lands there were a few who enjoyed partial immunity.
They received from the sheriff lists of debts due the crown from

[104] *Rot. hund.*, I, 237; II, 7.
[105] *Ibid.*, I, 372.
[106] *Ibid.*, II, 8; *Placita de quo warranto*, pp. 183, 253.
[107] *Rot. hund.*, II, 172.

tenants of their baronies and collected the money. The lord possessing this franchise could not prevent the sheriff from entering his barony to serve original writs or make arrests, but he could insist that the royal officer be accompanied by a baronial bailli.[108]   This privilege was called "extract of writs." While it was usually a mere adjunct to return of writs, some lords such as the bishop of Bath, the earl of Warwick, and the Moions of Dunster possessed it without the higher franchise.[109]

From the financial point of view, the franchises of return of writs and extract of writs must have been pure liabilities. They imposed a heavy burden on the baron's officers and yielded no return. But from the point of view of power and prestige they were of great value. The lord who could ban the king's officers enjoyed an obvious position of dignity—he had the form if not the substance of independence. Moreover he could delay the execution of the orders of the royal government. If his baillis failed to act, the sheriff could get a writ authorizing him to ignore the franchise, but the process might take a long time. While the lord's police power in arresting felons was subject to the oversight of the sheriff, in practice the supervision exercised by a royal officer who could not enter the liberty must have been extremely limited.

There is one more point to be mentioned in connection with the judicial and police powers exercised by barons in their fiefs. The hereditary possession of public office often had the effect of giving a lord privileges he might not have possessed otherwise. The Empress Matilda granted Geoffrey de Mandeville the office of royal justice in Essex. No other justice was to act in that shire except a peer of Geoffrey's who might be sent to sit with him. King Stephen extended this grant to cover London and Middlesex and Hertfordshire.[110]   The effect of this was to make Geoffrey absolute master of his own lands in those shires to say nothing of giving him great power over other tenants-in-chief and their fiefs. Geoffrey's fall brought an end to his privileges, and the county justices occasionally

---

[108] *Ibid.*, I, 288; *Bracton's note book*, III, 383.
[109] *Ibid.*, *Rot. hund.*, I, 171, II, 125.
[110] J. H. Round, *Geoffrey de Mandeville* (London, 1892), pp. 88-93, 140-144.

found under Henry I and Stephen never appeared again. But lesser hereditary offices continued to be of importance.

Along with the office of justice Geoffrey obtained the position of sheriff in the same four shires.[111] His contemporary, Miles of Gloucester, was hereditary sheriff of Gloucestershire.[112] The death of Geoffrey ended his hereditary shrievalties, and King John persuaded the Bohun successors of Miles to give up their claim to hold the office in Gloucestershire.[113] Earl William of Salisbury and his wife Ella during the reigns of John and Henry III made several attempts to establish their right to be hereditary sheriffs of Wiltshire, but they were unsuccessful.[114] The only hereditary shrievalty to survive into the thirteenth century was that of Worcestershire held by the Beauchamps of Elmley.[115] It seems clear that the possession of this office gave its holder powers equivalent to those covered by the franchise of return of writ free from the supervision of a royal sheriff.

Far more important than the hereditary sheriffs because of of their vastly greater number were the hereditary possessors of hundreds and wapentakes. There were private hundreds in Anglo-Saxon times, and the Norman kings increased their number. The Angevin monarchs were equally generous. All of them made hereditary grants of royal hundreds and wapentakes. In theory the possession of a hundred should not have increased a baron's power in his demesne manors as he presumably already possessed equivalent jurisdiction there. It would simply serve to give him *infangentheof* in the lands of his vassals which lay in his hundred.[116] But some lords of hundreds had exceptional powers. Thus the earl of Gloucester held the hundred of Chadelinton, Oxfordshire. Although view of frankpledge was a function of the sheriff, the earl shared it with that official in only two manors—in most of the hundred he held the view alone.[117] In other cases the lords of hundreds

[111] *Ibid.*
[112] *Ibid.*, p. 11.
[113] *Rot. chart.*, p. 53.
[114] *Bracton's note book*, III, 248-249.
[115] Round, *Geoffrey de Mandeville*, pp. 313-315.
[116] *Placita de quo warranto*, p. 751.
[117] *Rot. hund.*, II, 736.

could insist that the sheriff could enter only in company with their bailli, and some could bar that official entirely.[118]

When the holder of a private hundred was not an important landholder, the office was probably valued chiefly as a source of revenue. But when it was held by a baron with extensive lands in the hundred, it greatly strengthened his position. He gained definite judicial and police power in the lands of his vassals. Where fiefs were compact as in Sussex, much of the baron's authority outside his demesne was derived from his possession of the hundreds.[119]

In discussing the various franchises held by English barons I have centered my attention on the prestige and power which their possession conferred. But it is important to remember that franchises were an important source of baronial revenue. Unfortunately it is usually impossible to isolate completely franchisal from other revenue, to say nothing of obtaining figures on the value of individual franchises. As a rule all one can do is to find a figure labelled in the accounts as " pleas and perquisites." Not only is there doubt as to just what this heading covered, but also in all probability it did not always include the same items. I believe that ordinarily it covered all the judicial revenues collected by the officer who rendered the account. Thus it could include the profits from feudal and manorial as well as franchisal jurisdiction. On the other hand when individual demesne manors were leased at a fixed farm, the profits from the manorial and perhaps from the minor franchisal jurisdiction were probably included in the farm. But despite the unsatisfactory nature of the figures obtainable it seems worth while to give an idea of the relation between the sums accounted for under " pleas and perquisites " and the revenue from other sources on a few baronies. This will at least furnish an indication of the importance of franchisal revenue.

Let us first glance at two palatine earldoms. In 1241 the pleas of the justiciar of Cheshire, those of the sheriff, and the chattels of felons and fugitives yielded a total of about £158.

[118] *Placita de quo warranto*, p. 382; *Close rolls, 1227-1231*, p. 170.
[119] *Placita de quo warranto*, p. 751.

The minor pleas of the hundreds and manors came to about
£50 more. The demesne manors of the county palatine yielded
in that year £528.[120]   In 1214 the manors of the bishop of
Durham brought in £1,255 while his pleas yielded about
£600.[121]   These figures are for the bishop's whole barony—
not for the palatinate alone as in the case of Chester. To turn
to less privileged baronies, in 1212 the honor of Berkhamsted
yielded £304 from its manors and £109 from pleas.[122]   In the
same year the lands of the constable of Chester outside Cheshire, chiefly the baronies of Pomfret and Clitherhoe, brought
in £346 from demesne manors and £158 from pleas.[123]   At
about the same time the honor of Perche rendered in two years
£335 from its demesne and £380 from pleas.[124]   In 1241 the
Fitz Alan barony of Clun yielded £35 from its pleas as against
£150 from all other sources while the same house's barony of
Whitchurch brought in £58 from its Shropshire estates and £29
from its pleas in that county.[125]   These were all highly privileged fiefs. Let us compare them with a few baronies enjoying
less exalted franchises. In 1211 the fief of the Beauchamps of
Elmley yielded £130 from its manors and £36 from pleas.[126]   In
1209 the Tony lands in Holland rendered £76 from manors
and £10 from pleas.[127]   In 1212 the Fossard barony yielded
£278 from manors and mills and £56 from pleas.[128]   The
Pomeroy barony for three quarters of a year brought £72 from
manors and £26 from pleas.[129]   In 1185 the baronies of Mus-
camp, Musard, Lovetot of Sheffield, and Fitz Herbert yielded
respectively £55, £47, £66, and £121 from manors and £13,
£6, £21, and £9 from pleas.[130]

These figures and others that could be cited show conclu-

[120] *The great roll of the pipe for the twenty-sixth year of the reign of King Henry the third* (ed. H. L. Cannon, New Haven, 1918), pp. 120-122.

[121] *Pipe roll 16 John*, Public Record Office, E 372-60.

[122] *Pipe roll 14 John*, *ibid.*, E 372-58.

[123] *Ibid.*

[124] *Pipe roll 12 John*, *ibid.*, E 372-56.

[125] *Pipe roll 26 Henry* III, pp. 8-9.

[126] *Pipe roll 13 John*, Public Record Office, E 372-57.

[127] *Pipe roll 11 John*, *ibid.*, E 372-55.

[128] *Pipe roll 14 John*, *ibid.*, E 372-58.

[129] *Pipe roll 10 John*, *ibid.*, E 372-54.

[130] "Pipe roll 31 Henry II," *Pipe roll society*, XXXIV, pp. 11, 116, 117, 239.

sively that the income from pleas formed an important part of
the revenue from most baronies. I am inclined to believe that
a large part of this income came from pleas held under franchises. I should like to be able to say that the ratio between
revenue from pleas and from manors varied in accordance with
the franchises held by the barons. The figures seem to indicate
vaguely a relationship of this sort, but they do not do so clearly
enough to justify a positive statement. The figures show wide
variation in the comparative value of pleas from barony to
barony. I might add that in an individual barony the revenue
from this source could vary greatly from year to year.

CHAPTER V

FEUDAL RESOURCES

An extremely important part of a baron's resources consisted of the feudal obligations owed to him by his vassals. Unfortunately it is difficult to define these obligations exactly, to say nothing of discovering their actual value to the baron. Usually one finds simply the formal statement that a mesne fief is held by the service of so many knights. We know that the duties of a mesne tenant to his lord varied from barony to barony and even within the same barony. It is equally certain that the essential nature of these obligations changed with the passage of time. Yet the documents that permit one to look behind the formal screen of the words " by the service of so many knights " are too few and too scattered to allow much scope for generalization. In short it is usually fairly easy to learn how many knights owed service to a baron, but most difficult to discover the value of the services.

The basic obligation of a feudal tenant to his lord was military service. Three types of military service are mentioned in English documents. Mr. Stenton cites a statement of Richard de Chandos of Snodhill in Herefordshire that a vassal owed him service *in exercitu et chivalchia et custodia.*[1] The first two obligations were more commonly called *expeditio* and *equitatio.* The *exercitus* or *expeditio* was clearly the feudal host summoned by the king or by a lord who did not owe a contingent to the royal army. There is overwhelming evidence that in the twelfth and early thirteenth century the marcher lordships and the Isle of Wight owed no service in the general feudal levy of the realm.[2] Moreover it appears that the English tenants of some marcher baronies were exempt. The knights holding of the honor of Chester, of the Tony lords of Elvael, and of the

[1] *English feudalism,* p. 175.
[2] The marcher lands of the baronies of Striguil and Gloucester were exempt from scutage. (*Red book of the exchequer,* I, 67, 156.) Such lordships as Pembroke, Gower, and Montgomery did not appear on scutage lists. In 1194 the knights of the Isle of Wight fined to be exempt from scutage according to custom. ("Pipe roll 6 Richard I," *Pipe roll society,* XLIII, 218.)

Mortimers of Wigmore do not appear in lists of fees paying scutage.[3] In all these cases I believe the vassals performed their service in the host when they obeyed their lord's summons to protect his fief from the king's enemies. This service *in exercitu* corresponded to the service in the *ost* so common in French documents.

The relation between the barons and their vassals in regard to service in the royal host has already been discussed in detail. Here I merely wish to give a brief summary from the point of view of baronial revenue. During the Norman period the barons of England made provision for supplying their contingents to the king's army by granting fiefs to knightly tenants. If a baron had just enough knights to fill his *servitium debitum*, his only expense was the cost of his own service. If he had not enough knights, he was forced to hire some from his other resources. But suppose a baron had enfeoffed more knights than he owed—how could he profit from the royal summons to the host? Mr. Stenton has shown that there is clear evidence that barons collected scutage from their vassals in the Norman period. I believe that when a baron who had more knights than he needed was summoned to the host, he led his contingent and collected scutage from the rest. This would account for the fractional fees granted before the death of Henry I. In short it seems likely that before scutage was collected from lay baronies by the crown, barons had used it to make a profit from their extra knights. This same profit accrued to the baron when the king collected scutage based on the old *servitium debitum.*

In the case of a large and under-assessed barony this profit could be considerable. The Bigod earls of Norfolk owed 60 knights and had enfeoffed 162. If a scutage was levied at twenty shillings a fee, the earl made £102. The Mandevilles profited to the extent of £44 and the earls of Devon £74 at the same scutage rate. If Mr. Farrer's estimate of the fees held of the Warren barony is correct, the earl made £80 on a

---

[3] This is not quite certain for John's reign. Some Tony and Mortimer fees appear on the lists, but I cannot discover that they ever paid. Later these baronies lost their exemption. They were assessed for scutage under Henry III and owed service under the new quotas established in his reign.

twenty-shilling scutage.[4]   These were, of course, exceptional cases.   Most barons made only a few pounds if anything from excess knights.   But the profits of these few great lords may well have tempted Henry II.   The Bigods and Mandevilles were forced to accept greatly increased assessments.   The earls of Devon apparently were obliged to give way for a time, but continued to claim their former low assessment with varying success.   As far as I can discover no attempt was ever made to increase the *servitium debitum* of the Earls Warren.

It seems highly probable that the king was not the only one to look with a greedy eye on the profits drawn by the barons from scutages.   The mesne tenants may well have felt that they should share the benefits of under-assessment.   I can find only one clear case of such a claim.   The abbey of Bury St. Edmunds owed 40 knights to the host and had enfeoffed 50.   In 1196 the knights maintained that when a scutage was levied at twenty shillings per fee each knight owed only sixteen shillings.   In short the ten extra knights wanted to divide the scutage due the crown with the other forty and thus absorb the abbot's profit.   Abbot Samson insisted on his right to the full twenty shillings from every fee, and eventually the vassals gave way.   It is interesting to notice that the first to surrender was Roger Bigod, earl of Norfolk, who even under his increased assessment made £37 profit from a scutage.   The last to give way was Aubrey de Vere, earl of Oxford, who had no extra knights on his own barony.[5]

By the beginning of the thirteenth century the service *in exercitu* owed by a mesne tenant to his lord had become simply a matter of scutage payments.   The baron made the best bargain he could with the crown and then levied scutage from his vassals.   This lack of any real connection between the service owed the baron and that due from him to the crown became clear when the new service quotas were established.   A baron might then perform his full service to the crown with two knights and collect scutage from twenty or thirty fees.   If the

---

[4] *Honors and knights' fees*, III, 307.

[5] Jocelin de Brakelond, *Chronica de rebus gestis Samsonis abbatis monasterii Sancti Edmundi* (ed. John L. Rokewode, *Camden society*, XIII, London, 1840), pp. 48-49.

baron obtained more from his tenants than it cost him to furnish his service or pay a fine, he came out ahead. I suspect that in general those lords who had twenty or more fees profited. The really great barons like the earls of Gloucester must have done quite well. The earl held some 450 fees which would bring in £900 from a scutage at forty shillings a fee. It may well have been the thought of sums like this that moved the three Edwards to make their unsuccessful attempt to collect both scutage and service.

The transformation of service *in exercitu* into scutage payments had important effects on the feudal organization of the barony. As long as every knight's fee was expected to produce a fully-armed knight, the feudal hierarchy was unlikely to grow very complicated. But the introduction of scutage made subinfeudation much simpler. It was comparatively easy to pass scutage payments through the hands of numerous mesne lords. Theoretically there was no limit to the number of mesne lords who could be placed between the baron who held fifty fees and the tenant who held 1/200 of a fee. But practically, as the system grew more complicated, it became more and more difficult to enforce the payment of scutage. It was extremely difficult to follow the thread of service due from mesne lord to mesne lord to the actual tenant in demesne. Early in the thirteenth century there is evidence that the barons were tending to solve this problem by ignoring the mesne lords and attempting to collect directly from the holder in demesne.[6] Before the middle of the century the crown was encouraging this process. The *Inquest of knights' fees* of 1242 practically ignored the mesne lords.[7] It lists the men who held the estates of the barony in demesne and the service each owed, but it rarely indicates the lords who came between the tenants and the baron. So far as scutage was concerned the mesne lords had ceased to be of interest to the barons.

In summary one might say that scutage was an irregular and conditional source of baronial revenue. Obviously it could only be collected when the king summoned the feudal levy. By the

---

[6] *Curia regis rolls*, VII, 184; *Bracton's note book*, III, 165-166.
[7] *Book of fees*, II, 637-1111. This problem still existed in 1285. *Statutes of the realm*, I, 78-79.

time of John a baron could not levy scutage from his vassals unless he had a royal writ *de scutagio habendo.* Bracton points out that the baron was entitled to his scutage only after he had performed his service to the king or made a satisfactory fine.[8] With the abandonment of the feudal levy scutage came to an end as a source of baronial income.

The exact nature of the feudal service called *equitatio* or *chivalchia* is far from clear. Mr. Stenton points out that it corresponded to the French *chevauchée.* He then states " It seems certain that the *chevalchia* of French documents denoted, not military service, but the duty of escorting an immediate lord or the king from place to place. . . . " Mr. Stenton bases this conclusion on references supplied by a Mr. Lewis C. Loyd.[9] As these references are not given, it is difficult to criticize the statement, but I have grave doubt of its accuracy. Luchaire felt certain that *chevauchée* was military service—he simply questioned how often it was clearly distinguished from service in the host.[10] In the *Coutume de Touraine-Anjou* it is clearly a form of warfare.[11] It would take a great deal of evidence to convince me that *chevauchée* in French legal terminology did not mean a military expedition. At the same time in contemporary usage it could mean, as the instances collected by Godefroy show, any expedition on horseback. As a matter of fact as far as France is concerned I can see little use in trying to separate these meanings. When a French baron felt the need of an armed escort of vassals, his purpose was, I suspect, hostile to someone. After St. Louis and his successors had begun to discourage private war, a *chevauchée* might well be a peaceful journey, but before that I have little doubt that it was usually a hostile raid.

When one turns to England, the problem becomes more involved. Mr. Stenton is clearly correct in his belief that no English king permitted the waging of private war.[12] But I feel

[8] *De legibus,* II, 114.
[9] *English feudalism,* p. 175.
[10] Achille Luchaire, *Manuel des institutions françaises* (Paris, 1892), p. 196.
[11] " Coutume de Touraine-Anjou," *Les établissements de St. Louis* (ed. Paul Viollet, *Société de l'histoire de France*), III, 24; " Usage d'Orlenois," *ibid.,* I, 519.
[12] *English feudalism,* pp. 13-14.

far from certain that the king could always prevent hostilities between his barons. A passage in the *Leges Henrici* seems to me to assume the existence of private warfare. It states that if a lord has vassals who hold also of another lord with whom he is at war, he can forbid his men to protect his enemy's fief against him.[13] Whatever may have been the practice in time of peace, the situation must have been far different in periods of civil strife. Then certainly the baron would need the service of his knights to protect his fief or to raid his neighbor's. It seems incredible that a baron of the Norman period could not call his vassals to his banner except when the king summoned the feudal host. I might add that in the case of Richard de Chandos cited above the need for the service of his knights was particularly acute. His lordship lay in the borders of Herefordshire, and I have no doubt that the *chivalchia* service owed him was used to repel Welsh inroads or perhaps avenge them by counter-raids. In short I believe that in time of peace *equitatio* service could be performed by escorting the lord on a journey, but that in time of war it meant military service against the lord's foes.

A question of extreme interest is to what extent the mesne tenants followed their lords when the latter rose against the crown. There seems to be no doubt that English legal theory required the vassals of a rebel baron to support the king against their lord. Yet as late as the second half of the thirteenth century the *Dictum de Kenilworth* indicated that a vassal of Simon de Montfort who had followed him in his revolt was considered to have committed a less serious offence than one who was not bound to him by feudal ties.[14] It seems likely that feudal tradition inclined men to view leniently the vassal who stood by his lord even in an illegal cause.

Unfortunately it is extremely difficult to obtain any information about actual practice in this connection. During the Norman and early Angevin periods there were many baronial revolts, but rarely can one find the names of the rebels below the leaders. Only in the case of the great baronial rebellion

[13] *Leges Henrici*, c. 59, 12.
[14] *Dictum de Kenilworth*, c. 29, Stubbs, *Select charters*, pp. 419-425.

against King John is adequate information available. We have the names of all the freeholders who took part in that rising.[15] Among the mesne tenants whose feudal connections I have been able to establish seventy-one were vassals of rebel barons against forty-seven who held of loyal lords or of honors in the hand of the crown. But perhaps of even greater significance is the fact that I have been unable to discover the feudal connections of the vast majority of the rebels listed. This seems to indicate that they were men of little importance in the lower reaches of the feudal hierarchy. Many perhaps were free tenants who did not hold by knight service. If I am correct in this conclusion, it seems certain that these men were in the rebel ranks as mercenary troops. In short I believe that the rebel army that opposed John and the Regent William Marshal was composed of a few great men—barons, honorial barons, and important mesne lords—and their hired followers. Some of the latter may have served as knights, but the majority must have been classed as serjeants. Thus the evidence does not indicate that feudal obligations played a major part in this revolt.

The fact that the barons who rebelled against John did not rely chiefly on their vassals does not, of course, mean that the same situation had existed in earlier revolts. I suspect that the key to the solution of the problem lies in the nature of the vassal's relationship to his lord—whether it was personal or chiefly legal and financial. In the Norman period when a vassal expected to ride in his lord's contingent to the royal host, he was inclined to obey the lord's call to arms for all purposes. The lord was the customary captain of his band of vassals, and they did not worry much about where he was leading them. But when service in the host had become a matter of paying scutage, the vassal lost the habit of following his lord to war. If he merely paid money when the lord served the king, why should he take up arms when the lord was engaged in rebellion?

The third type of service mentioned by Richard de Chandos, *custodia*, was castle-guard duty. This service might be due

---

[15] This list is obtained from the writs ordering the king's officers to return the lands of repentent rebels. *Rot. claus.*, I, 297 *et seq.*

either at a royal castle or at the baron's own stronghold. In the Norman period groups of baronies were required to furnish garrisons for such royal fortresses as Dover, Northampton, Norwich, Rockingham, and Windsor. In the twelfth century the crown began to accept money in place of service in time of peace.[16] By the end of the thirteenth century actual performance of castle-guard duty in a royal castle was probably extremely rare. The service had become a money rent due to the constable of the castle. As long as the baronies maintained their integrity, castle-guard dues were collected by the barons from their tenants and turned over to the king's officer. If the money was in default, the crown distrained the baron.[17] As the number of knights demanded for castle-guard duty was based on the old *servitium debitum*, barons who had enfeoffed more knights than they owed could make a profit. The abbot of St. Edmunds drew £4 7s. a year from this source.[18] But when one considers that the baron was responsible for the whole sum due from his barony and had to collect as best he could from his tenants, it seems probable that he lost more often than he gained. For instance, it is clear that the abbot of St. Edmunds was rarely able to persuade the earl of Norfolk to pay the castle-guard due from his three fees.[19] Castle-guard rents remained in existence long after the disintegration of the baronies. Apparently they sometimes rested proportionally on all the manors that had formed part of the original fief and sometimes on the ancient *caput* alone.[20]

If a baron's tenants did not owe castle-guard service at a royal fortress, he expected them to perform this duty in his own castle. Although the available evidence may indicate that this statement requires some qualification, I believe that the exceptions are more apparent than real. It is impossible to prove that every baron of the Norman period had a castle, but I am convinced that possession of a castle was practically a requisite of baronial rank. A fourteenth-century inquisition states that

---

[16] Painter, "Castle-guard."

[17] *Calendar of inquisitions post mortem*, II, 207-208.

[18] Jocelin de Brakelond, p. 49.

[19] *Ibid.; Red book of the exchequer*, I, 394.

[20] *Calendar of inquisitions post mortem*, IX, 10; Round, "Castle-guard," pp. 157-158.

the De Clares had never taken castle-guard dues from their tenants.[21] This might be taken to mean that the tenants of the Clare barony had never owed castle-guard, but it seems more likely that actual service at the castle of Clare had become obsolete, and no system of commutation had been established. Mr. Stenton is certainly correct in his belief that outside of the Welsh and Scots marches actual castle-guard service in private strongholds had practically disappeared by the thirteenth century. Hence as most of our information on the subject comes from thirteenth- and fourteenth-century records, our evidence is largely confined to those baronies where the service had been commuted into money payments. The large number of castles at which this fragmentary material allows one to establish the existence of castle-guard service convinces me that it was a regular obligation of the tenants of most English baronies.

Two broad types of arrangements for garrisoning castles are found in England—permanent and emergency. While these types were used for both royal and baronial strongholds, comparatively few barons had enough vassals to supply adequate permanent garrisons for their castles. Four baronial castles, *caputs* of important baronies, are known to have had strong permanent garrisons—Hastings, Lancaster, Richmond, and Tickhill. At only two of these is the exact size of the garrison known. Richmond was held by forty-two knights during the summer when danger from the Scots was greatest and by twenty-six in winter. Hastings had a regular permanent garrison of fifteen knights. A number of other baronial castles were supplied with small permanent garrisons. As examples one might cite Alnwick, Pevensea, Proudhoe, Skipton in Craven, and Skipsea.

In all probability most barons were forced to be content with providing adequate garrisons for their castles in time of war. Although Wallingford castle was the seat of a barony containing about one hundred fees, the tenants owed castle-guard duty only in time of war.[22] The same was true of the equally large fief held by the earls of Warwick.[23] In the case of small

[21] *Calendar of inquisitions post mortem*, V, 350.
[22] *Calendar of inquisitions post mortem*, III, 173; *Rot. hund.*, II, 777-778.
[23] *Calendar of inquisitions post mortem*, IV, 9, 10; V, 399.

baronies it was absolutely necessary to limit the service to time of war if an adequate garrison was to be mustered. As I have suggested above our knowledge of the arrangements at fortresses which were garrisoned only in war is extremely limited. By the time material becomes plentiful, the services had become obsolete.

A baron did not rely solely on his knightly vassals for the defense of his castle. In the Norman and early Angevin periods the constableship was often, perhaps usually, a hereditary office held by an important mesne tenant.[24] The baron could provide a porter, a watchman, and one or two men-at-arms by granting parcels of land as serjeantries.[25] Sometimes freeholders attached to the manor on which the castle stood owed guard duty.[26] In other cases the burghers of a town were obliged to perform castle-guard service in the lord's stronghold.[27] Apparently in some fiefs the tenants were expected to furnish peasants to act as watchmen in their lord's castle. Except in the case of burghers of a town, it is doubtful if any of these devices could produce a sufficient garrison for times of war. But in peace a constable, a few serjeants, and some watchmen were adequate for the purpose. If an emergency arose, this skeleton force was reinforced by the baron's vassals.

The barons who had provided permanent garrisons for their castles began the practice of commutation at about the same time as did the crown. Presumably at first money was accepted in time of peace and service demanded in time of war. But as the personal tie between lord and vassal grew weaker, commutation was extended. The lord garrisoned his castle with paid soldiers and considered his tenants' castle-guard payments as one of his sources of revenue. At Alnwick the castle-guard dues amounted to £14 a year, at Belvoir to £26 18s, at Hastings to £20, at Lancaster to £36 15s, and at Tickhill to £30.[28] If I

---

[24] Stenton, *English feudalism*, pp. 78-80.

[25] *Calendar of inquisitions miscellaneous*, I, 14-15; *Calendar of inquisitions post mortem*, IV, 235; *Book of fees*, I, 120.

[26] *Calendar of inquisitions post mortem*, IV, 10.

[27] " A terrier of Fleet, Lincolnshire " (ed. Miss N. Neilson in *Records of the social and economic history of England and Wales*, IV, London, 1920), p. 105.

[28] *Calendar of inquisitions post mortem*, VIII, 232-233, X, 32; *Calendar of inquisitions miscellaneous*, I, 256; *Book of fees*, II, 1150; " Pipe roll 13 Henry II," *Pipe roll society*, XI, 101; *Pipe roll 26 Henry III*, p. 47.

am correct in my estimate that 50 Yorkshire fees of the honor of Richmond owed one-half marc each and about 130 fees in other shires ten shillings each, the sum of the wards due to Richmond castle must have reached £80.

It seems essentially improbable that castle-guard service owed only in time of war was ever commuted into money payments. In all likelihood it simply grew obsolete and unenforceable. I make this statement despite the fact that such services are sometimes given a value in inquisitions. Thus in 1272 the wards owed at the castle of Clun in the Welsh marches in time of war were valued at £6 15s.[29] But the hundred rolls speak of these obligations in terms of so many days of service with no mention of money payments.[30] Apparently the £6 15s simply represents an evaluation of these services in terms of money.

On some baronies the obligation of supplying or at least feeding watchmen in the lord's castle was commuted. The tenants of the honor of Tickhill paid small sums for feeding the watch in addition to their regular castle-guard dues.[31] There are other cases where the purpose of the payment is not specified except that it is for the guarding of the castle, but the sums are so small that they must have represented the cost of watchmen rather than commutation of castle-guard duty.[32]

The changes which took place during the twelfth and thirteenth centuries in the essential nature of the English mesne tenant's obligations of host, *chevauchée*, and castle-guard are of fundamental importance in the history of the barony. From the Norman Conquest to the sixteenth century the political status of the feudal barons and the Parliamentary barons who succeeded them was based primarily on military power. The threat of armed rebellion was their protection against attempts on the part of the crown to curb their political authority. This political power backed by military force safeguarded their eco-

---

[29] *Close rolls, 1268-1272*, p. 506. This valuation was not used in arriving at the total value of the barony, *ibid.*, p. 511.

[30] *Rot. hund.*, II, 76-77.

[31] *Book of fees*, II, 1150.

[32] *Rot. hund.*, II, 492-493; *Calendar of inquisitions post mortem*, IV, 267, V, 243.

nomic and social privileges. In short throughout this long period the position of the barons in English society rested on a combination of economic, political, and military power, but the development and preservation of the first two depended to a great extent on the effectiveness of the latter.

In the eleventh century the military importance of a baron depended on the number of his knightly vassals and the strength, number, and strategic location of his castles. The vassals followed their lord to the royal host and to perform guard duty in the king's castles. In time of civil strife they aided him in defending his fief or raiding an enemy's. Usually, I believe, they joined him if he chose to revolt against the king. They acted as garrison in the baron's castle. Often they supplied watchmen for the castle and were responsible for keeping it in repair. In general the number and strength of the baron's fortresses were governed by the number of vassals he had to garrison and maintain them. Throughout the Norman period the military power and hence the general importance of a baron could be measured fairly accurately by the number of knights' fees in his barony.

By the end of the twelfth century the personal military relation between lord and vassal had been seriously weakened. When a baron served in the royal host, he led a contingent far smaller than that required by his old *servitium debitum*. In John's reign it seems clear that this contingent was usually composed of the baron's relatives or of hired knights. The cost of supplying this force to the crown was offset to a greater or lesser extent by the scutage received from the baron's vassals. As we have stated above what evidence there is suggests that the same situation existed in respect to the armies led by the barons who rebelled against John. They were essentially forces of hired knights and serjeants. It seems likely that actual performance of castle-guard service lasted to a later period. Certainly it was being performed in royal castles early in Henry III's reign. But by the end of the thirteenth century it seems to have disappeared outside of the Welsh and Scots marches. Thus by 1300 at least the military services owed by vassals to their lord had either disappeared as in the case of *chevauchée* or been commuted to money payments. The baron of the early fourteenth century could still collect scutage to aid him in supplying his contingent to the king's army. He might still have castle-guard dues to help pay for the garrisoning of his castle. But the knights and serjeants who followed him in war and held his strongholds for him were serving for pay.

To summarize one can say that from the beginning of the thirteenth century the military resources of the English barons ceased to be feudal in the sense that they consisted of services performed by fief-holders. A baron's military power depended on the money he could find to hire soldiers and build and maintain fortresses. His feudal rights were important only as they served to swell his revenue. As we shall see some feudal privileges were valuable sources of money income. But it is interesting to notice that the ancient military obligations of host, *chevauchée*, and castle-guard were never transformed into important assets. Scutage came to an end with the disappearance of the royal feudal levy. As a royal writ was required to levy scutage, *chevauchée* never became a source of money income. While castle-guard dues swelled the coffers of a few barons, they were in a decided minority. Thus the military power of the barons rested on resources having no connection with the ancient feudal military system. It was replaced by essentially non-feudal contracts between the lords and their men.[33]

In addition to performing the various types of military service the vassal was obliged to attend his lord's feudal court. In the Norman period the *curia* of a baron was an extremely important body. It settled all civil disputes between lord and vassal or between vassal and vassal. If a vassal failed to perform his service, the court authorized the lord to distrain him. If two tenants-in-chief of the baron had a quarrel over land, the case was heard in the baronial court. The many questions that could arise over inheritance, dower, wardship, and marriage lay within the jurisdiction of the *curia*. Feudal custom as it was to be applied in the barony was moulded in the baron's court.[34] I have been unable to find any indication of

[33] For an example of such a contract see Denholm-Young, *Seignorial administration in England*, pp. 167-168.

[34] For a discussion of the importance of baronial courts in the Norman period see Stenton, *English feudalism*, pp. 24, 44-45.

the importance of the revenue in money derived from baronial courts in the Norman period. If the value of these courts in the eleventh century bore the same relation to their value in the thirteenth that the power and competence of the court in the early period bore to its power and competence in the later, they must have been extremely valuable assets to the baron in the Norman period.

The legislation of Henry II struck fatal blows at the baronial *curia*. The establishment of the " writ of right " subjected to royal control its jurisdiction over disputes concerning the ownership of free tenements. The grand assize removed many, perhaps most, of these cases to the royal courts. The use of the writ *praecipe* to transfer cases from baronial to royal courts was prohibited by *Magna Carta*, but this could do little more than delay the decline of the feudal *curia*.[35] Writs were soon developed to carry disputes over dower to the king's courts.[36] If a baron refused to accept the homage of a man who claimed to hold a fief of him, a writ could be obtained to bring the question before a royal court.[37] Henry II moulded feudal custom as used in the various baronies into the common law and gave it into the custody of his justices. The baronial courts rapidly lost both their business and their significance.

The only important function of the baronial courts not directly affected by the innovations of Henry II was their power to authorize distraint of tenants who failed to perform their services. But even here the introduction of the writ ordering the sheriff to release chattels taken in distraint gave that royal officer complete supervision over this function of the feudal courts. Only the most highly privileged barons retained their control over feudal distraint. As a matter of fact it appears that this innovation led indirectly to the end of the baronial courts' authority in this respect. Since distraint was supervised by the sheriff or by a baron as franchise holder, the lords saw no need to consult their courts. When service was in default, the lord made distraint without asking the approval of his *curia*. If he acted unjustly, the vassal had recourse to the sheriff or franchise holder.[38]

---

[35] *Magna carta*, c. 34.   [36] Glanville, *De legibus*, p. 90.   [37] *Ibid.*, p. 128.
[38] Pollock and Maitland, *History of English law*, II, 574-575.

By the middle of the thirteenth century the baronial feudal
courts did little more than receive writs of right and hear the
initiation of pleas that would be settled in the royal courts.
As these functions cannot have been of much interest to the
barons, these courts would probably have disappeared very
quickly had they not had some financial value. In 1263 the
court of the honor of Gloucester for its fees in Gloucestershire
and Somersetshire was worth £5 6s 8d a year.[39] In 1264 the
court of the honor of Leicester was valued at £10 2s.[40]
Undoubtedly some fees were collected for the limited functions performed by the courts, but I suspect very strongly that
the chief source of revenue was fines for non-attendance.[41]
There is evidence that the barons were attempting to develop
this asset. The first chapter of the *Provisions of Westminster*
states that no lord could force his vassal to attend his court
unless the vassal or his ancestor had performed such service
before 1230 or it was specifically mentioned in the charter of
enfeoffment.[42]

Here again we find the disappearance of personal relations
between lords and vassals. In the eleventh century the baron
and his men had worked together in his *curia* to solve the questions of feudal custom concerning the barony. The innovations
of Henry II had largely transferred this function to royal officials. From the vassal's point of view attendance at his lord's
court became simply a burdensome obligation. To the lord the
court was simply a source of income—and not a particularly
lucrative one. As in the case of military service the relationship
between lord and tenant by knight service had been placed
on a money basis.

In the eleventh century the barons of England used feudal
arrangements to provide themselves with administrative officers
as well as with soldiers and advisers. There were baronial stew-
ards, chamberlains, butlers, dispensers, constables, and mar-
shals. Not all these officials were present on every barony—

---

[39] *Close rolls, 1261-4*, p. 284.

[40] *Ibid.*, p. 408.

[41] *Historia et cartularium monasterii Sancti Petri Gloucestriae* (ed. W. H.
Hart, *Rolls series*), I, 35-36.

[42] *Statutes of the realm*, I, 8.

only the steward can be considered as absolutely indispensable. In the *Leges Henrici* he is the baron's recognized representative and chief administrator. There is not sufficient evidence to justify a categorical statement that these offices were always hereditary fiefs, but it is clear that they usually were. They were held as a rule by the baron's most important vassals—the honorial barons.[43]

During the second half of the twelfth century and the first half of the thirteenth these hereditary baronial officials either disappeared or were transformed into purely honorary officers. They were replaced by paid professional administrators. Paucity of available evidence makes it difficult either to date this change precisely or to trace the stages. What information exists for the period of transition is hard to use because of the vagueness of contemporary terminology. Take for instance the case of the most important of these officials, the steward. During the eleventh and twelfth centuries he was usually called *dapifer*. I have never found *dapifer* used for anyone who was not an important mesne tenant and the chief officer of his lord. But the title of seneschal that came into use in the early thirteenth century was much more loosely applied. The old *dapifer*, the chief of the baronial administration, was called a seneschal, but so were a number of lesser officials. One could be seneschal for a whole barony, for a few estates, or for the lord's household.[44] Thus the fact that one finds a man of no position called the seneschal of some baron does not prove that the hereditary seneschal no longer existed on the fief. This situation seems to have troubled the royal administration. Early in his reign King John decreed that the exchequer should not recognize as a seneschal any one who lacked the authority to pledge his lord's faith.[45]

Here and there one can catch a glimpse of the progress of this transformation in baronial administration. In 1204 the seneschal of the barony of Plympton was Robert d'Aumale, the chief mesne tenant of the barony and the descendant of a

---

[43] For an excellent discussion of baronial officers see Stenton, *English feudalism*, pp. 67-82.

[44] Denholm-Young, *Seignorial administration in England*, pp. 67-68.

[45] Roger of Hovedon, *Chronica*, IV, 152.

Domesday tenant-in-chief of the crown.[46] By the second half of the thirteenth century Mr. Denholm-Young finds this office exercised by professional administrators.[47] Some twenty-four baronial seneschals are mentioned in the memoranda roll of 1230. With one or two possible exceptions these were men of no feudal position in the baronies for which they served. Presumably they were hired officials.

Mr. Denholm-Young has clearly shown that after 1250 the baronies of England were administered by professionals—sometimes men of knightly rank and sometimes men of lower social position. I am inclined to believe that this practice was fairly general throughout the thirteenth century. First in all probability hired servants took over the functions of the butler and dispenser and the household duties of the chamberlain. The hereditary constable was replaced by a mercenary captain. Then the financial duties of the chamberlain and steward were given to men trained for such work. Eventually the hereditary seneschal was replaced by a professional.

The change from hereditary feudal to paid professional administrators cut the last personal bond between the baron and his vassals. The culmination of this process seems to me to mark the end of the feudal barony. Like most changes it was recognized rather slowly by contemporaries. Let me cite an example. In the early twelfth century a baron's importance was largely measured by the number of his knights' fees. When a barony was divided among co-heiresses or part of it was assigned in dower, the fees were apportioned by number. Two sisters divided the fees in half; a widow received one-third of the fees in dower. But by the last years of the thirteenth century the system changed. Knights' fees were evaluated in terms of money and distributed on that basis.[48] To me this marks the official end of English feudalism.

The disappearance of the feudal element from the relationships between members of the English gentle class requires emphasis because it is concealed from the casual glance. The

---

[46] *Curia regis rolls*, III, 138.

[47] *Seignorial administration in England*, pp. 75-77.

[48] *Calendar of close rolls, 1279-1288*, p. 156; *ibid., 1288-1296*, pp. 236-237; *ibid., 1296-1302*, pp. 437-439; *ibid., 1302-7*, pp. 190-191, 274-276, 511-513.

apparent structure of English society did not change. There were still barons who formed the top layer of the landed class. They were followed to war by knights and serjeants. They were summoned to Parliament and enjoyed extensive franchises. The prestige supplied by their political, military, and economic power made them the natural leaders of the lesser gentry. The sons and daughters of gentle families were brought up in the baron's household. But the basis of the system was no longer feudal. The men who followed the baron to war were paid soldiers. A seat in Parliament had little connection with tenure of an ancient barony. The gentle families who recognized the leadership of the baron and sent their children to be educated in his household might or might not be bound to him by feudal ties. Some barons held ancient baronies and still had tenants by knight service, but outside of the financial sphere their relationship to these tenants was the same as that to other gentlemen. And there were barons who did not hold baronies by tenure, who had no vassals, and yet they enjoyed the same prestige and power as the others. England in the fourteenth and fifteenth centuries had an aristocracy that lived as had the feudal class, but it was no longer feudal. Its resources were not based on the services due from fiefs.

Having discussed the feudal services that either disappeared or were commuted into money payments, we must now turn to those obligations of the vassal and rights of the lord that were from the beginning essentially financial. These include the lord's right to demand aids and relief, to marry the children of a deceased vassal, and to have custody of a mesne fief held by a minor. While the rights of marriage and custody were not financial in origin and retained other aspects well into the thirteenth century, they were thought of primarily as sources of revenue. Aid and relief were purely financial both in origin and English practice.

General feudal theory permitted a lord who was faced with necessary and unusual expense to ask his vassals to assist him in meeting it. It is conceivable that originally such assistance was often rendered in kind. Thus if a lord was planning a great feast to celebrate the knighting of his heir, he might ask

his vassals to contribute supplies. But in the early thirteenth
century when we first find adequate information about feudal
aids in England they were clearly money payments. What evidence there is suggests that they had been from the time of the
Conquest. Although these aids were essentially feudal, English
lords had no hesitation in demanding them from free tenants
who did not hold by knightly tenure.[49] This inconsistency did
not trouble Glanville who emphasized the feudal nature of
the obligation by insisting that the aid demanded of a vassal
must be in proportion to the size of his fief.[50] Bracton, on the
other hand, was worried by this peculiarity in the custom of
the realm. He tried to solve the difficulty by saying that aids
were not services; that they were not due from the fief. They
were personal grants by a lord's man to assist him in his needs.[51]
This seems to me to be simply a rationalization of contemporary practice and a rather unsuccessful one at that. Aids were
assessed by knights' fees on those who held by military service
and by the value of the estate on those holding by other free
tenures. The system was as purely feudal as English society
would permit.

Obviously the most important questions relating to feudal
aids concern their amount and their frequency. Until the First
Statute of Westminster of 1272 all formal pronouncements as
to the sum that a lord could demand from a vassal as an aid
simply stated that it must be reasonable. Presumably that
meant that it must accord with the lord's need and the vassal's
ability to pay. I am inclined to believe that before the reign
of Henry III the usual rate per knight's fee was about the same
as the customary contemporary scutage rate. When the lord's
need was great and the crown was sufficiently interested to
assist him in distraining his tenants, the sums demanded could
be larger. Thus a higher rate per fee is found in the case of
an aid levied by William de Mowbray to help him pay his
debts to King John, and delinquent vassals were distrained by
the sheriffs.[52] When in the reign of Henry III the ordinary

[49] Stenton, *English feudalism*, p. 173.
[50] *De legibus*, p. 130.
[51] *De legibus*, II, 116.
[52] *Pipe roll 11 John*, Public Record Office, E 372-55.

scutage rate was raised to forty shillings, I suspect the barons sought to increase the aids demanded from their tenants. At any rate the First Statute of Westminster set the rate at twenty shillings for a knight's fee or for land worth £20 a year.[53]

The earliest detailed statement as to the occasions on which an English lord could demand aid from his vassals is found in Glanville.[54] This writer had no doubt that a lord could ask for an aid to assist him in paying relief when he succeeded to his fief. Feudal custom also allowed the lord to levy aid when he knighted his eldest son or married his eldest daughter. The author was inclined to doubt the legality of the common practice of demanding an aid to " maintain the lord in war," that is to pay his military expenses. Perhaps he felt that if the war had the king's sanction, the lord could collect scutage. But the author stated emphatically that there was no fixed rule about the occasions on which aid could be demanded. This seems to suggest that a lord could ask for an aid whenever he saw fit, and I suspect that this was true. The question would be whether or not he could collect it. According to Glanville he could distrain his tenants to pay by order of his *curia*. If that procedure were unsuccessful, he could seek a writ from the king or the justiciar ordering the sheriff to aid him. In short a lord could collect an aid only if he could get the approval of his court or the royal government.

In general the statement of Glanville agrees with what little is known about twelfth-century feudal custom in respect to aids. Contemporary charters mention the aids to help the lord pay relief, to knight his son, and to marry his daughter.[55] But they also usually include the aid to assist the lord in ransoming himself. As this was one of the three aids mentioned in *Magna Carta*, its omission by Glanville was probably an oversight. While these were the occasions that were generally recognized, Glanville's statement that there was no set rule is extremely important. When the lord was in need, he could ask for aid.

I am inclined to believe that the key to the history of the feudal aid in the late twelfth and early thirteenth centuries lies

[53] Stubbs, *Select charters*, p. 451.
[54] *De legibus*, pp. 130-131.
[55] Stenton, *English feudalism*, pp. 171-174.

in Glanville's discussion of the means by which a lord could force his tenants to pay. The final decision as to the propriety of a request for an aid obviously rested with the individual or group that could authorize effective distraint. Glanville wrote in a period of transition between two systems. He insisted that no royal writ was needed—that a lord could distrain with the consent of the *curia*. This clearly represented feudal tradition. The lord and his vassals gathered in the lord's court determined their mutual relations. But Glanville's preoccupation with this question of securing a royal writ seems to indicate that it was becoming a common practice. As we have seen, the legislation of Henry II had started the rapid decline of the feudal courts. The lords were inclined to ignore their courts and to seek the king's writ. This gave them the assistance of the royal officers in collecting the aid.

Now it is clear that the lord's *curia* and the royal government might have very different ideas about the occasions that justified the demand for an aid. The tenants would be inclined to object to any payment beyond those generally recognized by feudal custom. The crown had other interests. When a baron owed relief, a fine, or some other debt to the crown, the king was anxious to help him pay it. If for any reason the scutage paid by a lord's vassals did not suffice to enable him to perform the service required by the crown, the king was inclined to authorize him to levy an aid " to maintain him in the king's service." This conflict between the views of the crown and those of the mesne tenants is illustrated by an incident of 1207. The vassals of Robert de Mortimer of Norfolk were summoned into the king's court to explain why they had disobeyed a royal writ ordering them to grant their lord an aid to sustain him in the king's service in Poitou. They replied that they and their ancestors had been accustomed only to render aid to knight the lord's son, marry his daughter, or ransom his person. They did not wish to give any other aid unless the court felt that they should.[56] The rolls of John's reign show many royal writs directing tenants to aid their lords. Some of these simply gave the lord the assistance of the sheriff in distraining his

[56] *Curia regis rolls*, V, 39.

tenants to pay the generally accepted aids, but others ordered mesne tenants to grant aids to their lords for various purposes in which the crown had an interest.

In the fifteenth article of *Magna Carta* King John promised that in the future he would not grant any lord leave to demand an aid from his vassals except for one of three purposes—to ransom his person, to knight his eldest son, and to marry his eldest daughter for the first time, and that the aid allowed would be "reasonable."[57] This is a long way from the statement of Glanville. Here it seems to be taken for granted that an aid can only be levied with the king's leave. The aid to help the lord pay relief, which was the one Glanville considered most certainly legal, has been banned. But this clause in the charter simply represents the aspirations of the mesne tenants. The regent and his advisers dropped it in reissuing the charter. While this may well have been done to safeguard the royal revenue, one must remember that the Regent William Marshal was a great baron with a vital interest in feudal aids. At any rate the government of Henry III continued John's policy. Throughout his reign numerous writs were issued directing mesne tenants to give their lord an aid to pay his debts to the crown or to sustain him in the king's service. Orders to grant an aid to pay the lord's relief were still issued, but were rather uncommon. In 1249 a writ directing the vassals of Thomas de Scotney to pay an aid to assist their lord towards his relief gave as the reason for its issuance the fact that the king had learned by inquiry that Thomas could not possibly pay without help.[58] Bracton mentioned only two occasions on which an aid could properly be demanded—the knighting of the eldest son and the marriage of the eldest daughter. The king's writ had to be obtained before the levy could be made.[59] Moreover he specifically denied that a lord could ask his tenants to grant an aid to assist him in paying relief. The vassal paid relief for his own fief, and it was not proper to ask him to contribute to his lord's.[60] The First Statute of Westminster which settled the amount of relief mentioned the same two occasions as Bracton. It added the provision that a lord could not ask an aid to knight

[57] *Magna carta*, c. 15.
[58] *Excerpta ex rotulis finium*, II, 65.
[59] *De legibus*, II, 116.
[60] *Ibid.*, p. 247.

his son before the boy was fifteen nor to marry his daughter until she was seven. As boys were usually knighted at about twenty-one years of age and the minimum canonical age for the marriage of a girl was twelve, this restriction does not seem unreasonable. By this statute feudal aid became a fixed tax that a lord could levy at set times. The contest between crown and lords on one side and the mesne tenants on the other had ended in the latter's favor.

The lord's right to demand relief when a vassal was succeeded by his heir probably had its origin in the days before fiefs had become hereditary. It was then a payment for permission to succeed to the fief. Later it became simply a feudal service. On the continent there are clear traces of ·an early feudal custom which required a vassal to pay relief when his lord died, but there is no evidence that this practice was ever common in England. The only clear instance of a demand for relief at the death of a lord is the well known letter of William II to the vassals of the bishop of Worcester.[61] The wording of the letter suggests an arbitrary demand rather than a request for a customary payment. Yet it is difficult to believe that if the king could collect payments in one case, he refrained from similar demands from the tenants of other baronies. Certainly one document is too slight a base on which to build general conclusions. Mr. Stenton has pointed out that when a vassal's heir succeeded to the fief, he frequently sought the lord's confirmation of the original enfeoffment and that in all probability he usually had to pay for it.[62] I should like to point out that the payment of an aid to assist the lord in meeting the cost of his relief had much the same effect. Such an aid was undoubtedly at a far lower rate per fee than that customary for relief, but it was a payment to the new lord.

The *charter of liberties of Henry I* stated that " the men of my barons shall relieve their lands from their lords by just and legitimate reliefs." [63] According to the *Leis Willelme* the heir of a *vavassor* or mesne tenant should give his lord as relief his father's horse, hauberk, helmet, shield, lance, and sword. If

---

[61] Dugdale, *Monasticon*, I, 601-602.
[62] *English feudalism*, pp. 161-162.
[63] *Charter of liberties*, c. 2.

he could not do this, he was to pay 100 shillings. Land held at lease was to be relieved by paying one year's rent.[64] As I have indicated in discussing baronial reliefs, I believe that this passage reflects chiefly the antiquarian interests of the author of the *Leis Willelme*. But it does suggest that in the early twelfth century there was an inclination to regard 100 shillings as a reasonable relief for a knight's fee. At the same time I join Mr. Stenton in believing that if this was a standard which was generally accepted, it had but recently been established.[65] I have little doubt that in the eleventh century reliefs were settled by baronial courts and varied from barony to barony. I have found one case of a local rate of relief as late as 1171.[66] In all probability the definite standardization of the relief due from mesne tenants was part of the general process by which common law replaced the varying feudal customs of the baronies.

It is clear that this standardization had been established by the end of the twelfth century. The *Dialogue of the exchequer* states that when a barony was in the king's hands, its tenants paid relief at the rate of 100 shillings a fee.[67] Glanville says that the custom of the realm considered the reasonable relief for a knight's fee to be 100 shillings.[68] The pipe rolls of Henry II show that he demanded relief from tenants of baronies which were in his hands at this rate. But it is interesting to notice that *Magna Carta* suggests that the 100 shillings relief was not yet universal. It states that " the heir or heirs of a knight for an entire knight's fee by 100 shillings at most; and he who owes less gives less according to the ancient custom of the fees." [69] This clearly implies that on some baronies relief was paid at a lower rate. Perhaps this was simply intended to cover the small fees " of Mortain," but it could easily permit other variations. In general, however, one can say that by the end of the twelfth century the relief for a mesne fief was paid at the rate of 100 shillings a fee.

[64] *Leis Willelme*, c. 20, 2-4.
[65] *English feudalism*, p. 163.
[66] " Pipe roll 17 Henry II," *Pipe roll society*, XVI, 135.
[67] *Dialogus de scaccario*, p. 135.
[68] *De legibus*, p. 128.
[69] *Magna carta*, c. 2.

Aids and reliefs were very irregular sources of revenue. According to feudal custom as described by Glanville an aid could not ordinarily be asked more than three times in a generation. A lord could demand an aid when he succeeded his father. If he had a son and a daughter, he could insist on an aid to knight the former and to marry the latter. Once the aid to assist the lord in paying relief disappeared, the accepted occasions were reduced to two in each generation, and they depended on the lord's ability to produce a son and a daughter. In short after the Statute of Westminster of 1272, the most a lord could hope for from feudal aids was two grants of twenty shillings a fee in each generation. From relief the lord received 100 shillings per fee whenever a new vassal inherited. If there was a succession of childless brothers, he profited accordingly. But ordinarily he received 100 shillings from each generation. Thus one can say that in the late thirteenth century relief and aid gave the lord a maximum of £7 from each fee in every generation. When one considers that in this same period a knight's fee was presumed to be worth £20 a year, this is a fairly small return. Moreover it was fixed by law and could not be increased as landed revenues grew greater. By the fourteenth century these feudal revenues were of comparatively little importance in baronial economy. Only the great holders of knights' fees like the earls of Gloucester and Lancaster derived important sums from this source.

The lord's rights of custody and marriage were not essentially financial in origin. A fief was granted in return for certain services. A woman or a minor could not perform the most vital of these services. The lord could obviously insist that the economic resources represented by the fief be used to support an adult male capable of fulfilling the obligations due him. Feudal custom achieved this end in several ways. A male relative of the woman or minor might be given temporary control of the fief. More usual perhaps was to give the lord the enjoyment of the revenues of the fief until the woman was married or the minor came of age. This seems to have been the custom in Normandy, and it certainly was in England. The right of marriage was equally important in the feudal system. When the daughter of a vassal married, her husband obtained an interest in at least part of her father's fief. In short he became a tenant on the barony. Obviously the baron could not permit his foes to obtain such positions. Hence the lord had to give his approval before a vassal could marry his daughter. If a vassal died leaving female heirs, the same considerations made it necessary that the lord should choose their husbands. The same was true of the vassal's widow who would carry her dowry to a second husband. Thus the rights of custody and marriage were of decided political importance in the early days of feudalism.

I am inclined to doubt that the political considerations discussed in the preceding paragraph were ever of great importance in England. The royal prohibition of private warfare must have made it difficult for one subject of the English king to maintain that another subject was his enemy. The rights of custody and marriage soon became purely financial. But financial considerations must have often made it desirable for a lord to control the marrying of the widows, daughters, and sisters of his vassals. Suppose an important mesne tenant had a daughter who was to be his sole heir. He wanted to marry her to a tenant on another barony. That would mean that the lord lost his right of marriage over the females of the family holding that fief. This problem became more acute with the development of the doctrine of prerogative wardship. If the heiress of a mesne tenant married a tenant-in-chief of the crown, the lord lost both custody and marriage over that fief.

Feudal tradition gave the lord no control over the marriage of male heirs. It made no difference if a vassal's wife was the lord's foe. Even if the marriage made the heir a vassal of some other baron for his wife's lands, his liege homage remained to his original lord. But in the early thirteenth century when the right of marriage had become simply a matter of money, the king and his barons could see no reason for not profiting from the marriage of male heirs. By Bracton's time the sale of the marriage of a minor male in the lord's custody was an accepted feudal custom.

The right of custody was obviously a highly irregular source of income. Many generations could pass without a minor falling heir to a mesne fief. Then a boy of one might inherit and give the lord twenty years to enjoy the revenues of the fief. The value of the right of custody depended on the annual revenue of the mesne fief. In general they were not very valuable. A few exceptions seem worth noting. The fief held from the earls of Cornwall by the Cardinans was valued in the late thirteenth century at £300 and was assessed for scutage at seventy-one fees.[70] The Colombar family held a fief from the honor of Striguil valued at £199 in 1282.[71] The honor of Petworth which was a mesne tenement of the honor of Arundel was worth £132 in 1186.[72] The fief held by the Gresleys of Manchester of the honor of Lancaster yielded £115 in 1183.[73] But such great mesne fiefs were rare. Moreover most of them were held by men who were elsewhere tenants-in-chief of the crown and hence escaped the barons' custody. But even in the case of small·fiefs the right of custody could be valuable. A baron with many fees had a fair chance of having some income from this source most of the time. The value of the right of marriage also depended on the revenue from the mesne fief. The market price of a widow or an heir was determined by the annual value of the lands involved. One can easily imagine an impecunious lord hopefully waiting for the death of an important mesne tenant. At the very least it would mean a relief and a widow to marry. It might mean a long and profitable custody and the marriage of valuable heirs.

The rights of custody and marriage had one great advantage as sources of baronial income—their value rose with the revenues from land. By the end of the thirteenth century castle-guard dues, penalties for not attending court, aids, and reliefs had become fixed in terms of money at the rates prevalent in the late twelfth or early thirteenth centuries. Take a mesne fief with an annual value of £20 in 1200 and £35 in 1250 held for the service of one knight. At both these dates it would have yielded the lord perhaps ten shillings a year for castle-guard, £5 once a generation for relief, and two or three aids at £1 each generation. But its custody had increased in value 75 per

[70] *Rot. hund.*, I, 57.
[71] *Calendar of close rolls, 1279-1288*, p. 161.
[72] " Pipe roll 32 Henry II," *Pipe roll society*, **XXXVI**, 184.
[73] " Pipe roll 29 Henry II," *ibid.*, **XXXII**, 72.

cent, and presumably the value of the marriage of its lord or
lady had grown correspondingly. Hence custody and marriage
remained important to English barons long after other feudal
obligations had become insignificant. An inquisition *post
mortem* of 1263 on the lands of the earl of Gloucester divided
the knights' fees into two classes—those over which the earl
had the rights of custody and marriage and those held by tenants-in-chief of the crown.[74] When towards the end of the
thirteenth century we find knights' fees valued for division
among co-heiresses, it is clearly the rights of custody and marriage that are being considered. Aids and reliefs were collected
by the fee and all were of equal value, but the revenues from
custody and marriage varied with the value of the fief and the
level of profits from land.

[74] *Close rolls, 1261-4*, pp. 284, 286-288, 292.

Chapter VI

MANORIAL RESOURCES

Although great lords who possessed extensive privileges and a large number of knights' fees drew a considerable proportion of their income from franchisal and feudal sources, most barons obtained by far the largest part of their revenue from their demesne manors. This manorial revenue consisted of the income derived from the exploitation of the manorial demesne and from the free and unfree agricultural tenants who lived on the manor. Contemporary practice divided manorial income into several classifications. First came the rents received from free and unfree tenants. Then there was the produce of the manorial demesne—corn and livestock. Thirdly there was the revenue from the lord's mills. These were the chief items. Such additional sources of income as the fees charged for feeding pigs in the lord's woods were rarely of much importance. Finally, as I have pointed out in discussing franchisal revenues, part of the item usually designated as " pleas and perquisites " represented income that was essentially manorial. This included the profits of the manorial court and such perquisites as heriot. I have omitted these sources from my discussion of manorial income because I can see no way to separate them from the franchisal revenue. When an account covered an entire barony, the item " pleas and perquisites " probably consisted chiefly of income from franchisal and feudal courts, but when it applied to a single manor the revenue from the manorial court and manorial perquisites may well have formed an important part of the total under this heading.[1]

The proportions among the three chief items of manorial revenue varied greatly from barony to barony. Let us glance at several accounts from the reign of John. In 1212 the lands of the constable of Chester yielded £346 from rents, £196 from

[1] In *The Pipe roll of the bishopric of Winchester for the fourth year of the Pontificate of Peter des Roches, 1208-09* (edited under the supervision of Hubert Hall, London, 1903) the court revenues, called *de purchasiis*, are chiefly manorial in nature with franchisal income forming a small part of the total.

the produce of the manorial demesne, and £73 from mills. Fees for the pasturing of cattle and pigs came to £75.[2] In 1214 the honor of Berkhamsted brought in £120 in rents, £40 in demesne produce, £64 from mills, and £20 from pig feeding.[3] The honor of Knaresborough in 1206 yielded £46 in rents, £44 from the demesnes, and £120 from mills.[4] In 1214 the lands of the bishop of Durham produced £1,255 from rents, £309 from the manorial demesnes, and £365 from mills. The bishop's fief also yielded £134 in pasturage fees and various forest rights.[5]

Two of the three most productive sources of manorial revenue, rents and the income from mills, were fairly stable from year to year, but the returns from the exploitation of the manorial demesne fluctuated violently. They were affected directly by the hazards of agriculture—bad weather for crops and epidemics among the livestock. They also suffered from baronial impecunity. The lord was always tempted to obtain immediate revenue by selling too much stock. As a result the manorial demesne became understocked and failed to yield as much as it should. The inquest made in 1185 into the value of wardships and marriages in the king's custody shows this situation very clearly.[6] In the lands of the Arcy barony Nocton and Dunston manors were worth £16 unstocked and £27 stocked. Stallingborough stocked as it was was worth £16. If it were stocked to capacity, it would be worth £40.[7] This question of stock was a vital point in the debates between lords and vassals over wardship rights. The lord was inclined to sell too much stock, to waste the estate, and hence injure the heir. In the year 1203 William de Stutville died. The account of his lands for the first year shows £260 from rents, £367 from the sale of corn, and £455 from the sale of stock. The latter included 2,519 sheep and 1,016 lambs.[8] The proportions of the different items make it appear likely that the crown was wasting the estate as effectively as possible.

[2] *Pipe roll 14 John*, Public Record Office, E 372-58.
[3] *Pipe roll 16 John, ibid.*, E 372-60.
[4] *Pipe roll 8 John, ibid.*, E 372-52.
[5] *Pipe roll 16 John, ibid.*, E 372-60.
[6] " Rotuli de dominibus, pueris, et puellis," *Pipe roll society*, XXXV.
[7] *Ibid.*, pp. 2, 16.
[8] " Pipe roll 5 John," *ibid.*, LIV, 222-223.

Many barons followed the practice of letting most of their demesne manors at a fixed rent or farm. This not only relieved them of the necessity for supervising the exploitation of the estates but also gave them a stable manorial income. This practice seems to have been more general in the twelfth than in the thirteenth century. I suspect that the explanation is that the hereditary feudal baronial officers were inefficient supervisors, and the barons found it more satisfactory to farm their manors. This situation changed with the appearance of professional administrators. When hired officials became available, the lords tended to return to direct exploitation of their demesne manors. This remained true until the general commutation of service rents made it desirable to rent the manorial demesnes. When that took place, the lord was no longer an agricultural entrepreneur but simply a rent collector. If the sums for which manors were let at farm had been arrived at by honest bargaining on a purely business basis, these figures would obviously be the most useful for estimating a baron's revenue. They would represent average annual returns. But granting a manor at a low farm was a common method of rewarding a servant, and often a lord brought pressure to bear to induce the farmer to promise more than a reasonable rent. Nevertheless when only a single year's income is available, the amount of a farm is far more reliable than the actual detailed accounts.

The trend of manorial revenues is a subject of prime importance not only to the student of the barony but to the general historian as well. Manorial income was usually the chief item in a baron's revenue, and it was the only resource of most freeholders in a lower status. The average tenant by knight service was practically entirely dependent on his manorial income. Moreover as agriculture was the overwhelmingly dominant industry of mediaeval England, the return received by the landholders is of great significance in English economic history. I approach this subject with considerable trepidation. As Professor Postan is at work on a book on English manorial income, my conclusions must soon face those of a trained economic historian who has in all probability far more material available than I have. Nevertheless the subject is so vital to my purpose that I must do what I can.

Obviously one of the most crucial questions in connection with manorial revenue concerns the form in which it was received by the baron. It is usual to assume that in a pure manorial economy the income received by the lord consisted entirely of services and payments in kind. There would be no market for agricultural produce. The lord and his household would consume his income directly. As I have indicated earlier in this essay, I do not believe that this situation ever existed in any absolute form in England. The fact that danegeld was collected would alone prove that some money was in circulation in the eleventh century. Various passages in *Domesday Book* and in contemporary documents support this conclusion. Certainly by the time of Henry I a large proportion of the royal revenue was received in the form of money.

Nevertheless it seems clear that an English baron of the eleventh or twelfth century ordinarily expected to consume his manorial income directly. *Domesday Book* shows that most barons kept their larger estates in demesne and concentrated their demesne manors in geographical groups. In some baronies at least there was a castle in one manor of each group. Both these facts indicate that the baron expected to travel from group to group consuming his income as he went. Robert Grosseteste's counsel to the countess of Lincoln shows that this practice was still followed to some extent at least in the thirteenth century. He told the young lady to consult her seneschal after the harvest, to find out the store of grain in each of her manors, and to plan her periods of residence in her various seats accordingly.[9]

In short the question in regard to eleventh- and twelfth-century England does not concern the existence of a market for manorial produce but rather the size of the market. By the time of Henry I the English feudal class was able to pay in money scutage, relief, danegeld, and penalties imposed by the royal courts. The sheriffs and other farmers of royal estates paid the revenue into the exchequer in cash. When a barony was in the king's hands, its net revenue went to the crown in money. The feudal class was clearly selling some part of its

---

[9] *Les reules Seynt Roberd* in *Walter of Henley's husbandry* (translated by Elizabeth Lamond, London, 1890), p. 145.

surplus income in kind or was receiving some income in money. Some small part of the manors of England were selling their entire net production. But as long as the feudal class was consuming most of its income directly, no very extensive market was required. It is a far cry from this state of semi-money economy to the day when a baron can sell the produce of all his manors except those adjacent to his residence and use the money income to support his household. I can think of no means for dating the culmination of this development, but I suspect that it was going on all through my period. As the market for manorial produce expanded, the baron either received a larger part of his income in money or could easily turn it into money after he received it.

I emphasize this question of the form in which manorial revenue was received because an adequate comprehension of baronial resources requires a clear understanding of the distinction between income received in cash or easily turned into money and income evaluated in terms of money. *Domesday Book* gives an annual value in terms of money for every estate in England. But it is certain that there was no market large enough to absorb the produce of more than a tiny part of these estates. Many of the figures that I have used to attempt to establish the trend of manorial income are simply evaluations. Even when the figures represent actual money turned into the exchequer, the historian must consider them as evaluations in using them to determine baronial resources. In short my figures represent manorial productivity and the price level of manorial produce. They furnish little information on the amount of actual money that passed through the hands of the average baron.

The earliest figures on manorial values in England are those found in *Domesday Book*. The next source that supplies them in sufficient quantity to be of any use for my purpose is the pipe rolls. During the reigns of Henry II, Richard, and John they furnish practically all the information obtainable. Then in the reigns of Henry III, Edward I, and Edward II come a large number of varied sources—inquisitions, surveys, assignments of dower. I have by no means covered all the existing material in this last period, but have simply used what was available in print. I suspect that a study of the unpublished "ministers' accounts" and the full "inquisitions *post mortem*" would supply an enormous mass of information on this period. But for my purpose here it would not be worth the effort. I am interested in the long-term trend, and figures for the late thirteenth and early fourteenth centuries alone would be of little use.

For purposes of comparison I have established four periods based chiefly on the chronological distribution of my figures. The first is that of the earliest information available—the late eleventh century. The next covers roughly the early Angevin period, the years 1150-1220. The third runs from 1220 to 1250. The fourth goes from 1250 to 1350. The great length of this last period is due to the fact that while figures are available for the value of many individual estates during it, the cases where two figures are obtainable for the same estate are too few to justify dividing it into two periods. The basis of my discussion of the trend of manorial income is a list of 272 estates for which I can find values in at least two of these periods.

The figures on manorial income that I have found fall into three general classes. There are accounts presented at the exchequer by the custodians of manors in the king's hand. Then there are the farms at which manors were let. Finally there are estimates of the annual value of estates. An account shows more or less clearly the actual income produced by an estate in a particular year. But as it is rarely possible to obtain figures for the same estate for more than two or three consecutive years, bad weather, epidemics, understocking, and the general hazards of agriculture can seriously distort the result. For our purpose the farm is much more useful. It represents the sum that the farmer was willing to pay in order to enjoy the income from the estate. It was his estimate of the annual value less some profit for himself. Undoubtedly a lord would at times favor a servant by letting him farm a manor at less than its normal rent. Again the farm might be set high in the hope that the farmer could squeeze the sum out of the tenants. But in general farms probably represented business bargains. Their chief weakness from our point of view is that they had a tendency to become traditional and hence obsolete. The farms at which royal estates appear in the pipe rolls must be regarded with suspicion for this reason.

Estimates of manorial income are more difficult to deal with than accounts and farms. The primary question is how an estimate was arrived at. Maitland has pointed out that some Domesday valuations seem to have been based on an idea that an important estate should have a certain value.[10] In the hundred rolls a few estimates of annual income appear to have been obtained by assigning a set value to the knight's fee.[11] Estimates of this sort are, of course, worthless for our purpose. At the opposite extreme from valuations based on preconceptions that had little or no connection with actual manorial production were careful estimates of annual value based on a system generally recognized throughout England. There is clear evidence that the royal government had developed such a system by 1185.[12] Bracton explains the methods in use in his day at some length.[13] Obviously figures based on a general system of this sort are extremely valuable for our purpose. They represent carefully reached averages of manorial earnings. Between these two sorts of estimates one can find many different kinds ranging from local systems of evaluation to pure guesses by juries.

Unfortunately we do not know how the Domesday evaluations were arrived at. Presumably the Domesday survey was conducted primarily in order to examine the assessments for danegeld. Hence the application of a common method of estimating values would have been highly desirable. If any valid information about comparative assessments was to be, obtained, a valuation of £15 a year in Sussex had to represent about the same manorial income as one of £15 in Lincolnshire. But we have no evidence that any general system had been worked out or that there were men who knew how to apply one. Certainly the statements about the values in the time of Edward the Confessor cannot have been constructed in this way. In

[10] *Domesday book and beyond*, p. 473.
[11] *Rot. hund.*, I, 241, 277.
[12] "Rotuli de dominibus, pueris, et puellis," *Pipe roll society*, XXXV.
[13] *De legibus*, II, 219-220. See also *Statutes of the realm*, I, 242-243.

short it seems likely that the Domesday valuations represent simply estimates by local juries with no commonly recognized system to guide them. As a result they cannot inspire much confidence, but the student of the eleventh century must make the best of what material he can find.

With some few exceptions the estimates I have used for later periods are of the more reliable variety. There are the meticulous valuations made by the king's officers in the survey of 1185. Then there are estimates of annual value made when dower was assigned to a widow or a barony was divided among female heirs. These last are highly reliable—if they appeared doubtful some interested party objected. The only questionable estimates from this later period are those obtained from such sources as the hundred rolls. As I have pointed out above, some of these must be rejected at once as based on invalid preconceptions. But I have accepted others which seem to me to represent honest if shot-gun estimates by local juries. These figures have little value. Fortunately I have had to use very few of them.

There is one final difficulty in connection with my figures on manorial revenues. In the vast majority of cases I have simply the name of the manor with no description of it. Hence it is impossible to be certain that the estate for which I find an annual value in the thirteenth century is of the same extent as the one of the same name in *Domesday*. Although in general barons were inclined to keep their demesne manors intact, there were exceptions. In some cases it is clear that knights were enfeoffed with part of a demesne estate. Probably of greater importance were grants made in free alms. Many great barons granted whole manors to the church, but many more merely gave lands in their demesne estates. In short I have no doubt that in the long period between the compilation of *Domesday Book* and the late twelfth century when my next figures appear the area from which the lord received income was in most manors reduced in size. Thus if my figures showed a downward trend of manorial revenues, they would be very dubious.

To sum up, the nature of my figures prevents me from taking seriously any slight increase or decrease in manorial revenues— let us say that changes of 50 per cent or less would have little meaning. The practices of sub-infeudation on demesne manors and grants in free alms might well explain decreases in manorial values. But it seems to me that my figures are sufficiently reliable to make a pronounced general trend—one to which there were few individual exceptions—have decided significance. What the significance is poses another and even more complicated question.

As I have stated above, I have a list of 272 estates for which I have found income figures in at least two of my four periods. Comparing Domesday valuations with figures for the period 1150-1220 I find 141 estates have a median increase in value of 60 per cent. The average of the middle 25 per cent gives an increase of 67 per cent. Comparing Domesday valuations with those for the period 1220-1250, 36 estates have a median increase of 163 per cent. The arithmetical average of the middle 25 per cent is 175 per cent. Comparing Domesday with the period 1250-1350, 112 estates show a median increase of 240 per cent and an arithmetical average of the middle 25 per cent of 242 per cent. Comparing the period 1150-1220 with that of 1220-1250, 23 estates have a median increase of 51 per cent and an arithmetical average of the middle 25 per cent of 55 per cent. Comparing the period 1150-1220 to that of 1250-1350, 83 estates show a median increase of 100 per cent and an arithmetical average of the middle 25 per cent of 110 per cent. Comparing the period 1220-1250 to that of 1250-1350, 19 estates show a median increase of 28 per cent and an arithmetical average of the middle 25 per cent of 32 per cent.

These figures indicate that by 1220 the revenue from the average English manor expressed in terms of money had increased 60 per cent over its Domesday valuation. By 1250 an approximately equal increase had taken place—between 51 per cent and 64 per cent. Between 1250 and 1350 the growth in revenue amounted to only 28-32 per cent. Considering that comparatively few figures in my list are from the period 1330-1350, it might be more accurate to say that the increase of 28-32 per cent took place before 1330. These results are obviously extremely rough. I simply present them for what they are worth. They seem to show a steady increase in manorial revenues between Domesday and the early fourteenth century with the growth particularly rapid in the first half of the thirteenth century.

Obviously this general rise in manorial income in terms of pounds, shillings, and pence could have a wide variety of meanings. Let us dismiss at once the possibility that it represented nothing more than a change in the methods of estimating manorial values. While it is not inconceivable that one might devise a way to estimate the income of a manor so that it would appear to be nearly tripled in value without any real change taking place, the resulting figure would have no connection with reality and would serve no useful purpose. Moreover after 1150 this rise can be confirmed for a small number of manors by the use of accounts alone. We are left with three possibilities. The metal content of the money used may have fallen. The prices of manorial produce may have risen. The productivity of the land may have increased. Apparently the first of these three developments did not take place. There was no change in the metallic content of the penny, the sole actual coin, between the time of William the Conqueror and the reign of Edward III. Hence we must seek the meaning of our figures in one of the other possibilities—or a combination of both.

I have little doubt that the chief factor in the increase in manorial revenues in terms of money was a rising trend in the price of the produce of the manor. When the Domesday evaluations were made, towns and markets were comparatively few. There was little demand for agricultural products, and the price was low. We know that the twelfth century saw the appearance of new towns and presumably the growth in population of many old ones. We know that during this same period fairs and markets began to multiply. Both these developments continued with increased vigor in the thirteenth century. While some towns and markets were founded with an optimism which proved unjustified, it is clear that there must have been during these two centuries a large increase in the demand for agricultural products and a consequent increase in prices.

While I am inclined to believe that the general trend of manorial revenues grew out of the expanding market for the produce of the manor, increased productivity certainly played

11

some part in the process. Mr. Gray believes that there were improvements in the utilization of the land—shifts from the two-field to the three-field system.[14] Certainly during the twelfth and thirteenth centuries much land that had formerly been forest and waste was being turned to agricultural production. Along the borders of the forests of England land was being cleared for the plow. Vast stretches of waste land, especially in Yorkshire and Lincolnshire, were being turned into sheep pastures.

It is impossible to make any estimate of the amount of land cleared during our period. The entries in the pipe rolls of Henry II dealing with penalties imposed for clearing land in the royal forests show that such activities were carried on continually during his reign. In so far as one can judge from the sums pardoned to favored lords, the operations were on a small scale. In 1155 the Earl Warren was acquitted of £24 2s in Surrey and £20 10s in Essex.[15] At the rates mentioned in the *Dialogue of the Exchequer* this would mean between 892 and 1,784 acres cleared, but there is no way of knowing over how long a period this work was done.[16] In 1160 the king of Scots was acquitted of £6 in Huntingdonshire and in 1170 of £4 13s in the same shire.[17] The fact that the penalties were remitted to the barons does not mean that the clearing was done to add to their manorial demesne—they were expected to reimburse their tenants who had done the work and presumably paid the penalties.[18]

Scattered documents throw some light on land clearing. Richard I gave the bishop of Worcester permission to clear 614 acres of land in thirteen different manors. The work was only partially completed during his reign and was finished under John.[19] This seems to show how slow the process was. An extremely interesting illustration of land clearing and its effects appears in the accounts of the honor of Knaresborough in the

[14] Howard Levi Gray, *English field systems* (Cambridge, 1915), pp. 72-82.
[15] *Pipe roll 2 Henry II*, pp. 11, 17.
[16] *Dialogus de scaccario*, p. 103.
[17] " Pipe roll 6 Henry II," *Pipe roll society*, II, 34; " Pipe roll 16 Henry II," *ibid.*, XV, 95.
[18] *Dialogus de scaccario*, pp. 104-105.
[19] *Memoranda roll, 1230-1*, p. 51.

reign of John. In the early years of Henry II the manors of Knaresborough and Boroughbridge which formed the honor were farmed for £60.[20] In 1173 the honor was granted to William de Stutville.[21] When William died in 1203, he had these two manors let at farm for £175 a year.[22] The custody of the honor was then given to Hubert Walter, archbishop of Canterbury, and our next account appears after his death. In 1206 corn worth £26 was sold which had been seized on assarts. Fines of £68 were levied against those who had made the clearings.[23] If one assumes that the penalties were levied at the rate given by the *Dialogue*, this represents the clearing of between 1,360 and 2,720 acres from the forest of Knaresborough. In 1211 and 1212 the total revenue from the honor was £318 and £342 respectively.[24] One must not press these figures too far. I suspect the £175 for 1203 may not be comparable with the figures for 1211 and 1212. But it seems clear that between 1173 and 1212 the value of the honor had increased 470 per cent and that extensive clearing had played some part in the change.

Another agricultural development that must have greatly increased the income from some manors was the growth of large-scale sheep raising. Unfortunately very little information is available about the early history of this pursuit in England. The *Exon Domesday* shows that fair-sized flocks were kept in the eleventh century on various manors in Dorset and Somerset.[25] The royal officers who estimated the actual income and potential income of manors in the king's hand in 1185 were fully aware of the value of sheep. On estate after estate in Lincolnshire and other shires they point out that the income would be increased if flocks were put on the land or ones already there enlarged.[26] In general they appear to have be-

---

[20] William Farrer, *Early Yorkshire charters* (Edinburgh, 1914), I, 390.

[21] *Ibid.*, p. 391.

[22] " Pipe roll 5 John," *Pipe roll society*, LIV, 222.

[23] *Pipe roll 8 John*, Public Record Office, E 372-52.

[24] *Pipe rolls 13 and 14 John, ibid.*, E 372-57-8; Farrer, *Early Yorkshire charters*, I, 392.

[25] *Exon Domesday*, pp. 26, 27, 41, 42.

[26] " Rotuli de dominibus, pueris, et puellis," *Pipe roll society*, XXXV, 2, 6, 8, 10, 13-16, 20, 30, 44, 48, 55.

lieved that 100 sheep would add £1 a year to the revenue.[27] Some of the proposed flocks were large. Stallingborough was stated to be able to support 1,100, Redbourne 500, Noctun and Dunston 460.[28] The pipe rolls of Richard's reign show the crown purchasing large flocks to stock manors in Wiltshire and Sussex. In 1195 three Wiltshire estates received 500 each and the demesne of the honor of Arundel over 2,500.[29] In 1208 the demesne manors of the bishop of Winchester held over 17,000 sheep and sold 13,496 fleeces worth £124 9s 10d.[30] This represented about 5.8 per cent of the gross yield of the bishop's manors.

In all probability the greatest increase in sheep raising during the twelfth and thirteenth centuries was in Yorkshire and Lincolnshire.[31] Apparently the pioneer work was done by the Cistercian abbeys which turned vast stretches of waste into sheep-runs. For example in 1157 Henry II gave the abbey of Rievaulx a section of waste land near Pickering to use for folds and pasture.[32] A few years later a local landowner granted enough additional land to fold and pasture 1,000 sheep.[33] About 1300 Rievaulx seems to have owned some 12,000 sheep while Fountains, another Cistercian house, had 15,000.[34] Progressive lay lords followed the example set by the Cistercians. When William de Stutville died, the crown sold 3,575 sheep from his lands for £263 7s.[35] If this represented the natural increase of the flocks, Stutville must have been by far the greatest sheep raiser of England. But it seems more likely that the king was making all possible profit from the manors before turning them over to a custodian, and that the sales represented most of William's sheep. Denholm-Young states that in 1260 the count of Aumale's demesnes in Holderness held 7,000 sheep yielding some £200 a year.[36] In 1260 Robert de Tateshal,

[27] *Ibid.*, pp. 13-14, 30, 44, 48,

[28] *Ibid.*, pp. 2, 16, 20.

[29] " Pipe roll 7 Richard I," *Pipe roll society*, XLIV, 37, 45.

[30] *Pipe roll of the bishopric of Winchester, 1208-9*, pp. xlvi-xlvii.

[31] H. C. Darby, *An historical geography of England before A. D. 1800* (Cambridge, 1936), p. 242.

[32] Farrer, *Early Yorkshire charters*, I, 313-315.

[33] *Ibid.*, pp. 301, 303-304.

[34] Darby, *An historical geography of England*, p. 242.

[35] " Pipe roll 5 John," *Pipe roll society*, LIV, 222.

[36] *Seignorial administration in England*, p. 59.

a great Lincolnshire baron, agreed to deliver 70 sacks of wool at Boston fair.[37] Figuring 300 fleeces to a sack this would mean a flock of 21,000.[38]

In summary it seems clear that the first two centuries after the Conquest saw a large increase in the revenue obtained from most English manors. An expanding market for manorial produce brought higher prices. If wages also rose, it was of little concern to the lord who tilled his demesne through service rents—for him it was at most a problem in accounting. Only the few lords who had commuted these rents were disturbed by rising wages. Meanwhile on some estates more effective field systems, the clearing of new land, and the introduction of wool-growing had increased the productivity of the land.

Closely related to manorial income was that from natural resources not used for agriculture. In 1185 the fisheries of the honor of Striguil in the river Wye produced £10 12s 3d or about 10 per cent of the value of the honor's lands in Netherwent.[39] In 1214 the bishop of Durham drew £58 from this source.[40] While the Wye fisheries and those of the bishop were probably unusually valuable, many barons must have drawn some revenue from their fisheries. Income from mines was probably rare. In general the crown monopolized the profits from tin and lead. In 1214 the bishop of Durham received £534 as income from his mines, but he was a palatine lord and hence far from typical of English barons.[41]

The natural resource most commonly possessed by English barons was timber. In general it was carefully preserved as an important capital asset. The baron and his tenants needed wood for building and burning. The standing trees furnished food for the swine. The lord took the timber he needed and fees for pasturing pigs. But he did not, if he could avoid it, sell his timber. When the crown or other custodian was in charge of a barony, there was a natural inclination to waste the woods for immediate profit. Thus in two years John sold £209 1s 6d worth

[37] *Ibid.*, p. 58.
[38] Darby, *An historical geography of England*, p. 240 note 3.
[39] " Pipe roll 31 Henry II," *Pipe roll society*, XXXIV, 8.
[40] *Pipe roll 16 John*, Public Record Office, E 372-60.
[41] *Ibid.*

of the timber of the honor of Richmond.[42] In 1210 he sold £106 from Simon de Montfort's half of the honor of Leicester.[43] In the reign of Henry III an inquisition revealed extensive waste of the woodlands of the honor of Lewes by its custodian Peter de Savoy.[44] Moreover when a baron was under great financial stress the sale of his timber was a possible recourse. According to Matthew Paris when Simon de Montfort needed money for a crusade he sold " his noble wood of Leicester " for about £1,000.[45] Thus except for pasturage fees, which I included in manorial revenues, the woods of a baron did not contribute to his money income. Exceptions to this statement would be the palatine lords who handled their forests as the king did his. In 1241 the pleas of the forest in Cheshire yielded £16 18s. In 1214 the forests of the see of Durham brought in £92. In 1186 the Netherwent forests of the honor of Striguil were worth £5 8s 4d.[46]

In addition to their income from agriculture and the exploitation of the natural resources of their fiefs, some barons drew revenues from commerce and industry. The ownership of towns, fairs, and markets could be exceedingly profitable. The revenue from Bristol amounted to between 19 per cent and 26 per cent of the income of the earl of Gloucester in the twelfth century. In 1210 the borough of Leicester yielded 67 per cent of the total revenue of Simon de Montfort's half of the honor of Leicester. But Bristol and Leicester were unusually important towns to be in the hands of barons, and most baronial boroughs were much smaller. The earl of Gloucester's boroughs of Teukesbury and Thornbury yielded £12 and £32 respectively in the late twelfth century.[47] In this same period Arundel seems to have been worth about £32 and Dunster £21.[48]

As far as I can discover the twelfth and thirteenth centuries saw no general trend in the revenue from baronial boroughs.

[42] " Pipe roll 2 John," *Pipe roll society*, L, 88-89.

[43] *Pipe roll 12 John*, Public Record Office, E 372-56.

[44] *Calendar of inquisitions miscellaneous*, I, 4-5.

[45] *Chronica maiora*, IV, 7.

[46] *Pipe roll 26 Henry III*, pp. 120-121; *Pipe roll 16 John*, Public Record Office, E 372-60; " Pipe roll 32 Henry II," *Pipe roll society*, XXXVI, 203.

[47] " Pipe rolls 2 and 3 John," *Pipe roll society*, L, 127; LII, 54.

[48] " Pipe roll 25 Henry II," *ibid.*, XXVIII, 38-39; " Pipe roll 8 Richard I," *ibid.*, XLV, 198.

Some increased greatly in value, while others declined. Leicester was worth £172 a year in 1210 and £154 in the middle of the century.[49] Dunster yielded £21 in 1196 and £17 18s in 1279.[50] Arundel was worth £32 in the twelfth century and £23 19s in 1272.[51] On the other hand Teukesbury increased in value from £12 in 1201 to £169 in 1263, while the revenue from Thornbury grew from £32 to £131 in the same period.[52] The financial possibilities of a well located borough are shown by the case of the town of Ros in Ireland. Founded early in the thirteenth century by William Marshal, lord of Leinster, it was worth £52 13s a year in 1245.[53] In general the more valuable towns belonged to the crown, but a fair number of barons drew income from well situated boroughs.

The twelfth and thirteenth centuries saw fairs and markets generously distributed throughout England. Most barons had an annual fair and a weekly market on each of their more important demesne manors. While he was regent of England, William Marshal granted himself fairs or markets on five of his manors.[54] But most of these local fairs and markets were not very valuable. In 1201 the earl of Gloucester's fair at Warham was worth £1 8s.[55] In 1242 the fair at Clun yielded £18 8s.[56] In the late twelfth century the fair at Rayleigh in Essex was worth £3.[57] These fairs were probably little more than annual cattle sales. The great fairs like that of Boston were far more profitable. The honor of Richmond's share of the revenues from Boston fair varied greatly but were always considerable. In 1177 they amounted to £72, in 1180 to £61, in 1182 to £91, in 1183 to £184, in 1199 to £54, in 1200 to £71. Early in the reign of Edward I the honor was drawing £289 from this source.[58] The Tonys who also participated in Boston

[49] *Pipe roll 12 John,* Public Record Office, E 372-56; *Calendar of inquisitions miscellaneous,* I, 236.

[50] *Calendar of close rolls, 1272-9,* p. 540.

[51] *Close rolls, 1268-1272,* p. 505.

[52] *Ibid.,* 1261-4, pp. 284-285.

[53] *Calendar of patent rolls, 1364-7,* p. 271.

[54] Sidney Painter, *William Marshal, knight-errant, baron, and regent of England* (Baltimore, 1933), p. 270.

[55] " Pipe roll 3 John," *Pipe roll society,* LII, 54.

[56] *Pipe roll 26 Henry III,* p. 8.

[57] " Pipe roll 27 Henry II," *Pipe roll society,* XXX, 107-109.

[58] *Calendar of inquisitions post mortem,* II, 211. The earlier values are found in the pipe rolls.

fair received £106 from it in 1209.[59] Boston fair was probably by far the most valuable in the hands of lay barons, but several ecclesiastical lords, especially the bishops of Winchester, owned important fairs.

In addition to collecting rents from the tenants of his demesne manors and the burghers of his towns and forcing them to pay fees for the use of mills, ovens, pasture, and forest, a baron could levy tallage from them. Remarkably little precise information is available about the English manorial lord's right to tallage. Apparently in theory the villains could be tallaged at will and the free men for fixed sums on certain occasions, but actually custom probably limited the lord's right to tallage his villains. It is clear that in practice tallage was applied in various ways from shire to shire and manor to manor. There is some reason for believing that in Lincolnshire it was levied regularly at fixed amounts.[60] This was almost certainly not the case in most regions.[61] On manors that had once formed part of the royal demesne the lord could only levy tallage when the king did.[62] One finds a manor where the tenants pay tallage only when a new lord comes into possession.[63] In general, however, it seems likely that a lord could levy tallage when he needed money badly for some special purpose. An inquest of 1265 states that the Tony lords of Flamstead in Hertfordshire had never tallaged their men on this manor until the early thirteenth century. Roger de Tony was a strenuous knight who often lost horses and needed aid. Three times in ten years he tallaged his men. His son Ralph followed the same practice, but Roger, the present lord, asked aid too frequently.[64] While one may doubt the statement that earlier lords had never tallaged Flamstead, this document seems to give a good illustration of the usual practice. A document in the *Red book of the*

---

[59] *Pipe roll 11 John*, Public Record Office, E 372-55.

[60] In *Domesday book* and in some later valuations tallage was included in the estimates of annual value of many manors in this shire. See *Documents illustrative of English history in the thirteenth and fourteenth centuries* (ed. Henry Cole, *Record commission*), p. 347.

[61] I base this conclusion on the fact that tallage was not generally included in most estimates of value and does not usually appear in extents.

[62] Pollock and Maitland, *History of English law*, I, 562.

[63] *Calendar of inquisitions miscellaneous*, I, 64.

[64] *Ibid.*, pp. 99-100.

exchequer shows the tenants of the demesne manors of the earl of Arundel paying tallage when the earl went on the king's service in the Welsh marches, when he returned from a journey across the sea, and to help him pay his debts to the Jews.[65] The accounts on the pipe rolls show that when a baron died and his lands fell into the crown's custody, the king promptly levied tallage on the baron's men. In short tallage was an irregular levy of varying amount. Custom and the resources of the tenants obviously limited both its frequency and amount.

When it was levied, tallage could be extremely profitable from the baron's point of view. In 1200 the honor of Richmond yielded £280 in tallage or about 66 per cent of its annual revenue without Boston fair.[66] In 1203 the Stutville barony paid £165 to the crown and £11 to the bishop of Durham.[67] The total tallage came to about 25 per cent of the annual income. In 1209 part of the Tony barony yielded £66 in tallage or 29 per cent of its annual value.[68] A year later the manors of Simon de Montfort's share of the honor of Leicester paid £21 or 23 per cent of their value, but the borough of Leicester paid £200 or 116 per cent of its annual value.[69] In 1211 the barony of Beauchamp of Elmley was tallaged to the sum of £436 or 55 per cent of its revenue; £66 of this was levied on the suburbs of the burgh of Worcester.[70] In 1212 the lands late of Roger de Lacy, constable of Chester, paid £335 in tallage—an amount equal to 42 per cent of their annual value.[71] These were all tallages levied by the crown on lands in its custody, but what evidence there is indicates that the barons collected at just as high a rate. For instance in 1209 the bishop of Winchester collected £580 in tallage from his demesnes, a sum amounting to 40 per cent of their annual value.[72]

[65] *Red book of the exchequer*, II, cclxvii-cclxx.
[66] " Pipe roll 2 John," *Pipe roll society*, L, 91.
[67] " Pipe roll 5 John," *ibid.*, LIV, 223.
[68] *Pipe roll 11 John*, Public Record Office, E 372-55.
[69] *Pipe roll 12 John, ibid.*, 56.
[70] *Pipe roll 13 John, ibid.*, 57.
[71] *Pipe roll 14 John, ibid.*, 58.
[72] *Pipe roll of the bishopric of Winchester, 1208-9.*

Chapter VII

BARONIAL INCOMES

We have discussed at some length the history of the various sources of baronial revenue. Now it is necessary to turn to the actual income enjoyed by barons. For the period 1160-1220 I have secured figures showing the regular annual income of fifty-four barons. For the period 1260-1320 I have found similar data on twenty-seven barons. As these figures do not take into account the irregular feudal revenues, they are too low for the holders of numerous knights' fees, but they are the best that can be obtained. Finally, for purposes of comparison I have added Professor Gray's figures on baronial and knightly incomes in 1436.[1] These are based on the incomes which were acknowledged by the holders for purposes of taxation. While I have grave doubts of the incomes reported by a few lords, on the whole I am inclined to accept Professor Gray's view that the figures are fairly reliable.

The fifty-four barons for whom I have figures in the period 1160-1220 had revenues totalling £10,935 or an average income of £202. I estimate that there were about 160 barons in England during this period. If the barons for whose incomes I have figures represent a fair sample, and I believe they do, the total revenue of the tenurial barons would come to £32,805. Accepting Ramsay's estimates of the royal revenues, this would mean that the baronage as a whole had an income as high as Henry II enjoyed in his most prosperous years, well above the best that Richard ever reached, and about equal to John's in ordinary years.[2]

Although the average income of these fifty-four barons was £202, the median income was only £115. Seven barons enjoyed revenues over £400, eight between £300 and £400, three between £200 and £300, and sixteen between £100 and £200. Twenty had less than £100 a year. The highest individual income on my list is the £800 enjoyed by Roger de Lacy, con-

[1] H. L. Gray, "Incomes from land in England in 1436," *English historical review*, XLIX (1934), 607-631.
[2] *Revenues of the kings of England*, I, 191, 227, 261.

stable of Chester, at his death in 1210.[3] Next comes the £700
of Earl William of Gloucester in the reign of Henry II.[4] Earl
Robert of Leicester apparently had about £560 a year, Earl
William de Mandeville £504, and the lord of the honor of
Richmond about £500.[5] As all these lords held many knights'
fees, their totals would be increased by adding feudal revenues.
Earl William of Gloucester had about three hundred fees. This
would mean £1,500 a generation in reliefs alone, and if he
collected twenty shilling aids to knight his son and marry his
daughter, £600 additional would appear. But among these
great feudal potentates there appears a lord who had no feudal
income of any importance—William de Stutville. At his death
in 1203 he was drawing from his hereditary estates and his
honor of Knaresborough some £550 a year.[6] William's hereditary lands were assessed at eight fees, he owed three more for
Knaresborough, and he held about seventeen of the Mowbrays.
Although he was a baron of little importance in the feudal
sense, his income almost equalled that of the earl of Leicester.

This lack of any close relation between knights' fees and
income is perhaps the most striking feature of these statistics.
The earl of Devon who held well over a hundred fees had an
income of £385.[7] The De Vesci lords of Alnwick had £387 a
year, but only 36 knights' fees *in capite* and some 13 more as
mesne lords.[8] In Henry II's reign the palatine earls of Cornwall
and Chester, each of whom had some two hundred fees, had
incomes of £341 and £327 respectively, while the Earl Giffard
with less than 90 fees had £324 a year.[9] The Moion lord of
Dunster who held 50 fees had only about £50 a year—some £4
more than William Blundus who owed the service of 7 knights.[10]

[3] *Pipe roll 10 John*, Public Record Office, E 372-56.

[4] " Pipe rolls 30-34 Henry II," *Pipe roll society*, XXXIII-XXXVIII.

[5] " Pipe roll 26 Henry II," *ibid.*, XXIX; " Pipe roll 2 Richard I," *ibid.*,
XXXIX. " Pipe rolls 24-29 Henry II," *ibid.*, XXVII-XXXII. The figure for
the earldom of Gloucester includes Bristol. The estimate for Richmond includes
an average value for the fluctuating income from the fair of Boston.

[6] " Pipe roll 5 John," *ibid.*, LIV, 222-224.

[7] " Pipe roll 25 Henry II," *ibid.*, XXVIII, 15, 90, 109-110.

[8] " Pipe rolls 33-34 Henry II," *ibid.*, XXXVII-XXXVIII.

[9] " Pipe rolls 28-30 Henry II," *ibid.*, XXXI-XXXIII; " Pipe roll 33 Henry
II," *ibid.*, XXXVII; " Pipe rolls 22-34 Henry II," *ibid.*, XXV-XXXVIII.

[10] " Pipe roll 23 Henry II," *ibid.*, XXVI; " Pipe roll 31 Henry II," *ibid.*,
XXXIV.

It is extremely difficult to give these baronial incomes con-
crete meaning for the reader. Income can be evaluated only in
terms of prices, and mediaeval prices varied widely from place
to place and from year to year. Perhaps the best basis for
comparison can be provided by citing the theoretical and actual
incomes of members of the non-baronial classes. In the reign
of Henry II a knight was paid eight pence a day for service as
a mercenary soldier. By the time of John the usual rate was two
shillings.[11] Eight pence a day for a year comes very close to the
sixteen marcs a year income suggested as the minimum for a
knight by Henry II's " Assize of Arms." In 1185 the royal
officers making the survey of estates in the hands of the crown
estimated that Peter of Billingley who held one fee from the
archbishop of York could have drawn £11 a year from his fief
though actually it was bringing in much less.[12] In general one
can say that in this period 1180-1220 an annual income of
from £10 to £20 was required to support a man as a knight.
Late in the twelfth century Abbot Samson of St. Edmunds was
said to have declared that if he had had five or six marcs a
year to support himself as a scholar, he never would have
become a monk.[13] As Samson was a man of ample tastes, it
seems safe to assume that £4 would support a scholar in
reasonable comfort. Unfortunately it is impossible to find any
figures to indicate the incomes enjoyed by merchants or others
of the middle class. When William Cade, a strange combination of money-lender, merchant, and royal official died in 1167,
he left a fortune of £5,000.[14] In 1199 Nicholas Morel, apparently a merchant, claimed that the count of Flanders had
seized 2,000 marcs of his money.[15]

Further bases for comprehending the real value of baronial
incomes can be provided by citing the cost of items in the
standard of living suitable for a baron. In 1194 Richard I set
fees to be paid for the privilege of participating in tournaments
at 20 marcs for an earl, 10 marcs for a baron, and 4 marcs for

---

[11] Mitchell, *Studies in taxation*, p. 309.
[12] " Rotuli de dominibus et pueris et puellis," *Pipe roll society*, **XXXV**, 3.
[13] Jocelin de Brakelond, pp. 26-27.
[14] Ramsay, *Revenues of the kings of England*, I, 94.
[15] *Rotuli de oblatis et finibus*, p. 37.

a landed knight.[16] Richard de Clare, earl of Hertford, gave a
lady, presumably his mistress, an annuity of £10 a year.[17] William Marshal considered £30 a year in land and 200 marcs in
cash ample provision for his youngest daughter.[18] When in
1219 the constable of Newcastle seized the baggage of Earl
William of Salisbury, the earl valued it at 300 marcs.[19] John
Maltravers, an important mesne lord, claimed damages of £100
when his house and its contents were burned.[20] The silken robes
in King John's treasury at his death were valued at from 2½
to 3 marcs each while those of samite were worth £5. The best
emeralds in the same store brought £6 6s while sapphires were
valued at £11 and diamonds at £18. As the government was
short of ready money and used robes and jewels to pay its
obligations, these figures may well be below the usual prices.[21]
There is little or no information available as to the cost of the
castles of earth and wood with which most twelfth-century
barons had to be content. Probably they cost very little. But
stone castles were expensive. Henry II spent £1,396 in eight
years in building Oreford castle. As this was a royal stronghold, it was perhaps more elaborate than most barons could
aspire to. Wark and Chilham are better examples. These were
baronial castles which were temporarily in the king's hands.
He built keeps and perhaps other works at a cost of £357 and
£419 respectively.[22] It seems clear that a baron who wanted a
stone castle had to be able to spend a minimum of about £350.

For the period 1260-1320 I have figures on the incomes of
twenty-seven important English landholders. As these years
were in the midst of the transition from the tenurial to the
parliamentary baronage, it is difficult to describe them more
exactly. Six were earls. All but three were certainly tenurial
barons. Their total income was £18,048 giving an average
income of £668. The median income was £339. As I cannot
define the baronage during this period and have no idea whether

[16] Roger of Hovedon, III, 268.
[17] *Bracton's note book*, II, 48-49.
[18] Painter, William Marshal, p. 282.
[19] *Selden society*, LVI, 393-394.
[20] *Curia regis roils*, I, 380-381.
[21] *Compotus* of William Marshal, Public Record Office, E 364-1, M3.
[22] These figures are taken from the pipe rolls.

or not these individuals represented a fair cross-section, I shall make no further comparisons.

There seems little doubt that the richest baron in England in the late thirteenth century was the earl of Cornwall. Mr. Denholm-Young describes Earl Richard's wealth as " fabulous " without venturing any figures.[23] When Richard's heir, Edmund, died in 1301, his annual income was about £3,800.[24] I have no doubt that special concessions of one kind or another had supplied Richard himself with a larger revenue than his son, but it seems unlikely that it exceeded if it equalled the £5,170 that John drew from the short-lived palatinate given him by Richard I in 1189.[25] Had the great Marshal earldom survived intact into this period, its revenue would probably have been little less than that of Earl Richard. Walter Marshal apparently enjoyed at the time of his death in 1245 an income of £3,350 over half of which came from his lordship of Leinster.[26] Denholm-Young states that late in the thirteenth century Isabel de Fortibus, who was countess of Devon and Aumale, had an income of £2,500.[27] In 1263 the De Clare earl of Gloucester and Hertford had some £1,800 without counting his Welsh and Irish estates.[28] The earldom of Richmond in this period seems to have yielded between £1,500 and £1,700.[29] There is evidence that the last Earl Ferrars had an income of £1,333.[30] These are the large revenues on my list. From them one falls at once to the £537 of Thomas de Multon of Copeland, the £489 of the Courtenay lord of Okehampton, the £485 of Mortimer of Wigmore, and the £400 more or less of the Gresleys of Manchester, the Quency earls of Winchester, and the Bardolf lords of Wormgay.[31] As in the earlier period the

---

[23] *Seignorial administration*, p. 22.

[24] This figure is based on the dower assigned his widow. (*Calendar of close rolls, 1296-1302*, p. 426.) An addition of the values of lands known to have been in his hands supports this estimate of his income.

[25] Kate Norgate, *John Lackland* (London, 1902), pp. 27-28.

[26] *Calendar of patent rolls, 1364-7*, pp. 263-275.

[27] *Seignorial administration*, p. 23.

[28] *Close rolls, 1261-4*, pp. 284-293.

[29] Denholm-Young, *Seignorial administration*, p. 22; *Calendar of inquisitions post mortem*, II, 210-223.

[30] Denholm-Young, *Seignorial administration*, p. 22.

[31] Miss N. Neilson, " A terrier of Fleet, Lincolnshire," pp. 92-93; *Calendar*

Moion lords of Dunster are near the bottom of the list. Their £50 has become £194, but above them at £199 was the Colombar fief, a mesne tenancy of the earldom of Devon.[32] At the bottom of the list come the Tresgoz lord of Ewyas with £181, the Marmions of Tamworth with £168, and the Bassets of Weldon with £138.[33]

Comparisons between the values of a barony at different times must be used with extreme care. In general they are completely unreliable as indications of the trend of incomes from landed property. Rarely does one have sufficient information about a barony to make a proper allowance for alienations from the demesne—enfeoffments, marriage portions, and gifts in free alms. Doweries reduced the value of baronies temporarily. The existence of two dowagers would decrease the income to the lord of the fief by over 50 per cent. The chief value of comparisons of this sort lies in what they tell about the distribution of wealth and the varying fortunes of baronial families.

The three richest lords on my list for the period 1260-1320 held combinations of several ancient baronies. The earls of Cornwall held the former Dunstanville earldom of Cornwall, the honors of Wallingford, St. Valery, Eye, Berkhamsted. and Knaresborough, the shire of Rutland with its demesne manors, the manor of Kirkeaton with its appurtenances, and many single estates. Isabel de Fortibus was mistress of two important twelfth-century earldoms, Devon and Aumale. The De Clares ruled the baronies of Gloucester and Clare, half the ancient Giffard barony, and a share of the Marshal inheritance. A comparison of the annual values of the individual baronies in the complex fiefs in the two periods shows a wide variation in trend. The earldom of Cornwall had more than tripled in value since it had been held by the Dunstanville earls. Knaresborough had increased by 77 per cent. Wallingford and St. Valery brought in about the same income they had at the beginning of the thirteenth century, and Berkhamsted had fallen

of close rolls, 1288-1296, pp. 236-237; ibid., 1302-7, p. 176; ibid., 1279-1288, p. 156; Close rolls, 1261-4, pp. 407-408; Calendar of close rolls, 1302-7, p. 227.
    [32] Ibid., 1272-9, p. 540; ibid., 1279-1288, p. 161.
    [33] Ibid., 1296-1302, pp. 476-7; ibid., 1288-1296, pp. 255, 269-270.

from some £400 to £72. The earldom of Gloucester had risen
from some £400 to about £900. To glance at a few other
baronies, the value of the earldom of Richmond had tripled,
but the honor of Leicester and the Fossard-De Maulay and De
Vesci baronies had fallen slightly.

The chief importance of these figures is as a demonstration
of the essential instability of baronial fortunes. In the interval
between the periods 1160-1220 and 1260-1320 some houses
had waxed extremely rich through marriages that combined
several ancient baronies. Good fortune or good management
had vastly increased the income of other families from their
ancient lands. But some noble houses had seen their revenues
stand still or even decrease somewhat. Obviously these last saw
their comparative wealth and position greatly lessened. This
instability of family fortunes does much to explain the arbitrary system of issuing summonses to Parliament used during
the late thirteenth and fourteenth centuries. Tenure by barony
had been abandoned as a basis for issuing summonses. Hereditary Parliamentary barons had not appeared. The king called
those whom wealth and personal force made men of importance
in the realm, and both these factors varied from generation to
generation.

Let us now turn to Professor Gray's figures for the year 1436.
Although they deal with a time well beyond the period covered
by this book, their value for purposes of comparison seems to
justify their use here. I have modified Mr. Gray's figures
slightly by leaving out two peers for whom his estimates seem
dubious, dropping several widows dowered from extinct baronies, and estimating the income of the barony from the dower in
two cases. The result is forty-nine baronies with a total income
of £43,165, or an average of £881. Comparing the individual
incomes with those on the list for the period 1260-1320 we find
that the richest peer in England, Richard, duke of York, had
an income of £3,230 a year, or well below that of the earls of
Cornwall in the earlier era. Richard, earl of Warwick, with
£3,116 was rather above Isabel de Fortibus with £2,500. But
one must remember that the earlier list is incomplete and covers
only twenty-seven incomes. Thus when one considers that in
1436 there were four baronies with over £2,000 and in 1260-

1320 there were three, the top income levels seem about the same. As I am convinced that in the earlier period several lords for whom I have no exact figures had over £2,000—for instance the Earl Warren, Henry de Lacy, earl of Lincoln, and Edmund of Lancaster—there appear to have been fewer very wealthy lords in 1436.

The chief change between these periods seems to lie just below this level. On the list for 1260-1320 there are but three baronies with incomes between £500 and £2,000. Twenty-five of the baronies of 1436 come in this range. At the same time the poorest baron in 1436 had only £112 or less than the £138 of Basset of Weldon in the early period. In short the baronial incomes of 1436 cover about the same range as those of 1260-1320, but are graduated much more evenly. To put it another way in 1260-1320 the earl of Cornwall had an income 5.7 times the average of the list, while in 1436 the duke of York's revenue was but 3.6 times the average.

Finally, I would like to venture a comparison between the figures for 1160-1220 and those for 1436 with respect to the relative incomes of the king and his barons. If my estimate is reasonably correct, in the earlier of these periods 162 tenurial barons had an income about equal to that enjoyed by King John. Using my revision of Mr. Gray's figures we find in 1436 forty-nine Parliamentary barons with a total income of £43,165.[34] In 1411 the net revenue of the crown, after subtracting local expenses and annuities charged against the revenues of the shires and royal estates, was £48,366.[35] In 1416 it was £56,966, in 1421, £55,743, and in 1433, £35,432.[36] The low figure for 1433 was largely the result of large assignments of revenue to the king's creditors. In short, in the early fifteenth century the incomes of the crown and the Parliamentary baronage were about equal on the basis of these figures.

This comparison is of dubious validity. The Parliamentary

[34] Gray's total for the peers is £44,655. "Incomes from land in 1436," p. 619.

[35] *Proceedings and ordinances of the privy council of England* (ed. Harris Nicolas, *Record commission*), II, 7-10, cited in Charles Plummer's notes to Sir John Fortescue, *The Governance of England* (Oxford, 1885), p. 211.

[36] *Proceedings and ordinances of the privy council*, II, 172, 312-313; *Rotuli Parliamentorum*, IV, 433-434; *Plummer's notes* pp. 212-213.

baronage of 1436 formed a far smaller part of the English landholding class than did the tenurial baronage of John's reign. Moreover I doubt that one is justified in using the net royal revenue. I can see no reason why one should subtract annuities on the farms of the shires in arriving at the income of the crown and not those paid at the exchequer. Hence I shall present a comparison on a different basis. In 1436 there were 232 men in England with incomes over £100. Their total revenue came to £81,165.[37] This group seems to me to be reasonably comparable with the 162 tenurial barons of John's reign. Unfortunately it is difficult to discover the gross revenue of the crown in the fifteenth century. In 1433 it was about £57,000.[38] During the reign of Richard II it had averaged about £125,000.[39] But one must remember that the figures on net revenue showed 1433 to be a bad year. It seems clear that the Lancastrian kings had less income than Richard II. His revenue from customs averaged £47,000, while his successors seem to have had less than £30,000 from this source. On the whole it seems safe to say that in the early fifteenth century the king's revenue was about equal to that of his 232 richest subjects and about twice that of the peers. The relative incomes of the crown and the great landholders had not changed since John's reign, but the Parliamentary baronage of the fifteenth century had comparatively less than the tenurial baronage of the earlier period.

Before leaving the subject of baronial incomes it seems worth while to glance at the financial history of a few baronies about which reasonably adequate information is available. Let us first examine the fief called in the twelfth century the honor of Striguil. In 1086 William d'Eu held lands in nine shires valued at about £404. He held in demesne estates worth £164 a year in eight counties and had granted fiefs worth £240 in nine counties. In addition to his English lands he held the castle of Striguil, modern Chepstow, and some lands near it. The value of these marcher estates is hard to determine, but they probably brought in about £40 a year. Our next glimpse of the revenue

[37] Gray, " Incomes from land in 1436," pp. 622-623.
[38] *Rotuli Parliamentorum*, IV, 433-434.
[39] Ramsay, *Revenues of the kings of England*, II, 427.

from this barony is in 1185. William d'Eu had forfeited his lands in the reign of William II, and his barony had passed to the De Clares. In 1185 it was in custody with the heir of Richard fitz Gilbert de Clare, earl of Pembroke. The English demesnes had been almost completely dissipated. All that remained was a manor in Gloucestershire worth £4 and one in Hertfordshire yielding £20. The former estate was way below its Domesday value, the latter just equal to it.[40] In short, in all probability parts of these manors had been granted as fiefs. The marcher lands, comprising the demesne manors of Striguil, Tidenham, Magor, and Uske, were worth £85.[41] Thus the demesnes of the barony were worth £109 against the £164 of the Domesday demesne.

In 1189 the honor of Striguil passed to William Marshal on his marriage to Isabel de Clare. The next figures on its value come from the year 1245 when William's fourth son, Walter Marshal, earl of Pembroke, died without issue, and the barony was divided among his sisters and their heirs. The value of the two demesne manors in England had increased from the £24 of 1185 to £90. Caerleon and Trelleck had been added to the marcher demesnes. The whole value of the lands in Netherwent had risen from the £85 of 1185 to £458. The demesnes of the barony in both England and Netherwent were valued at £547 against the £109 of 1185.[42] In short, between Domesday and 1185 alienations from the demesnes had reduced the annual value of the barony. Between 1185 and 1245 the demesnes had been kept intact and in the marches increased. The revenue of the barony increased 400 per cent during this period.

Let us now turn to the chief part of the barony of Berkeley— the so-called liberty of Berkeley lying about the castle that was its seat. In 1086 Roger de Berkeley rendered to the crown a farm of £170 for this territory. In 1130 William de Berkeley accounted for a farm of £234. Against this he received a credit of £13 for an estate given to the queen.[43] Henry II took Berke-

---

[40] " Rotuli de dominibus et pueris et puellis," *Pipe roll society*, **XXXV**.
[41] " Pipe roll 31 Henry II," *ibid.*, **XXXIV**, 8-10.
[42] *Calendar of patent rolls, 1364-7*, pp. 263-275.
[43] *Pipe roll 31 Henry I*, p. 133.

ley away from the Berkeley family and granted it as a fief to
Robert fitz Harding, but a marriage alliance between the two
families gave the Berkeleys two estates in the liberty. One of
these, Dursley, became the seat of their barony.[44] Then, in
order to complicate the work of future historians, the new
lords of the liberty took the name of Berkeley. In addition to
the two estates given to the Berkeleys of Dursley, Robert fitz
Harding gave two more to his second son Robert.[45] Hence
when we find our next figures for the value of the liberty in
1194-5, it is considerably reduced in size. It was then worth
about £90 a year to its lord.[46] Then over a century and a half
later, in 1348, we learn that the whole Berkeley barony was
worth £554.[47] An allowance of £100 would be ample for the
lands outside the liberty. The next figure on the revenue of the
Berkeley barony is rather puzzling. In Mr. Gray's list based
on the assessments of 1436 James de Berkeley, lord Berkeley,
admitted an income of only £333. As dowers appeared on the
list, that cannot solve the problem. Apparently one must
either assume a period of depression on the Berkeley estates or
an understatement of his revenue by Lord Berkeley. At any
rate there was no permanent downward trend in the value of
the barony. In 1492 the liberty of Berkeley was valued at over
£500 a year and the entire barony at about £650.[48]

The baronies of Striguil and Berkeley were very different
from the feudal viewpoint. The former was assessed for scutage at sixty-five and one-half fees on its English lands alone—
the twenty-three fees in Netherwent were exempt. The Berkeley barony owed the crown the service of five knights in the
twelfth century. Under the reduced service quotas established
in the thirteenth century it owed three knights. Apparently the
Berkeleys never granted any knights' fees and performed their
service from the resources of their demesne. But from the
financial point of view both these baronies were important.
The Berkeleys were men of position in the period of transition

[44] *Calendar of inquisitions post mortem*, II, 380-381.
[45] " Pipe roll 6 Richard I," *Pipe roll society*, XLIII, 3.
[46] *Ibid.*, " Pipe roll 7 Richard I," *ibid.*, XLIV, 55-56.
[47] *Calendar of inquisitions post mortem*, XII, 195.
[48] *Calendar of inquisitions post mortem, Henry VII*, I, 333-334.

and later Parliamentary barons. I have no doubt the lords of Striguil would have shared this fortune if the barony had remained intact.

Let us now glance at a barony with a very different history. In 1086 Gozelin fitz Lambert was a tenant-in-chief of the crown in Lincolnshire. His fief was valued at about £33, of which he held £15 in demesne and £18 in knights' fees. In the twelfth century this barony was assessed at fourteen and one-half fees. In 1185 the lords of the fief, then known as the barony of Redbourne after its *caput*, held three estates in demesne. They brought in £13 16s but the king's officers believed they could be made to yield £25.[49] Then in John's reign there was a bitter dispute over the barony between an uncle and niece.[50] The niece won, but was forced to grant part of the demesne to her uncle. The demesnes were further reduced by grants in free alms—especially to Bullington priory. By 1212 the demesne of the barony had been reduced to the manor of Redbourne.[51] In 1321 an inquisition *post mortem* for Roger de Neville of Redbourne stated that he held a capital messuage, forty-two acres of arable, twenty acres of meadow and pasture, a ruinous windmill, and 17s 2¼d of rent.[52] By 1357 the rent roll had sunk to 30d.[53] In short, from the Conquest to the reign of John the lords of Redbourne were minor barons. In the fourteenth century they were small freehold farmers. The demesne of the barony had never been rich, and alienations had been heavy. As long as knights' fees were marks of prestige, the fourteen and one-half fees of the barony gave its lords a certain position. But by the fourteenth century the knights' fees were forgotten, and the lords were left with nothing but the sad remnant of their demesnes.

The decay that struck many small baronies during the early thirteenth century is also illustrated by the history of the Kentwell fief. Although we lack estimates of its annual value at different periods, the general process is clear. In 1166 Roger de

[49] "Rotuli de dominibus et pueris et puellis," *Pipe roll society*, **XXXV**, 7.
[50] *Curia regis rolls*, II, 218.
[51] Returns for Lincolnshire, *Book of fees*, I, 153-197.
[52] *Calendar of inquisitions post mortem*, **VI**, 174.
[53] *Ibid.*, X, 314.

Kentwell owed the king the service of ten knights. He had granted five knights' fees and owed five knights from his demesne.[54] By 1231 the Kentwells had reduced this demesne by granting five more knights' fees and by giving a carucate of land to the Hospitallers in free alms.[55] The lord of the fief, William de Kentwell, was deeply in debt to the crown for past scutages and fines in lieu of military service.[56] Not only was he unable to collect the service owed by seven of his knights' fees but he did not even know who held them. In 1231 a royal writ ordered the sheriff of Norfolk and Suffolk to enquire what fees had belonged to the Kentwell barony.[57] Another writ ordered the knights who held these fees to be summoned before the exchequer.[58] This document furnishes a list of those who held these seven fees in demesne, but it tells little about the mesne lords who held between William and the knights summoned. A court case of 1214 shows a fief of the Kentwell barony in the hands of a certain William de Wicheton who held it from William de Hastings who in turn held it from Aubrey de Vere, earl of Oxford, who held it from the chief lord, Gilbert de Kentwell.[59] If other fees of the barony were sub-infeudated to that extent, it is easy to see how the Kentwells had lost track of their fees.

Apparently the inquest held· in 1231 was of little benefit to William de Kentwell. In the inquest of knights' fees of 1242 the only fees listed as belonging to him were the three he had under his control in 1231.[60] In short seven of his ten knights' fees were of no benefit to him. When William died in 1244, he was stated to hold in demesne two carucates of land in his manor of Kentwell.[61] Later in this same year his heirs sold the manor to the king for £50.[62] In 1251 it was granted to

[54] *Red book of the exchequer*, I, 410.
[55] "Memoranda roll, 1230-1," *Pipe roll society*, XLIX, 45-46. *Rot. hund.*, II, 142.
[56] "Pipe roll 14 Henry III," *ibid.*, XLII, 340, 348, 352.
[57] "Memoranda roll, 1230-1," *ibid.*, XLIX, 61.
[58] *Ibid.*, pp. 45-46.
[59] *Curia regis rolls*, VII, 184.
[60] *Book of fees*, II, 919.
[61] *Calendar of inquisitions post mortem*, I, 11.
[62] *Calendar of patent rolls, 1232-1247*, p. 446.

William de Valence to hold for the service of one knight. Its value was stated to be £17 a year.[63] Had the Kentwells kept intact the demesne they held in 1166, they might well have remained men of importance. As it was they granted too many fees and lost control of them. They were left with their sadly reduced demesne and the service of three knights.

We have followed the fortunes of two baronies which increased sufficiently in value to allow their lords to retain, perhaps even to improve, their comparative position among the great landholders of England. We have seen two others the value of which decreased so greatly that their lords became simple gentlemen or in the case of the barony of Redbourne mere small farmers. Let us now glance at one that changed little in value between the thirteenth and fifteenth centuries.

In 1086 Ralph de Pomeroy held a barony worth £101 a year. His demesne had an annual value of £78 and he had granted fiefs worth a total of £23. In 1208 the demesne of Henry de Pomeroy brought in about £113 a year.[64] In 1496 the estates of Richard de Pomeroy were valued at £185.[65] Between 1086 and 1496 the chief manor of the barony, Berry Pomeroy, had increased in value from £12 to £133, but the revenue from the demesnes as a whole had little more than doubled. In my list of baronial revenues for the period 1180-1220 the Pomeroys stood at just about the median. If they enjoyed in 1436 about the same income they did in 1496, they had less than any peer except Lord Clinton and had just about the average income of the richer knights. The Pomeroy lands had increased in value, but not enough to enable them to hold their comparative position. Average barons in the early thirteenth century, by the early fifteenth they were average knights.

A discussion of the revenues enjoyed by barons has little meaning unless it is combined with an examination of baronial debt. It seems likely that by far the major part of this debt originated in expenditures connected with the barons' political position. While some lords may have lived beyond their means through over-indulgence in fine clothes, rare foods, chivalric

[63] *Calendar of charter rolls*, I, 352.
[64] *Pipe roll 10 John*, Public Record Office, E 372-54.
[65] *Calendar of inquisitions post mortem, Henry VII*, I, 514.

largesse, and gaming, I suspect that during our period few got deeply involved through such extravagance. A few impecunious barons may have gone into debt attempting to rival the way of life of their richer peers, but in general baronial incomes probably amply covered the comparatively primitive standard of noble living. It seems equally unlikely that many barons fell into debt through gifts for pious purposes. Some minor lords like the Nevilles of Redbourne certainly reduced their gross income to a serious extent by too generous grants of land to the church, but I can find no evidence that the giving of large sums in cash was common.

The only pious activity that looms large as a possible source of baronial debt was crusading. Miss Beatrice Siedschlag in her *English participation in the Crusades 1150-1220* cites a number of cases of barons who are known to have mortgaged their lands to finance a crusade.[66] She also points out that some dozen crusaders appear on the list of debtors of the Jew Aaron of York.[67] As most of these men took part in King Richard's expedition, the fact that Aaron died in 1186 while Richard did not start for the Holy Land until 1190 makes it improbable that the loans in question were made to finance the crusade. Only in the case of Earl Robert of Leicester, who had made an expedition to Palestine in 1179, does it seem likely that the debt was incurred for this purpose, and Earl Robert's political troubles in England could easily account for his financial embarrassment. To conclude, there is no doubt that barons borrowed money in order to go on crusades. But none of the really heavy burdens of debt borne by barons in our period can be traced with any confidence to this source.

The political expenditures that led barons into debt were of several distinct types. One of these consisted of the ordinary feudal obligations—relief, aid, and military service. Another comprised commitments that were essentially speculative such as the sums offered for marriages, custodies, franchises, and offices. As we have seen in a previous chapter, relief, even

[66] Beatrice N. Siedschlag, *English participation in the Crusades, 1150-1220* (Privately printed, 1939), pp. 94-95. See also under individual crusaders in Appendix A.
[67] *Ibid.*, p. 88.

when kept within the limit regarded as reasonable, was a heavy burden. Few barons could hope to pay it at once without borrowing. Aids and scutages were probably not serious burdens when the baron could collect from his vassals. But it is clear that frequently the baron found it difficult to force his vassals to pay and hence went into debt himself. Moreover, the records show that when a baron chose to perform his service, he rarely had enough ready cash to support his contingent on the campaign and was obliged to borrow for this purpose.[68] As a rule debts contracted in connection with the ordinary feudal services were small and were paid off reasonably quickly. Only occasionally did they pile up to a serious extent.

Speculative ventures were far more common as the source of heavy debts. When a baron fined with the crown for the custody of a fief, the right to marry an heiress, or to enjoy a disputed inheritance, his object was likely to be power and prestige as much as money income. Even if the speculation was successful, he often found it difficult to pay the money promised. When the speculation was unsuccessful, he became hopelessly involved. Suppose a baron paid a large sum for an heiress who died within a year or two after the marriage without bearing him a child. He still had to pay the fine offered for her and did not enjoy the revenue from her lands.

While ordinary feudal dues and speculative fines were the chief sources of the political debts incurred by barons, there were other varieties. Barons who committed offences against the law were punished with heavy financial penalties. The king's forgiveness for political crimes could be purchased, but the price was usually high. A baron who was a royal official could fall behind in the payments due the crown. Sometimes at least they paid large sums to avoid rendering an account.

When a baron owed the crown a sum larger than he could produce at once, he had two obvious courses. He could simply fail to pay, or he could borrow the necessary money. In the twelfth century practically the sole source of loans was the usurer, Jew or Christian. While most of the money-lenders were Jews, a few Christians practiced this profession. By the

---

[68] See lists of loans in *Rotuli de liberate ac de misis et praestitis* (ed. T. D. Hardy, *Record commission*) and in the various pipe rolls.

thirteenth century devices had been found which permitted Christians to loan money profitably without committing usury. Perhaps the most common was the purchase at a low price of wool for future delivery. This method was used by the Regent William Marshal to raise the money needed to pay the indemnity promised Louis of France and seems to have been popular with the Italian merchants later in the thirteenth century.[69]

The Jewish money-lenders were in reality simply one of the means by which the crown drew revenue from the feudal class. The Jews and their property were completely at the king's mercy. He could drain off their current profits by tallaging at will. When a Jew died, the crown seized his chattels, cash, and notes. Sometimes the king allowed the Jew's heirs to buy two-thirds of the notes; sometimes he simply collected the debts himself. The king did not hesitate to interfere in the relations between the Jew and his knightly debtor by forgiving part or all of the debt, forcing a reduction of the sum owed, or changing the conditions of a mortgage.[70] In short to borrow from the Jews was to incur an indirect debt to the crown.

Let me give an example to illustrate the relation between debts owed the crown and those due the Jews. In 1164 Walter de Amundeville, an important vassal of the bishop of Lincoln, was removed from the shrievalty of Lincolnshire. His payments to the exchequer on the farms of the county and the town of Lincoln were in arrears to the extent of £312. In 1165 the pipe roll states that he owed the £312 and a penalty of £100 presumably imposed for some offence committed while sheriff. But Walter had paid off this large debt. He had turned over the entire sum to Isaac the Jew, a royal creditor.[71] Then in 1191 on the roll of debts due to Aaron the Jew appears the name of Walter's heir Joscelin de Amundeville as owing the considerable sum of £268 18s.[72] Now it is impossible to prove

---

[69] *Patent rolls, 1216-1225*, pp. 114-115; *Denholm-Young, Seignorial administration in England*, pp. 58, 60. Mr. Denholm-Young does not speak of loans repaid by delivery of wool, but a transaction of this sort seems to me the only possible explanation for some of the arrangements cited by him. For another apparent case of this kind see *Memoranda roll, 1230-1*, pp. 46-47.

[70] " Pipe roll 4 John," *Pipe roll society*, LIII, 118; " Pipe roll 10 Richard I," *ibid.*, XLVII, 165; *Rotuli de oblatis et finibus*, p. 400.

[71] " Pipe roll 11 Henry II," *Pipe roll society*, VIII, 35.

[72] " Pipe Roll 3 Richard I," *ibid.*, XL, 19.

the connection between the debt to Aaron and the payment to Isaac, but it seems highly plausible. At any rate the Amundevilles now owed the crown £268 18s. Joscelin made less than no progress in paying it off. In 1208 the barons of the exchequer were ordered to seize his lands to distrain him to pay £272 owed as a debt to Aaron.[73] If this order was ever carried out, it had no great effect. In 1230 the bishop of Lincoln as custodian of the minor heir of Joscelin's son Peter answered for £166 owed by the Amundevilles to the crown.[74] Obviously this financial history of the Amundevilles is not complete. Other debts beside that to Aaron may have formed part of the sum owed in 1230. But the general relation between debts to Jews and to the crown seems clear.

In all probability throughout our period a fair proportion of the English baronage was always in debt to the crown. In the early twelfth century William de Mandeville owed the king over £2,000.[75] The pipe roll of 1130 shows a large number of barons in debt—some very heavily. The troubles of Stephen's reign wiped out these old accounts and the early rolls of Henry II contain few debts beyond current obligations. But as Henry's reign advanced, baronial debts piled up on the rolls. King Richard raised the level of fines demanded by the crown and imposed more and heavier money penalties. As a result the list of old debts increased rapidly.

During the reigns of Henry I, Henry II, and Richard I the debts owed by barons to the crown were often extremely large, but they do not appear to have been so out of proportion to the revenues of the baronies that there was little or no hope that they would be paid. This situation changed in John's reign. As we have seen in an earlier chapter, he demanded utterly fantastic sums which added materially to the accumulation of old debts on the rolls. In the year 1230 some eighty barons were in debt to the crown for other than current obligations. Some of the sums were enormous. Nicholas de Stutville owed £1,163 in addition to £9,998 left over from John's reign. Wil-

---

[73] *Rotuli de oblatis et finibus*, p. 419. I cannot account for the increase of the debt.

[74] " Pipe roll 14 Henry III," *Pipe roll society*, XLII, 295.

[75] Farrer, " Itinerary of Henry I," no. 153.

liam de Albini of Belvoir owed £3,308, Giles de Erdinton
£3,437, Reginald de Cornhill £2,362, and William de Lancaster £6,508.[76] The unreality of these amounts is shown by the
annual payments demanded. Giles de Erdinton was expected to
pay £5 per year at which rate his debt would have been cleared
up in 1917.[77] Paying £40 a year William de Lancaster would
have been free of debt in 162 years.[78] These were, of course,
unusual cases. Most of the eighty odd barons who were in debt
in 1230 owed from one to six times the annual income from
their fiefs.

To the historian of the barony the chief question that arises
in connection with these debts due to the crown concerns their
effect on the political and economic position of the baronial
debtors. This effect obviously depended largely on the means
available to and used by the crown to enforce payment. Our
earliest example is the debt of £2,210 owed to Henry I by
William de Mandeville. King Henry seized three of William's
demesne manors, Sawbridgeworth, Wealdham, and Walden,
to be held until the debt was paid and turned them over for that
time to Eudes, the royal sewer.[79] Apparently the obligation
was never cleared up. When in the year 1156 Henry II created
William's grandson, Geoffrey, earl of Essex and granted him
the family fief, he expressly included these three manors and
released his grandfather's mortgage on them.[80] As Earl Geoffrey later granted at least a part of Sawbridgeworth to Warin
fitz Gerold who then held most of the barony of Eudes the
sewer, it seems likely that a promise to do so may have been
part of the agreement with King Henry.[81] At any rate William
de Mandeville's debt deprived his house of three valuable
estates for a generation.

There are a few cases similar to that of William de Mandeville. An ancestor of the Foliot lords of the barony of Wardon
lost heavily while gambling with either Henry I or Henry II

[76] "Pipe roll 14 Henry III," *Pipe roll society*, XLII, 112, 233, 274-275, 298,
332.
[77] *Ibid.*, p. 233.
[78] *Ibid.*, p. 332.
[79] Farrer, "Itinerary of Henry I," no. 153; *Honors and knights' fees*, III, 225.
[80] Round, *Geoffrey de Mandeville*, pp. 235-236.
[81] Farrer, *Honors and knights' fees*, III, 225-226.

and was obliged to give a manor as security for payment. In the reign of Henry II Robert Foliot fined for the manor. When he failed to pay, Henry seized it.[82] Robert de Chokes was obliged to surrender a manor to Henry II when he was unable to pay £40 of arrears on his relief.[83] Thus in some cases temporary or permanent seizure of part of the baron's demesne was the crown's means of collecting unpaid debts. Equally drastic measures were occasionally taken by King John. Heavy debts owed the crown were at least the excuse for John's campaign against the De Briouse family.[84] Thomas de Multon was confined in prison for failure to pay.[85] Joscelin de Amundeville, William de Montaigu, and others had their lands seized temporarily for debts owed the Jews which had become obligations to the crown.[86] Henry III sometimes forced the vassals of a debtor who had died to assume his obligation.[87] In general, however, the king was obliged to resort to far milder devices. The crown could occasionally risk alienating a baron by using strong measures to collect debts due it, but to do so frequently was politically impracticable. While no monarch could hope to keep all his barons contented, the stability of the king's government depended on his ability to maintain enough baronial friends to over-awe his foes. When he failed to do this, he faced a baronial revolt. Hence as a rule when a baron became hopelessly in debt to the crown, a compromise was made. Sometimes the king simply forgave the debt in whole or in part. In other cases fixed annual payments within the baron's means were agreed upon. The nature of the compromise reached depended to some extent on the debtor's ability to pay, but probably even more on his political importance. A powerful lord with strong castles, well-armed followers, and a wide circle of friends and relatives need not worry much about his debts.

The conclusion seems inescapable that a baron's political and

[82] *Curia regis rolls*, VIII, 6.

[83] *Ibid.*, V, 233.

[84] Kate Norgate, *John Lackland*, pp. 287-288.

[85] *Rot. pat.*, p. 85b.

[86] *Rotuli de oblatis et finibus*, pp. 419-420; *Pipe roll 13 John*, Public Record Office, E 372-57.

[87] *Pipe roll 26 Henry III*, pp. 74-75.

economic positions were completely interdependent. While his gross income was governed to some extent by the foresight and ability with which he exploited the resources of his fief, it depended also on the political power that enabled him to obtain exemptions and privileges. If he were in debt to the crown, as some 60 per cent of the barons of England were in 1230, his net income depended on the nature of the financial arrangement he could make with the king. Here obviously political power played a predominant part.

CHAPTER VIII

CONCLUSION

In conclusion it seems desirable to attempt a brief summary of the history of the English feudal barony. The barony was introduced into England by the Conqueror. It was a feudal subdivision of the realm superimposed on the Anglo-Saxon shires and hundreds. As a feudal unit it owed certain obligations to the king as suzerain of the barons of England, and its component lands bore their share of the burdens imposed on the shires and hundreds by the king as successor to the Anglo-Saxon monarchs. The baron and his vassals were members of the feudal hierarchy and English landholders. In the first capacity they performed military service; in the second they paid or avoided paying danegeld. Their privileges were as complex in origin as were their obligations. They enjoyed the personal rights of the French feudal aristocracy. Their power over the non-feudal inhabitants of their lands and their relations with the government of the shires and hundreds were expressed in Anglo-Saxon terms, but the interpretation of these terms was strongly influenced by Norman conceptions.

During the reigns of the four Norman kings the barons strove to maintain and extend their power under the conditions outlined above. They debated with the crown about their feudal obligations. They tried to reduce or to avoid completely the public burdens due from their lands. They did what they could to encroach on the authority of the sheriffs and the popular courts over which those officials presided. In Anglo-Saxon times the lands held by great ecclesiastics had enjoyed essential immunity from the king's local agents, and this privilege was retained after the Conquest. The existence of these rights gave the lay barons a practical objective at which to aim, but the great lords were probably equally influenced by continental conceptions of the political powers suitable to a baron.

Before the death of Henry I the barons made little progress —in fact they probably lost ground. A few great laymen apparently obtained immunity from the sheriffs and as a result

191

enjoyed the sheriff's powers and perquisites in their lands. These same lords probably avoided the payment of most public obligations due from their estates. But most barons were forced to be content with the limited privileges given them by the Conqueror. Moreover the introduction by Henry I of royal itinerant justices must have made usurpation of privileges and immunities far more difficult.

Unfortunately we know little or nothing of baronial history during Stephen's reign. We see great lords like the count of Aumale, the earls of Chester, Leicester, and Norfolk, and the Lacy lords of Pomfret building concentrated groups of castles to secure military control of the regions in which their lands lay. Geoffrey de Mandeville obtained immunity from the king's justices by securing his own hereditary appointment as justice in Essex and Hertfordshire and London and Middlesex. It is clear that there was little effective royal government, and as a result usurpation of privileges must have been easy. In all probability a few barons approached the status enjoyed by their French contemporaries while lesser men made good progress in that direction.

On the economic side the reign of Henry I probably saw the beginning of the process that was to destroy the feudal barony. A limited market for produce existed and was slowly growing. Barons occasionally accepted scutage instead of military service from their vassals. The crown exacted scutage from ecclesiastic barons and in some cases at least permitted commutation of castle-guard service. But despite these signs of change the relations between king and barons and barons and mesne tenants were still essentially feudal. The baron's officers were vassals who served by hereditary right. His army was the feudal levy of his lands. He and his men were still bound together by the close personal relations that grew out of the feudal bond.

One other feature of baronial history in the Norman period seems worthy of notice. The hereditary right of a family to its fief and the rules governing such inheritance had not become so deeply imbedded in custom as they were to be later. The revolts against William II and Henry I resulted in the confiscation of many fiefs. Often the seized baronies were granted to new lords. Such drastic action was extremely rare under the early Angevin kings when the vested interests of the baronage had grown stronger. Again the Norman kings frequently permitted the division of baronies between brothers. In one case Henry I went so far as to give a fief to a baron's second son because he was " a better knight " than his elder brother. Not even King John would have dared to treat the customs of inheritance so casually.

The hand of King Henry II bore heavily on his English barons. He deprived them of their offices as sheriffs and constables of royal castles. Whenever an opportunity arose, he razed their own fortresses. Grants of lands and privileges made by King Stephen, the Empress Matilda, and Henry himself to purchase baronial support in the civil war were largely ignored by the new king. Many barons were forced to accept higher *servitia debita*. If Henry did not institute prerogative wardship, he certainly insisted on his right to it. He apparently revived the practice of selling the marriage of male heirs in his custody. The introduction of original writs greatly reduced the value of the right of immunity from the sheriff. One of these writs permitted the sheriff to supervise feudal discipline through control of distraint. The introduction of the writ of right established royal control over action for freehold in baronial courts, and the grand assize removed many such cases to the royal tribunals.

The barons seem to have scored only a few minor victories over this aggressive monarch. Danegeld was abandoned. The king did not succeed in raising the service quotas quite so much as he wished. His new jurisdiction over weights and measures was largely given over to the barons and their men. But with the possible exception of the abolition of danegeld these gains were of slight importance. In 1173 the exasperated baronage rose in revolt under the standards of Henry, the young king, and Earl Robert of Leicester. The failure of this rebellion allowed Henry to raze many baronial castles and in general to break the power of those who opposed him. In all probability the last years of Henry II saw the royal power in England at the highest level it was to reach before the Tudor period.

The reigns of Richard, John, and Henry III were a period of transition. The relations between king and barons and between

13

barons and mesne tenants were adjusted to changing circumstances and in the process gradually lost their feudal nature. The fundamental developments which eventually destroyed feudalism were economic. The increase in the volume of trade led to the growth of the towns which in turn enlarged the market for agricultural produce. A greater demand for Flemish and Lombard cloth made its makers seek more English wool. The actual production of the land in England increased. Moreover the expanding market brought a rise in the price level.

Perhaps the most important result of a higher price level was the increase in the cost of waging war. Rising prices combined with improvements in military equipment made knights more expensive. The king could no longer expect the barons to furnish their full quotas of fully armed men. At the same time he ceased to be satisfied with scutage payments at the traditional rates. Hence from 1190 to 1240 the service performed or the commutation paid by a baron was arrived at by separate bargains for each campaign. Fortunately for the barons the system was stabilized by the mutual acceptance of new quotas at a time when the crown was weak. As a result while the barons continued to owe personal service, the contingents of knights which they led to the host were reduced enormously. During this same period the barons resisted vigorously all attempts by the crown to increase their feudal financial obligations to correspond with changed economic conditions. I suspect that this was one of the chief reasons for John's quarrels with his barons. Henry II, Richard, and John had seriously depleted the royal demesne by generous grants to servants and favorites, and hence the crown profited comparatively little from increasing agricultural income. John knew that the revenues of most of his barons were expanding rapidly, and he wanted a share. The result was his attempt to collect very high reliefs and to demand heavy fines on every possible occasion. Certainly *Magna Carta* indicates that the king's financial exactions were the barons' major grievance.

The reign of Henry III saw the barons victorious in the struggle to limit their feudal financial obligations to the traditional amounts. The £100 relief, which had been customary under Henry II and Richard and which was definitely established by *Magna Carta*, was actually reduced to 100 marcs. While the barons were not entirely successful in their claim that feudal aids could not exceed twenty shillings a fee, they never rose over forty shillings. With the exception of the profits from wardship and marriage the feudal revenues of the crown rapidly lost their importance. Customs duties and non-feudal levies supplied the crown with money—feudal aids were a mere pleasant windfall. Edward I and Edward II made some attempt to revive the feudal sources of revenue. The former for a time restored relief to the £100 level. Both monarchs tried to force the barons to pay scutage in addition to serving in the host or offering a fine, but the attempt was unsuccessful. While feudal aids continued to be collected occasionally, the feudal relationship between king and barons practically came to an end with the abandonment of the feudal host.

While the most significant developments in the history of the English barony during the thirteenth century stemmed from economic change, other factors played a part. Henry II had fundamentally altered the very bases of the English judicial and police systems. The popular courts of the shires and hundreds and the feudal courts of the barons were rapidly losing all important functions. The enormous extension of the judicial business of the royal courts upset the established balance of power between crown and barons. Hence a general read-justment was necessary. Throughout the reigns of John and Henry III the barons strove to limit as much as possible the encroachment of the royal courts on their authority and to gain what power they could at the expense of the local courts. A few very great lords obtained private justices and assizes. Others were able to hamper the royal justices by means of the privilege of return of writ. The provision of *Magna Carta* limiting the use of the writ *praecipe* was an attempt at a gen-eral restriction of the royal courts. This struggle terminated in a baronial victory when the crown was forced to acknowl-edge that additions to the powers of its courts could come only through statutes passed by a Parliament dominated by barons.

They were equally successful in encroaching on the powers of the sheriffs and the courts these officials presided over. Many barons obtained exemption from suit at the courts of shire and hundred and the right to view frankpledge. Others usurped these privileges during the frequent periods of civil turmoil. At the death of Henry III a fair number of barons were well on the way towards establishing their fiefs as effective sub-divisions of the realm for judicial purposes. This process was probably stopped by the *quo warranto* proceedings instituted by Edward I and continued by his successors, but little of the ground gained was surrendered. To a very considerable extent the barons and their mesne tenants fell heir to the judicial and police powers of the sheriffs and the local courts. In all probability a careful study of the late fourteenth and the fifteenth centuries would show the barons in turn being replaced by the rising justices of the peace.

The economic and political developments described in the preceding few paragraphs had extremely important effects on the internal history of the barony. The rise in the cost of knights modified greatly the relations between the baron and his vassals. In most cases it was not practical for the baron to apportion his reduced quota among his men. It was far simpler to take their scutage payments and hire knights to perform the service. Thus for a mesne tenant tenure by knight service became in reality tenure by scutage. At the same time the royal courts were rapidly depriving the baron's feudal courts of all business of any significance, and the barons summoned these bodies largely so that they could collect fines from those who failed to appear. Moreover the barons were replacing the hereditary officers drawn from their mesne tenants with paid officials. In short the personal relationship between lord and vassal disappeared. The lord simply collected certain money revenues from his tenants by knight service.

As the price level rose, the feudal revenues received by the barons from their vassals became comparatively less important. Scutages, aids, and reliefs were fixed in amount and could not be increased as incomes from land grew larger. While the evidence is by no means conclusive, I am inclined to believe that the same was true of the profits from franchises. The revenue that built strong castles, hired well-armed retainers, and supported luxurious living came more and more from the demesne manors. But in this respect many a baron could hardly equal, much less be superior to, his more prosperous mesne tenants. In short, tenure by barony soon had little meaning in terms of wealth, power, and prestige and rapidly became obsolete.

A friend and former colleague who has been kind enough to read this manuscript questions my conclusion that the feudal barony came to an end in the fourteenth century. Obviously this depends to a great extent on what one means by feudal. By 1350 the king no longer summoned the feudal host. Reliefs and feudal aids were an unimportant part of the royal revenue. When the king held a meeting of the Great Council or of Parliament, he did not restrict his individual summonses to men holding baronies by tenure. The barons' relations to their vassals were almost entirely financial. Their officials and soldiers were paid retainers. Finally the possession of a tenurial barony did not make a man a baron in the eyes of his contemporaries. There were still barons and baronies, but I cannot call them feudal.

INDEX

A

Aaron, 184, 186-187.
Abingdon, abbot of, 47 n.
Achard, Peter, 103.
Aid:
   feudal, 34, 36, 48, 50, 64, 141-146,
     150-151, 184, 195;
   non-feudal, 42, 48, 50, 64, 90, 195.
Ailsbury, manor of, 81.
Aincurt, barony of, 21, 28, 29, 36, 37,
   88, 105.
Aincurt, Walter de, 34.
Albini, Ely de, 52, 53.
Albini, Robert (Ralph ?) de, 30.
Albini, Robert de, of Cainhoe, 59.
Albini, William de, 188.
Alms, grants in, 159, 160, 181, 182.
Alnwick:
   barony of, 116, 176;
     lords of, see Vesci;
   castle of, 132, 133.
Amundeville, Joscelin de, 186, 187,
   189.
Amundeville, Peter de, 187.
Amundeville, Walter de, 186.
Anjou, count of, 32.
Ap Adam, John, 53.
Aquitaine, duchess of, Eleanor, 32.
Arcy, barony, 27, 28, 30, 153.
Armitage-Smith, S., *John of Gaunt*,
   113 n.
Arsic, barony of, 25 n.
Arundel:
   barony of, 53, 150, 164;
     lords of, see Arundel, earl of;
     Shrewsbury, earl of;
   earl of, 105, 117, 169;
     William de Albini, 59;
   town of, 166, 167.
Assize of arms, 172.
Assize of bread and ale, right to en-
   force, 96-97, 100, 102, 193.
Assize of Clarendon, 97 n., 98, 100,
   110.
Assize of Northampton, 111.
Assize of *ultima praesentatione*, 35.

Ault, Warren O., 11;
   *Court rolls of the abbey of Ramsey
     and of the honor of Clare,* 11 n.;
   Private jurisdiction in England, 11 n.
Aumale, count of, 52, 116, 117, 164,
   192;
   barony of 53;
   Baldwin de Bethune, 84, 108-109;
   Stephen, 110.
Aumale, Robert de (11th century), 18,
   24.
Aumale, Robert de (13th century),
   139.

B

Bailli, baronial, 116, 117, 119, 120.
Balliol, John de, 62.
Balon, barony, 43.
Bampton, barony of, 23 n.
Bardolf, Hugh, 174.
Baring, F. H., *Domesday tables,* 75 n.
Baron, meaning of term, 14-15.
Baronial demesnes, 22, 27-28, 37, 152-
   169.
Baronial incomes, 43, 44, 55, 57, 170-
   190;
   compared to royal, 170, 177-178;
   1160-1220, 170, 171;
   1260-1320, 170, 173-176, 177;
   1436, 170, 176-177.
Baronics, nature of in eleventh cen-
   tury, 16-18.
Barons:
   desires of, 12-13;
   Parliamentary, 15, 16, 47, 52-56,
     134, 176, 177;
   tenurial, see Tenure, by barony.
Barony, meaning of term, 15-16.
Basset of Weldon, barony of, 88.
Basset, Ralph, of Drayton, 52.
Basset, Ralph, of Weldon, 175, 177.
Bath, bishop of, 119.
Bayeux, barony of, 36.
Bayeux, bishop of, 17 n., 23, 75, 82.
Beauchamp of Elmley:
   barony of, 122, 169;
   family, 120.

199

14

Printed in Great Britain
by Amazon